PALGRAVE POCKET CONSULTANTS

Palgrave Pocket Consultants are concise, authoritative guides that provide actionable solutions to specific, high-level business problems that would otherwise drive you or your company to employ a consultant. Written for aspiring middle to senior managers working across business at any scale, they offer solutions to the most cutting-edge issues across modern business. Be your own expert and have the advice you need at your fingertips.

Available titles:
ATTRACTING AND RETAINING TALENT
Tim Baker

MYTH-BUSTING CHINA'S NUMBERS
Matthew Crabbe

RISKY BUSINESS IN CHINA
Jeremy Gordon

Forthcoming titles:
CREATING A RESILENT WORKFORCE
Ivan Robertson and Cary Cooper
MANAGING ONLINE REPUTATION
Charlie Pownall
THE WORKPLACE COMMUNITY
Ian Gee and Matthew Hanwell

Series ISBN 9781137396792

About the Author

Gary Bowerman is Director of Scribes of the Orient, an Asia-based marketing and communications agency. He previously held key positions at leading travel, trade and consumer publishing companies in the UK, was a researcher for Rough Guides and managed the post-9/11 re-launch of a quarterly magazine for the American Society of Travel Agents. In China, where he has lived and worked since 2004, he was Shanghai co-editor for *Zagat*, and spent two years as Editor in Chief of *Shanghai Business Review*. Since co-founding Scribes of the Orient in 2008, Bowerman has worked closely with travel and tourism brands in China, across Asia and worldwide. This has given him unique insights into the mindset of Chinese travelers and the approaches of brands and destinations seeking to connect with them.

Business Opportunities from the Chinese Travel Revolution

The New Chinese Traveler

Gary Bowerman
Director and Co-Founder, Scribes of the Orient Ltd,
Hong Kong, Shanghai, Kuala Lumpur

© Gary Bowerman 2014

All rights reserved. No reproduction, copy or transmission of this publication may be made without written permission.

No portion of this publication may be reproduced, copied or transmitted save with written permission or in accordance with the provisions of the Copyright, Designs and Patents Act 1988, or under the terms of any licence permitting limited copying issued by the Copyright Licensing Agency, Saffron House, 6–10 Kirby Street, London EC1N 8TS.

Any person who does any unauthorized act in relation to this publication may be liable to criminal prosecution and civil claims for damages.

The author has asserted his right to be identified as the author of this work in accordance with the Copyright, Designs and Patents Act 1988.

First published 2014 by
PALGRAVE MACMILLAN

Palgrave Macmillan in the UK is an imprint of Macmillan Publishers Limited, registered in England, company number 785998, of Houndmills, Basingstoke, Hampshire RG21 6XS.

Palgrave Macmillan in the US is a division of St Martin's Press LLC, 175 Fifth Avenue, New York, NY 10010.

Palgrave Macmillan is the global academic imprint of the above companies and has companies and representatives throughout the world.

Palgrave® and Macmillan® are registered trademarks in the United States, the United Kingdom, Europe and other countries.

ISBN 978–1–137–39728–7

This book is printed on paper suitable for recycling and made from fully managed and sustained forest sources. Logging, pulping and manufacturing processes are expected to conform to the environmental regulations of the country of origin.

A catalogue record for this book is available from the British Library.

A catalog record for this book is available from the Library of Congress.

Typeset by MPS Limited, Chennai, India.

Contents

List of Tables / vii
Preface / viii
List of Abbreviations and Acronyms Used / x

    Introduction: Beyond the Middle Kingdom: The Makings of a Travel Revolution / 1

1 Building a Brand New Industry: From ADS to the New Tourism Law / 14

2 Going Global: China's New Travel Class Spreads Its Wings / 32

3 Magnetized by Macao: Creating a Global Tourism Phenomenon / 50

4 The Purchasing Prerogative: Hong Kong and Shopping Tourism / 67

5 Sun, Sea, and Shopping: China Goes to the Beach / 79

6 Lights, Camera, Action: Chinese Tourism on TV and Film / 95

7 All Around the World: Tourism Marketers Target China / 105

8   A Place to Stay: Checking-in with
    Chinese Travelers ╱ 124

9   Taking Flight: China's Aviation Revolution ╱ 142

10 The Media Game: Publishing for the
    Modern Traveler ╱ 159

11 Smart Travel, Chinese Style: Trip Planning
    and New Technology ╱ 174

12 Keeping It Local: Fast Trains, Ski Slopes
    and the New Macao ╱ 185

13 The Resort Revolution: Chinese Weekenders
    in Search of Style ╱ 201

14 Economics in Action: Business Travelers
    Explore New Frontiers ╱ 209

Index ╱ 223

List of Tables

 I.1 China outbound travelers, 2000–2013 ∕ 2
 3.1 Macao inbound arrivals from mainland China, 2003–2013 ∕ 51
 4.1 Hong Kong arrivals from mainland China, 2002–2013 ∕ 72
14.1 China RMB appreciation versus international currencies, 2004–2014 ∕ 218

Preface

Over the last two years, the subject of Chinese outbound travel has risen high on the world's news agenda. Producers of TV documentaries and discussion shows and the writers of newspaper columns, magazine articles and online blogs are eagerly seeking to engage viewers, readers and casual observers about a phenomenon that is, unquestionably, effecting change across the global travel industry. This book seeks to address some of the critical questions that interested parties are asking about the *The New Chinese Traveler*, and attempts to explain the subject in a national, regional and international context.

The Introduction and Chapters 1 and 2 address the causal economic and societal factors that are pushing the expansion of Chinese tourism. Mass travel beyond the Chinese mainland is a relatively new phenomenon, and Chapters 3, 4 and 5 explore how three key destinations, Macao, Hong Kong and Hainan Island, have been used as tourism training grounds for outbound holidaymakers. All three hot spots are governed by China, but are locations that have introduced the concept of international travel, and are, concurrently, being used by the government to test tourism concepts that might be rolled out across China, Asia and the world.

The next part of the book discusses Chinese tourism in action. Chapters 6, 7 and 8 assess the range and scope of marketing and engagement strategies being implemented by international tourism providers and hoteliers to entice and retain Chinese visitors. The impact of a dramatic increase in air connectivity in China over the past decade is the subject of Chapter 9, while Chapters 10 and 11 go behind the scenes of two crucial facilitators of Chinese travel: the media and travel planning technology.

Intensifying demand for overseas tourism has prompted a proactive response by China's domestic travel industry. Private investors and entrepreneurs are now seeking to direct the future of tourism at home and overseas, and this development is discussed in Chapters 12 and 13. Finally, Chapter 14 focuses on Chinese business travel and global tourism economics.

As I write this Preface, I am sat on a train headed to Venice. In the last week, I encountered young Chinese tourists shopping at the Gucci store in Rome, photographing the Duomo in Florence and eating pasta on a *trattoria* terrace in Siena. These encounters occurred in early June, not a month normally associated with Chinese outbound travel, which has hitherto been closely aligned to the nation's mandated public holidays. This underscores a point I have tried to emphasize in the following pages – that Chinese outbound travel is a dynamic and fluid story. This book provides a snapshot in time to help readers understand the developmental trends over the past 20 years, and to look ahead at how the Chinese travel revolution might further evolve in the coming years.

I would like to thank Paul French, with whom I discussed this topic over numerous curries and beers in Shanghai and London, and who finally persuaded me that our musings merited conversion into a book. Numerous other people helped me with the research process, most notably my Shanghai-based business partner, Amy Fabris-Shi, and my KL beer buddy, Matthew Crabbe – both of whom encouraged me to shape and channel my thoughts instead of boring them interminably on the topic of Chinese travel. Special thanks also to the editor, Tamsine O'Riordan, and editorial assistant, Josephine Taylor, whose advice and expertise made the publishing process smoother and less fraught than it might otherwise have been.

This book is dedicated to the passengers and crew of Malaysia Airlines Flight MH370, and their families in China, Malaysia and around the world, and to all the victims, and their families, of the MH17 tragedy.

Gary Bowerman
Italy, June 2014

List of Abbreviations and Acronyms Used

ACI – Airports Council International
ACTE – Association of Corporate Travel Executives
ADS – Approved Destination Status
ASEAN – Association of South East Asian Nations
ASEAN AEC – ASEAN Economic Community
ASTA – American Society of Travel Agents
CAAC – Civil Aviation Administration of China
CAPA – Centre for Aviation
CCTV – China Central Television
(CNNIC) – China Internet Network Information Center
CITS – China International Travel Service
CLIA – Cruise Lines International Association
CNTA – China National Tourism Administration
COMAC – Commercial Aircraft Corporation of China
CRH – China Railway High-Speed
CTC – Canadian Tourism Commission
ETC – European Travel Commission
FIT – free independent travel
FTZ – Free Trade Zone (China)
GBTA – Global Business Travel Association
GDS – Global Distribution System
HNWI – High Net-Worth Individual
IATA – International Air Transport Association
ICBC – Industrial and Commercial Bank of China
IIE – Institute of International Education
IVS – Individual Visit Scheme (Hong Kong)

KTB – Kenya Tourism Board
KTO – Korea Tourism Organization
LATCB – Los Angeles Tourism & Convention Board
LCC – low-cost carrier
LEED – Leadership in Environmental & Energy Design
MICE – meetings, incentives, conferences and exhibitions
MTR – Mass Transit Railway (Hong Kong)
NBA – National Basketball Association (US)
NDC – New Distribution Capability
NDRC – National Development and Reform Commission (China)
OECD – Organization for Economic Cooperation and Development
PATA – Pacific Asia Travel Association
PSS – Passenger Services System
REIT – real estate investment trust
SAR – Special Administrative Region (Hong Kong and Macao)
SARFT – State Administration of Press, Publication, Radio, Film and Television (China)
SARS – Severe Acute Respiratory Syndrome
SLTPB – Sri Lanka Tourism Promotion Bureau
STDM – Sociedade de Turismo e Diversões de Macao
TCM – Traditional Chinese Medicine
UNDP – United Nations Development Programme
UNESCO – United Nations Educational, Scientific and Cultural Organization
UNWTO – United Nations World Travel Organization
WFOE – Wholly Foreign Owned Enterprise (China)
WTO – World Trade Organization
WTTC – World Travel and Tourism Council

Introduction
Beyond the Middle Kingdom: The Makings of a Travel Revolution

Heading towards the 100 million benchmark

Thursday, 9 January 2014 was an unremarkable news day. Dennis Rodman had just sung *Happy Birthday* to North Korean leader Kim Jong-un, "Polar Vortex" was acquiring "political issue" status, and anti-government protests paralyzed Bangkok. Otherwise, the international media struck a parochial tone. The London-based *Financial Times* ran with the European Central Bank maintaining benchmark interest rates, the *New York Times* focused on revelations about the New Jersey Governor, *The Australian* discussed the alleged mistreatment of asylum-seekers, and the Singapore-based *Straits Times* reported the kidnapping of the mother of a local supermarket CEO.

Just after 10 a.m. local time, however, China's Xinhua state media agency published a statistics-based story that electrified the news wires, and would be commented upon globally throughout the following days, weeks and months. In 2013, 97 million Chinese had traveled beyond the Middle Kingdom (*zhong guo*, 中国) – and the inevitable conclusion was that more than 100 million would follow suit in 2014. Indeed, the figure was shortlived. One week later, the China National Tourism Administration (CNTA) upgraded the 2013 outbound total to 98.2 million. Either way, it was news of genuine global importance.

The 98 million Chinese outbounders improved upon the 2012 figure by 18 percent, or around 15 million people – roughly equivalent to the combined population of Norway and Sweden – according to the CNTA.

To place the 100 million projection for 2014 into a different context – figures from the Word Bank show that only 11 countries in the world (including China) had a total population of more than 100 million at the end of 2012. See Table I.1 for numbers of Chinese outbound travelers 2000–2013.

The subsequent excited opinion columns and analytical features across the planet confirmed a diagnosis that had been pending for some time. The tourism industry was now officially addicted to a transformative new stimulant. It's called China, and the world is transfixed. Just as in the retail, finance, manufacturing, and property sectors – and pretty much any other industry you could care to mention – the expanding international influence of China's economy has destinations worldwide salivating at the potential revenues to be earned, and, equally importantly, the tourism-related jobs to be created, from China's expanding class of aspirant holidaymakers.

Table I.1 China outbound travelers, 2000–2013

Year	Travelers (millions)
2013	98.2
2012	83.2
2011	70.3
2010	57.4
2009	47.6
2008	45.8
2007	41.0
2006	34.5
2005	31.0
2004	28.9
2003	20.2
2002	16.6
2001	12.1
2000	10.5

Note: Based on border crossing figures, including to Hong Kong and Macao.
Source: China Tourism Academy/China National Tourism Administration.

From Auckland to Kuala Lumpur, and London to Zanzibar, calculations are constantly being revisited about just how many and how often Chinese travelers might arrive via planes, trains and automobiles – from which cities they will come, how much money they will spend and where they will stay. Numbers, too, are being crunched to deduce what they plan to do and buy, and their preferred modes of transport.

And what about next year, and the year after? Will those same Chinese visitors return for a second trip? Will they bring the extended family, or head instead for pastures new? Are they replaceable? Is there an even longer line of "second mover" travelers at the airport gates of Beijing, Shanghai, Guangzhou, Tianjin, or Chengdu waiting to replace those first movers who have been there, done that and posted their photos on social media? The tourism industry's quest for answers to these questions intensified on 9 January 2014, but as seasoned China observers always caution: the response to one question rarely achieves more than sparking a tangential set of new queries.

We don't know a great deal about the composition of the 2013 outbound figures, which is often the case with Chinese official statistics as they are neatly rounded up to make them harder hitting and more easily consumed by the local and international media. But even in the absence of drilled-down data, it is evident that, as in recent years, the majority of Chinese tourists traveled within Asia during 2013. Hong Kong and Macao were the primary destinations, which may seem a little odd given China's "One country, two systems" governance that has been applied since sovereignty of Hong Kong and Macao were handed back by the UK (1997) and Portugal (1999), respectively. Both Hong Kong and Macao are classified in Chinese travel accounting as "international" destinations and require visas for PRC citizens.

Beyond the immediate Asian map, Australia, New Zealand, North America, and Europe are popular with experienced Chinese travelers, while wealthy adventurers are now dispersing to the polar south, the equatorial center and the arctic north to spend their holidays. But, as we shall see later in this book, making qualified predictions about the future patterns of outbound travel from a continent-sized country with a population of around 1.4 billion people is at best tricky.

One thing that analysts mostly agree upon, however, is that China is having a transformative impact on the way the global tourism industry operates, finances and promotes itself. The multi-layered strategies being put into place by tourism providers to cater to Chinese travelers will develop tangentially. Earning a "winning share" of the Chinese market is a white hot subject of debate that is unlikely to take flight any time soon, particularly as most projections indicate that – pending an economic downturn, which can never be discounted – Chinese outbound volumes and annual outbound spending are locked on an upward curve. In whatever form and scope to which it may evolve, the Chinese Travel Revolution is only just beginning.

The twenty-first century Red-and-Gold Rush

China's 2013 outbound travel figures were released on the same day as Beijing's English-language *Global Times* newspaper published comments from tourism experts in China urging the government to add more official vacation days to offset the worsening travel congestion that occurs at airports and on trains and roads during the nation's two annual Golden Week holidays. The timing of the article was deliberate, as the mass pre-Spring Festival migration (known as *chunyun* 春运) was about to commence. Across the next month, hundreds of millions of Chinese would be heading home to spend the 2014 Chinese Spring Festival – the largest and most culturally important holiday of the year, which officially began on 31 January – with their families.

As the mass migration began, China's National Development and Reform Commission (NDRC) predicted that up to 3.6 billion trips (with 258 million rail tickets expected to be sold) would be made by trains, planes and automobiles during the full 40 days of the designated holiday transport period. This prediction represented an increase of 200 million from 2012. Yes, you read that correctly: an extra 200 million trips were predicted in little more than a month – which is akin to adding the total population of Brazil to China's 2014 Spring Festival travel equation.

Discussing the Chinese domestic holiday travel situation at this early point in the story is deliberate. China's overlapping relationship between domestic and outbound tourism is largely directed by the state-mandated holiday system and the still evolving private paid-leave entitlements, so that holidaymakers have restricted windows for travel, whether domestic or outbound. Until a more flexible paid leave system is implemented, the bottlenecks that exist for domestic travel during the Spring Festival are likely to carry over, particularly during the shorter May Day break and the October National Day Golden Week vacation – as increasing urban affluence and less familial pressure to spend those holidays at home presage an ever greater number of outbound travelers. Consequently, extra strains will be exerted on transport pressure points, particularly in mass travel destinations like Hong Kong, Macao, Hainan Island, and Tibet, plus regional hotspots like Bali, Thailand, Singapore, and increasingly in Japan, Taiwan, South Korea and, possibly, even North Korea.

This brings us back to the issue of Golden Week outbound travel, and more specifically to the Spring Festival, which in 2014 ran from 31 January to 6 February. The global response to the issuance of China's 2013 travel statistics was immediate, calculated and opportunistic. More than ever before, the figures confirmed that the China Red-and-Gold Travel Rush is breaking barriers – and tourism administrators began discussing an auspiciously golden future.

In a skillful piece of political timing, French Foreign Minister Laurent Fabius waited just four days after the 2013 figures were released before flying to Beijing and announcing, on 13 January, that France would expedite travel visas for Chinese travelers with a turnaround period of just 48 hours. France's new visa policy would begin two weeks later, on 27 January 2014, the 50th anniversary of bilateral Sino-French relations, and four days before the official start of the 2014 Spring Festival Golden Week. "Paris veut doper le tourisme chinois en France" (Paris seeks to boost Chinese tourism in France) exclaimed the French daily newspaper *Libération*. France is Europe's leading destination for Chinese tourists, attracting around 1.5 million in 2013.

A few days later German car manufacturer Mercedes-Benz – not previously known for its travel agency credentials or aspirations – announced it was creating a luxury travel brand based in Shanghai to offer "a range of high-grade travel packages focused on fascinating European locations as well as unique events," according to a company statement. The target market for the partnership venture with HH Travel, a division of Ctrip International, China's largest online travel agency, was clear: "China offers great potential for products of Mercedes-Benz Travel, as it is a fast growing market for international, guided tours with sophisticated ambitions," said the launch statement.

Foreign tourism providers were now lining up to make pronouncements, launch policy initiatives and issue press releases. Spanish Prime Minister Mariano Rajoy declared that Spain had broken the benchmark of 60 million annual visitor arrivals 2013, and had welcomed 35 percent more Chinese visitors than in 2012. Meanwhile, in Barbados Prime Minister Freundel Stuart, declared the island's "great interest in seeing Chinese nationals traveling to Barbados." It was, in all likelihood, the most obvious political statement he will ever make.

Fashion Show, the largest retail center in Las Vegas, and Grand Canal Shoppes at The Venetian Las Vegas provided cardholders of China UnionPay – China's largest payment card system, which accounted for around 80 of purchases by Chinese tourists in 2013, according to a UnionPay report – with a Chinese New Year gift bag including "Lucky Draw" tickets and an auspicious red envelope containing a gift card during the Spring Festival. They were not alone. Airport duty-free and high street department stores worldwide unveiled red and gold storefronts decorated with equine imagery to welcome the Year of the Horse, and exclusive promotional discounts for Chinese shoppers.

The response to the 2013 outbound figures in China was similarly rapid. The country's largest telecom operator, China Mobile, slashed its Wi-Fi roaming fees for Chinese subscribers traveling in 80 countries and regions, including Hong Kong and Taiwan. Air China's first scheduled nonstop flight to Honolulu departed from Beijing, and Hainan Airlines, China's fourth largest carrier, launched its first direct service between China and Bali.

Behavioral economics in action

China's outbound tourism surge may be in a nascent phase, but its impact has been closely tracked for the past decade as the industry's "next best thing." But over the last two years, its thrusting momentum, allied with the continued expansion of Chinese domestic travel, has raised important strategic and infrastructure questions for global governments, tourism boards, destination marketers and convention bureaus. One simple dilemma pertains: are you ready to deal with the Chinese tourism force headed your way?

In fact, 2012 was the real benchmark of what may be to come. In that year, according to the China Tourism Academy, China overtook Germany and the US to become the world's largest outbound tourism market, with an estimated 83 million overseas trips made by Chinese citizens. China also became the highest-spending tourism nation, splashing out USD 102 billion while overseas (which increased to USD 128.7 billion in 2013) according the United Nations World Travel Organization (UNWTO).

The broadening scope of Chinese tourism has catalyzed two interesting marketing phenomena. Tourism providers who had already devised "China ready" strategies were tending if not to tear them up then to heavily re-focus them, while those who had prevaricated fell even further behind the cashed-up travel bandwagon departing from the Middle Kingdom. The tens, soon to be hundreds, of millions collecting their boarding passes at airports from Beijing and Kunming to Shanghai to Xi'an do so in the knowledge that they are the central players in the global tourism game, with rafts of new cash-generating initiatives awaiting them in the transit and arrivals lounges.

The vastness of China's population, the rapid rate of urbanization and striking middle-class income growth in recent years, plus a proven willingness to spend big when overseas, have forced a planetary rethink about travel dynamics. China is the fulcrum of this new world order. The China Outbound Tourism Research Institute, for example, estimated that Chinese travelers would make 114 million border crossings and spend USD 140 billion in 2014, while brokerage house CLSA Asia-Pacific

Markets predicted that by 2020 annual outbound Chinese tourists will reach 200 million. Yes, that's the entire population of Brazil once again tossed into the mix.

With intensifying frequency, a tourism board official somewhere will unveil plans to "capture a larger share of the strategic China travel market," while a copywriter drafts a press release boasting of a double-digit increase in Chinese arrivals during the previous month. Elsewhere, a conference company is working on the sales strategy for a seminar discussing "the future of the Chinese travel boom," and a radio producer is calling travel editors to ask them to analyze a consultancy report about Chinese consumer spending on foreign shores.

Meanwhile, hotel marketers are trawling Chinese social media sites, such as Weibo and Weixin (also known as WeChat), in search of inspiration for their consumer campaigns, and an airline executive is flying into a central Chinese city of whose existence he was blissfully unaware a decade ago to negotiate landing rights. Back at his departure point, the airport duty-free store has recruited a Nanjing-based company to train Chinese-speaking sales staff, while the retail director is reassessing inventory for the upcoming Golden Week. In a government office, a heated discussion is under way about the relative merits of axing versus relaxing the criteria for Chinese visa applications. Across the street, a luxury brand executive is negotiating with an event management company about the cost of a Chinese New Year gala sponsorship at a US university. Six floors down, a consultant economist is perfecting a new algorithm-based projection of Chinese outbound spending patterns in 2100.

At the same time, Chinese construction workers are building a luxury beachside resort in the Caribbean, while off-duty flight attendants from a Chinese airline are shopping on Sunset Boulevard. On a remote island, a Chinese movie star you may never have heard of is marrying a TV host in a ceremony paid for by the local tourism board. Meanwhile, in a private lounge at Beijing airport, two bleary-eyed travel writers are waiting to fly to Glasgow, where a Chongqing-born Cambridge graduate who owns a UK-based tour agency has arranged a Rolls-Royce transfer to a Scottish castle recently converted into a Ming Dynasty-themed boutique hotel.

Other less obvious aspects of the Chinese Travel Revolution are worth considering. Chinese investors already own some of the world's most iconic hotels and are turning their attentions to wine estates, French chateaux and luxury villas. Ningbo-based Geely owns the manufacturer of the iconic London black cab, while the Sunseeker yacht from the James Bond movie *Quantum of Solace* is part of the Dalian Wanda Group, which is building a new hotel in London. For the record, the distance between Ningbo and Dalian is around 1,250 kilometers, about the same as Berlin to Belgrade.

Chinese tourism is, in a sense, a real-time study of behavioral economics. Wherever we travel, the "China factor" infuses the present and the future. Airport signage companies are adding Chinese characters to their repertoires. Hotel general managers are examining the costs of hiring extra Mandarin-speaking sales staff. Aircraft designers are working to cater for Chinese travelers who prefer carrying their luggage onto a plane, rather than checking it into the hold, and cruise-ship operators are juggling their route schedules to assign larger ships to East Asian ports. Airline loyalty card managers are devising digital blasts to sign up more Chinese members, while everyone from car-hire companies to ATM providers are re-synching their systems to accept China UnionPay cards. In summer 3014, Chinese police were deployed on the streets of Paris to help protect big-spending tourists from pickpockets and bag snatchers.

In addition to the logistics of travel, the "tourism + shopping" coefficient is being reconsidered. Chinese travelers may not have invented "shopping tourism" – anyone who remembers the Japanese outbound travel surge in the 1980s knows that – but they are elevating it to a cash-popping art form. A research note by Morgan Stanley predicted Chinese vacationers could splash out USD 194 billion in 2015. On high streets, in malls and outlet villages, retailers are ordering and displaying quantities of stock unthinkable three years ago. Similarly, retail brands are not just upgrading their Chinese websites, they are tailoring their services and products to appeal to street-savvy shoppers from China's largest cities, and are launching ever-more daring promotions via Chinese social media.

For these reasons, Chinese tourism is a visible representation of the so-called "Chinese economic dream," a subject about which we read in newspaper articles and which we see on TV documentaries. But technical discussions about the Chinese government acquiring foreign debt, the sovereign wealth fund purchasing overseas assets or whether the renminbi is becoming a global reserve currency are less buzz-worthy and digestible than stories about Chinese travelers arriving in ever-greater numbers to a nearby town or tourism attraction.

Behavioral traits, spending patterns and destination preferences have attained "trending" status. Bold headlines and captioned images of Chinese travelers taking photos in Times Square, buying souvenirs at Harrods or clothes at Galeries Lafayette, climbing the Sydney Harbour Bridge or an Alpine pass in Grindelwald, dining by the harbor in Cape Town, marrying at the South Pole or fighting on a flight from Thailand are accessible depictions of China's economy "going global."

Olympic ambassadors and Mr Li's trip to the UK

In 2005, I attended a seminar presentation in Shanghai given by Michael Payne, former Commercial Director of the International Olympic Committee and author of the book *Olympic Turnaround*. His recollections about a group of Chinese in a land not their own were compelling. After the Cold War-era mass political boycotts of the 1980 Moscow Olympics, retaliatory withdrawals threatened not just the 1984 Los Angeles Games, but the entire future of the near-bankrupt Olympic movement.

After frantic negotiations, China was persuaded to send a team to the LA Games – the first time it had done so for a summer Olympic Games since 1952. The 216 Chinese athletes may not have realized, but their participation was crucial in securing global commercial sponsorships and TV deals. As they entered the Coliseum Stadium for the opening ceremony a mass roar echoed around the arena. American fans understood that the visiting Chinese athletes had probably saved the Olympics.

Fast forward two decades, and Chinese tourists are being similarly cast in the fiscal spotlight by tourism providers eager to monetize the

"Chinese Dream." China's government understands this fact, which is why it has been so concerned to legislate for ensuring "ambassadorial" behavior by its outbound citizens. In addition to financing the tourism economies from Australia to Zambia, Chinese officials hope they will contribute to a general reprogramming of the global consciousness about a nation that is widely perceived as ambiguous and abstruse.

Although the phrase "behind the Bamboo Curtain" is rarely used today, elements of that image's Cold War implications, of a suspicious, Communist-governed, Western world-hating sleeping giant have proved hard to shift among foreign politicians and populations. Hence, international tourism is often debated in terms of "hard" and "soft" power – the former being the actual reality of millions of Chinese citizens spending time and money overseas, and the latter being the evocation of nation-building pride such trips generate.

Chinese travelers who ventured overseas during the 1980s and 1990s will tell you that common perceptions about their country were of a populace dressed in blue Mao suits and overly salted takeaway food. Few people they encountered back then understood that Beijing and Peking were two iterations for the same city, that Sichuan cuisine is as different from Cantonese cooking as chicken madras is from coq au vin, or why Chinese travelers had better mobile phones and Sony Walkmans than Europeans (the reason being the prevalence of cheap, high-quality imports from Japan).

This back-story is as compelling as the drama of the cash-fuelled present. Having worked closely with the Chinese tourism industry for a decade, the inspiration for this book was neither the seismic socio-economic strides made this millennium, nor the bear-hugging embrace from tourism bodies. The inspiration was Mr Li.

In late 2006, I moved into the Blackstone Apartments, a Baroque 1920s gem on Fuxing Road in Shanghai's former French Concession. A few days later, a knock on the door signaled my first visitor. Mr Li entered wearing a warm winter coat (the central heating systems of historic buildings in Shanghai were removed on Mao's orders shortly after 1949 on account of southern China below the Yangtze River officially having a sub-tropical climate) and a polite smile. He clasped some aging Polaroid photos and asked if he could show them to me.

Mr Li was among China's first generation of independent traveler. In the 1980s, he obtained a visa to study in the UK, and set off on a journey of exploration. He flirted with education, but mostly worked in restaurants to scrape together money to travel. His photos – which would today be called "selfies" – bore witness to stops in London, Bath, Bournemouth and places in France and Belgium that he could not now name. He had visited my home city, Oxford, but didn't have enough money to buy camera film. As he opened the door to leave, he thanked me for taking time to view his visual memories. "Those few months were the best of my life," he smiled.

EXPERT INSIGHT: MARTIN CRAIGS, CEO, PATA

An experienced airline industry marketer and advocate, Martin Craigs was appointed CEO of the Pacific Asia Travel Association (PATA) in October 2011. Headquartered in Bangkok, PATA is a membership association that supports the development of travel and tourism industry in the Asia Pacific region.

PATA has monitored Chinese outbound travel for many years. How do you view the development in both a regional and global context?

The increase of China's outbound tourism is a direct result of the increase in the strength of China's economy. This trend will continue to grow over the years. In addition, the recent pollution in North China has contributed to this trend, as more Chinese travelers prefer to take their vacations internationally than domestically. Regionally and globally, there will be more tourists from China and all destinations need to be prepared. A major and crucial challenge going forward is the carrying capacity of the destinations.

Today, the main subjects of inquiry from our members include the understanding of Chinese travel habits, how to reach Chinese tour operators and how to reach the market. As a destination, the more you learn the better service you can provide.

In 2013, PATA held its annual Travel Mart in Chengdu. Why was that city chosen, and what did delegates learn from the event?

Chengdu is one of the fastest growing cities in China with excellent facilities for an international event. It offers many hotels that meet international standards and an ambitious hub airport plan. PATA previously held the event in Beijing and Hangzhou, and it was a good opportunity to stage our first trade show in southwest China.

PATA Travel Mart delegates, both members and non-members, had the opportunity to network with good-quality buyers from almost 50 countries. During the workshop, they were updated on the changes in the structure, demand and expectations of Chinese outbound travelers. There might be a slowdown in the growth of outbound Chinese travelers, but the demand for specific types of holidays – especially island vacations – will continue to grow.

Chapter 1
Building a Brand New Industry: From ADS to the New Tourism Law

From Zheng He to "inelastic demand"

In November 2013, a celebrity-loaded reception in Beijing was promoted as a celebration of the 15th anniversary of liberalization of China's outbound travel market. Organized by Top Travel, a glossy Chinese-language travel magazine, the event, called "100 bigger worlds," featured a charitable initiative by a coterie of Chinese pop stars and TV actors to raise funds to send children from deprived backgrounds on an overseas travel-and-study program.

Media attention about the event was sparse, which was surprising given its central tenet: Chinese outbound tourism is a thriving industry that has been built from the ground up in less than two decades. The achievements in this short period of time are a source of pride to the Chinese government, which refers to overseas travel as a social benefit created by its economic development policies.

Politics aside, the growth figures are impressive – outbound tourism numbers doubled from 2009 to 2013, while more border crossings were made from China during the first nine months of 2013 than in the whole of 2011. According to official figures, 10.5 million border crossings were made from China in 2000. Fourteen years later, more than 100 million outbound trips will have been made. No country has ever witnessed such explosive tourism growth, and visa-free access is now being used to induce further expansion. In June 2014, the China Tourism Academy said China passport-holders could, at the time, visit 81 countries and regions without a pre-arranged visa or by collecting a visa on arrival.

Chinese exploration is nothing new, of course. Chinese merchants traveled across Asia when Rome ruled Europe, and, in his book *1421*, Gavin Menzies claims that the Ming dynasty Admiral Zheng sailed to North America 600 years ago. More recently, Chinese emigration since the eighteenth century is evidenced by the Chinatowns established from London to San Francisco, Kolkata to Johannesburg and Buenos Aires to Melbourne. These Chinese districts feature shops, restaurants, clan houses, temples and churches. Sustained emigration also created South East Asia's sizeable Chinese diaspora, most notably in Singapore, Malaysia, Indonesia and Vietnam.

But, with the exception of a small number of tour groups in the late 1980s and 1990s, mass-scale Chinese travel is a twenty-first century phenomenon. Recent Chinese tourism has come to be viewed in three, rather narrow, categories from the elite super-wealthy who buy properties, yachts and, occasionally, foreign companies on their travels; to the burgeoning middle class spending their disposable cash on experiential travel; to package group tourists on shopping tours around Asia, Europe the US. While those categorizations tell some of the story, ten defining trends over the past decade expand those easy definitions into a more rounded picture.

(1) Domestic tourism is developing on a diversified scale that is simply impossible to fathom if you don't live in a rapidly urbanizing, economically expanding nation of around 1.4 billion people.
(2) Travel to Hong Kong and Macao (both officially categorized as international destinations) has, hitherto, been the significant contributor to outbound travel from China.
(3) Chinese travelers have generally tended to visit at least one Asian destination before graduating to longer haul trips to Europe, Australasia or North America.

(4) Travel to visit family and friends living or studying overseas has been a strong contributory factor to long-haul travel.
(5) Affluent Chinese travelers are increasingly displaying "inelastic demand" and are happy to travel wherever the calling takes them.
(6) The majority of outbound travel – beyond weekend destinations like Hong Kong and Macao – has been focused around the state-mandated Chinese public holidays.
(7) Chinese tourism has integrated with experiential advances that have improved the travel experience for travelers worldwide. Savvy Chinese tourists now have high service expectations, and the challenge for tourism providers is to anticipate how to cater for the further evolution of the Chinese travel dream.
(8) China has, unquestionably, assumed leadership status in the future shaping of global travel, air transport and hospitality, and related industries like retail, infrastructure and real estate.
(9) Given Chinese travelers' propensity to spend, there has been a monumental conversion from a cash-based economy to one dominated by card purchasing. Virtually no one used a credit or debit card in China a decade ago. In early 2014, its banks had issued around 4.2 billion cards (around three times the nation's total population). Combined with the growing prevalence of "electronic wallet" mechanisms and a stratospheric rise in online shopping, urban Chinese now favor invisible cash exchanges to banknotes – and this has made overseas travel less complicated during a period when the RMB remained non-exchangeable.
(10) The application of technology has made Chinese travel more easily monitored and metric-related, but it has also contributed to a dynamism and, fluidity that render it a highly unpredictable story.

Approving the world's travel destinations

China has created the world's fastest-growing tourism sector with assiduous care over the past two decades. Now that more than 100 million Chinese are traveling annually, it's hard to conceive that outbound tourism didn't really exist in China until the late 1990s. Before then, those who traveled into the outside world were mostly officially sanctioned businessmen, government members, diplomats and university students. Some leverage was provided for approved tour groups, but it was minimal.

The growth of tourism did not occur in a vacuum, of course. Experience from industrializing nations from the early nineteenth century onwards proved that economic growth and increased urban affluence catalyze the desire to explore beyond work and home. For this reason, China established the Golden Week public hoidays in 1999 to provide mandated time for workers to spend as they chose – whether that be with families and friends and/or embarking on tourism trips around their homeland. As more people became able to afford overseas trips, the government explored ways to administer and control both the volumes and the flight paths. It conceived a phased process of approving overseas destinations for Chinese groups.

Approved Destination Status (ADS) was a ubiquitous buzz phrase during the first decade of the new millennium. The Chinese media frequently teased readers with trails of upcoming ADS agreements with new destinations, while grateful foreign governments flourished press statements announcing that they had found their tourism Holy Grail: confirmation by the Chinese government that their nation would join the list of approved destinations for Chinese group travelers.

The ADS acronym seems dated now. Almost 150 tourism destinations had signed up by the end of 2013, and China's outbound market has matured beyond a reliance on packaged tour groups through state-approved agencies. But back in the early 1990s when ADS was first introduced for destinations in South East Asia, including Malaysia, Singapore, and Thailand, it heralded the start of the Chinese travel revolution. It was the stamp of approval that would, two decades later in 2013, result in those three nations each receiving record numbers of Chinese visitors: Malaysia (1.79 million), Singapore (1.24 million), Thailand (4.7 million).

The ADS program also set the wheels in motion for today's wider tourism dispersion. Businesses worldwide that welcome Chinese visitors – from the Cornell Museum of Glass in New York and the Prado

Museum in Madrid to wine tour operators in Tuscany and DMZ guides in South Korea; and from the beachside restaurants of Nusa Dua and Cancun, to the safari parks of the Serengeti and the dive boats of the Great Barrier Reef – know that none of this would have happened without the managed effect of the ADS program.

China's ADS policy was created to account for the growing propensity of Chinese citizens to travel abroad, but it also imposed strict mechanisms to control travel movements. Even today, only certified ADS travel agencies are allowed to promote and organize outbound tour groups, assist with the visa application process and make payments to foreign parties. Foreign governments signing up to receive ADS groups became able to promote their country within China as a tourism destination, but were required to liaise only with approved travel agencies and tourism authorities. Being granted ADS status did not initially permit a nation to welcome independent travelers, or to set up its own travel agency mechanisms.

The ADS process was rolled out gradually. Early members included South Korea which joined in 1998; Australia and New Zealand joined in 1999 and were the first countries outside Asia to do so; and Japan joined in 2000. In 2003, Germany became the first EU nation to receive ADS recognition. A swathe of European countries – including Austria, France, Iceland, Netherlands, Poland and Spain – followed in 2004, the same year as Jordan, Kenya, and Zambia. The UK signed up in 2005, as did Chile, Peru and Russia; and the US joined in 2007 (effective from 2008) – the same year as Bangladesh, Monaco and Morocco. Canada was a relative latecomer, signing the agreement in 2010, a year in which Micronesia and Serbia also put pen to paper.

The use of ADS as a policy tool was discussed in a research paper published by The Hong Kong Polytechnic University (HKPU) (*PolyU Study Finds Chinese Outbound Tourism Policy a Form of Diplomacy, January 2014*). Written by Dr Tony Tse of HKPU's School of Hotel and Tourism Management, the paper notes that few countries in the world have a public policy on outbound tourism, and the Chinese government "uses tourism as a form of 'soft' diplomacy in its dealings with other countries." In particular, Dr Tse notes, the withholding of ADS status was an important political and economic leveraging tool. It has since been noted by some commentators that China continues to exploit the soft power opportunities by encouraging countries to sign bilateral visa-free agreements to avoid losing out in the scramble for its big-spending tourists.

Dr Tse's paper argues that the government also used outbound tourist flows as economic support mechanisms, in particular to Macao after the return of sovereignty in 2009, and to Hong Kong following the economic setbacks after the handover to China in 1997, after which the economy was bolstered in 2003 by the Individual Visit Scheme. Dr Tse also cites South Korea, Sri Lanka, Thailand and the UK as examples of how "the development of Chinese tourism can be seen as a manifestation of positive political relationships," with Chinese tourists being "unofficial diplomats building the soft power base." To benefit, Dr Tse concludes, destinations must learn what Chinese travelers want and "understand the policy and politics at play."

China, outbound tourism and the WTO

China was approved to join the World Trade Organization (WTO) on 11 December 2001, and was duly required to open up much of its economy and integrate it with global commercial-legal mechanisms. Some industries and sectors were opened and some tariffs were reduced more quickly than others, and a spate of trade disputes between China and other WTO member countries surfaced in the ensuing years. The primary result of WTO membership over the past 13 years, however, is that China has become the planet's largest exporter and second-largest economy.

Beyond China, the world became accustomed to – if not always enamored by – the "Made in China" label (even if that often meant "assembled in China using components from other countries"). Consumers gratefully purchased exported items ranging from clothes, car parts and furniture to smartphones, widgets and wheelbarrows at prices considerably lower than they might otherwise have expected.

One requirement of China's WTO accession was the reform of its closeted travel sector. This proved to be a slow process. Wholly Foreign Owned Enterprises (WFOEs) were permitted from 2003 for hotel projects, and some foreign travel companies were entitled to establish joint-venture (JV) travel agencies in Beijing, Guangzhou, Shanghai, Shenzhen, and Xi'an. The Beijing-based *Morning Star* was established in 2001 and American Express teamed up with China International Travel Service (CITS) in 2002. More JV travel agencies focused on corporate travel followed but the licenses did not permit foreign firms to enter China's most coveted tourism sector: outbound leisure travel.

In July 2003, new rules enabled foreign firms to own more than 50 percent of a JV travel agency with a Chinese company provided they met certain conditions: notably registered capital of RMB 4 million for the JV, and the foreign operator needed to prove gross sales of USD 40 million for a JV, or USD 500 million to set up a WFOE. These conditions set the bar high, and enabled only established global players to become involved in the Chinese travel agency sector. Still, foreign participation was excluded from the management of overseas leisure travel.

Six years later, in May 2009, China's State Council and the CNTA adopted the New Regulations on Travel Agencies. This represented a significant revision to previous policy governing foreign investment by permitting the establishment of WFOE travel agencies, lowering the registered capital threshold for establishing a travel agency and lifting the restrictions with regard to establishing branches by foreign-invested travel agencies. Two critical connected elements of China's travel infrastructure remained protected, however: the travel sales distribution network and the management of outbound travel.

Travel agents worldwide rely on a handful of computerized systems that aggregate airline flights, hotel bookings, package tours, cruise trips and other travel services. These networks, called Global Distribution Systems (GDS), were the bedrock of the travel industry in the pre-Internet era. They were used to make all bookings and to maintain stability of pricing – since demand and supply are easy to control through aggregated systems. Travel agents made bookings on behalf of their traveler clients (who did not have access to GDS), thereby ensuring a cozily unimpeachable supply chain.

And then the Internet happened. Online travel agents like Expedia recognized that travelers wanted control over their own bookings and the prices they paid. The advent of independent online travel agencies imperiled the *modus operandi* of the GDS in established markets, although travel agencies still rely on their offerings.

In China, the judicious marshaling of tourism development by Beijing rendered the GDS system central to managing outbound travel. Travel agents and airlines sanctioned to make overseas bookings for clients used the same GDS, operated by a Beijing-based, state-built company (now listed on the Hong Kong Stock Exchange) called TravelSky, which was incorporated in 2000. Overseas package tours booked anywhere in China were processed though TravelSky's centralized computer system.

In 2013, the Civil Aviation Administration of China (CAAC) relaxed the regulations, and a slow, partial change was implemented to license overseas GDS operators, like Singapore-based Abacus and Madrid-headquartered Amadeus, to collaborate with approved Chinese travel agents. Primarily, this enabled the selling of flights offered by foreign airlines, plus hotel bookings and outbound travel services by approved tour operators. Operationally, such situations – which are burdened with caveats like "knowledge transfer" and "technological integration" – are embedded with difficulties in China. Both Abacus and Amadeus had to secure a billing and settlement plan (BSP) certification from the International Air Transport Association (IATA). Neither company was expected to be fully operational until late 2014 at the earliest.

They are entering an arena dominated by TravelSky, an entrenched, well funded and technologically ambitious company, which has benefitted from years of state protection from competition, has the Chinese domestic flight and travel agency booking system tied up, and has entered partnership agreements with some foreign GDS suppliers. TravelSky remains partially owned by the holding companies of Air China, China Eastern Airlines and China Southern Airlines – China's three largest commercial airlines. In recent years, it has established subsidiaries across Asia, plus Europe and the US, and has expanded its services to meet new local and global trends in travel booking. In April 2013, HP Enterprise Services announced it was working with TravelSky to develop a Passenger Services System (PSS) called New Compass.

Liberalization of tourism policy is also attracting new market entrants. In January 2014, German automaker Mercedes-Benz chose Shanghai to unveil its new Mercedes-Benz Travel brand. China is the first location for its foray into the premium travel sector. In partnership with HH Travel, a subsidiary of Ctrip International, it offers "high-grade travel packages focused on fascinating European locations plus unique events." To deliver the trips, Mercedes-Benz has teamed with Eurotours, the largest inbound agency in Central Europe. The target clientele is "travel-loving, sophisticated customers in the Chinese market," according to a company statement.

From Zhengzhou to Luxor: Chinese tourists behaving badly

What is the difference between a "riot" and "chaos"? That may sound a rudimentary vocabulary question, but consider it from the prism in which Chinese travel currently exists. It is a defining trend story of our era, and every aspect is scrutinized and evaluated, particularly the behavior of Chinese holidaymakers.

Speaking with Chinese travelers during the research for this book, contrasting feelings were apparent. The freedom, desire and financial capacity to travel are wholeheartedly embraced. Everyone with whom I spoke enjoys exploring the world beyond Chinese borders, and wants (and plans) to do more of it. But Chinese travelers are implicitly aware of the media spotlight being being shone brightly on them, both in their homeland and worldwide. As with all themes that achieve "breaking story" status, every angle is reported, and those angles are mostly negative.

Let's return to the "riot" versus "chaos" question. In February 2014, heavy snow across China at the end of the Spring Festival holiday caused flight delays and cancellations, reduced train speeds and closed highways at a time when hundreds of millions of people were returning to the cities where they live and work. The enforced closure of Xinzheng airport at Zhengzhou, the capital city of Henan province, was widely reported when up to 2,000 grounded passengers reacted angrily. International media headlined their ensuing actions in late evening as "a riot," while Chinese state media more delicately termed the events – which involved throwing water bottles and smashing bulletin boards and computers – as "a chaos." The English-language edition of state media agency Xinhua reported the events at Zhengzhou in the second part of a travel disruption story focused on the extra 760 trains being deployed to alleviate the snow-related transport difficulties. A difference in emphasis, no doubt, but it would be churlish to argue that the Chinese media does not report negative stories about travel behavior, or just buries them inside other stories.

While newspaper editors worldwide scan the wires daily for Chinese travel stories to amuse and bemuse readers, the media in China also covers tourism stories with a telephoto lens, but it chooses its targets with meticulous care. When a story about poor behavior needs emphasizing, the media does so – usually in an overarching thematic way, rather than focusing on one particular event. Headline-making behavior by Chinese citizens overseas tends to be portrayed in terms of a collective national, rather than personalized, reaction. The Chinese media is not tasked with sparking outrage since it is tied to the government's vision of a "Harmonious Society." Examining stories about Chinese travel behavior must be approached within that paradigm.

Overseas comportment is a hot issue. Speaking to Chinese friends, a common comment is "many Chinese travelers aren't very sophisticated yet." The "yet" rejoinder suggests an educative timeline – that a large proportion of Chinese tourists have minimal or no experience of the outside world, and are still learning about international travel and foreign cultures. Many found their feet through the security of a package tour – and group travel, by any definition, is often accompanied by insular, inwardly focused behavior. Relentless price bargaining in stores, loudness in restaurants and hotel lounges, line jumping, and brusquely barging for photo opportunities in front of famous landmarks and store logos are commonly lodged criticisms.

The most notorious recent story was the graffiti etched on an ancient Egyptian temple at Luxor by a Chinese teenager from Nanjing. The phrase "Ding Jinhao was here" was portrayed, in China and beyond, as the epitome of disrespect by a Chinese tourist. Graffiti at domestic tourism sites in China, particularly the Great Wall of China, had been a rising controversy for some years – to the extent that tourism officials have considered introducing electronic graffiti boards – but the personal name-carving on foreign soil resulted in angry postings on Chinese social media. Netizens decried the boy's thoughtless actions as harming the nation's international reputation. Chinese media weighed into the debate, and for several months in 2013 the issue challenged many of the underlying precepts of the Chinese Dream.

Other behavioral examples sparking ire included two Chinese passengers fighting on a flight from Beijing to Zurich resulting in the plane being forced to return, swimmers in Hainan taking photos beside a dying dolphin, and allegations that Chinese touts were selling counterfeit tickets to Chinese visitors outside the Louvre in Paris. Numerous articles were also being published, both in Hong Kong and in China, about the disrespectful attitude of some Chinese visitors on shopping and sightseeing tours to Hong Kong.

Such coverage precipitated mutterings of the phrase "Ugly Chinese," which was used in a similar context to the predecessor "Ugly American" and "Ugly Japanese" tags. Both had entered the travel lexicon in previous decades to describe American and Japanese travelers who were tagged for their boorish behavior and dismissive attitudes. Such media labeling is easy to apply – but less easy to remove. In a country that is only beginning to establish its role on the international stage, the negative connotations being attached to Chinese tourism were troubling.

In 2013, the issue of tourist behavior had consumed public debate to such an extent that Chinese vice premier, Wang Yang, made a speech imploring that "improving the civilized quality of citizens" would help "build a good image" for China beyond its borders. Such a direct statement from a senior leader implied two things. Firstly, the government was sufficiently concerned about the preservation of its coveted harmonious society to make the actions of Chinese travelers an on-the-record issue of public order. Secondly, some form of governmental intervention was pending.

Legislating for more harmonious tourism

China's leaders had hitherto been dealing with more pressing developmental issues in the powerhouse sectors of banking, manufacturing, construction, shipping, and real estate – plus managing the 2008 Olympics in Beijing and 2010 World Expo in Shanghai and attempting to reduce endemic corruption at local governmental level. So, being a relatively new industry, Chinese tourism had not previously been a subject of political discourse.

But as China's growth rate began to slow, and with a stated objective of moving China's economy towards a more self-sustaining platform, tourism assumed greater importance. Planning for the previously disparate sectors of inbound, outbound and domestic tourism began to overlap, forming a developmental Venn diagram.

The origins of these connective nodes can be traced back to late 2002, when Shanghai secured the right to host the 2010 World Expo. Ostensibly, the billions of dollars invested in urban infrastructure and transportation projects enabled China to showcase Shanghai as its most globalized city, but the six-month Expo also served another purpose. It brought the world to Shanghai, in the full knowledge that the more than 180 participating nations would spend heavily to educate, enchant and intrigue the 73 million mostly Chinese visitors about their destinations, cultures and cuisines.

That's exactly what happened. Governments from around the world hired star-name architects to design eye-catching national pavilions filled with historic treasures, video imagery of tourism attractions and freebie giveaways of local delicacies and handicrafts. Some nations flew in celebrity chefs, fashion designers and sports stars to greet the Chinese media and local consumers. Essentially, the 2010 Shanghai World Expo was the largest tourism exhibition in history – and its single target was the new Chinese traveler.

There were other tangible benefits, too. Myriad trade and commercial contracts were signed, a multitude of political leaders and VIPs were snapped with broad grins in Shanghai, and the city's ambition to become a global financial center by 2020 was relentlessly communicated. The global showcase also eased open the gates at Shanghai's two upgraded and expanded airports – with a slew of new flight routes announced in the following months to connect China's most international city with the world. A drip-down effect was the desired result, with increasing affluence encouraging urbanites from Nanjing to Nanning to Ningbo to covet similar outbound travel opportunities as the Shanghainese.

By 2013, Chinese outbound travel had acquired such momentum that it was now a policy issue at the highest level. In April of that year, President Xi Jinping stated during his keynote speech at the Boao Forum for Asia that China would most likely export more than 400 million tourists in the next five years. This unexpected statement was the first time a Chinese leader had publicly spoken in such clear terms about outbound tourism – a surefire confirmation of its economic and social significance.

Consequently, it was no surprise when, on 1 October 2013, the Chinese government implemented the heavily signposted Tourism Law of the People's Republic of China, which had been approved on 25 April 2013 at the 12th National People's Congress.

The timing was assured, coinciding with the China National Day Golden Week holiday that commemorates the 1949 founding by Mao Zedong of the People's Republic of China. It also marks China's largest annual travel exodus. The new law was a clear statement to tour operators, travel agencies and outbound vacationers that the government was stepping up its regulation of the tourism sector, which is considered a central tenet of efforts to direct more sustained consumer input into the nation's economic growth.

In anticipation of the new Chinese Tourism Law, state-run China Central Television (CCTV) broadcast videos promoting etiquette for overseas travelers. This followed a similar slew of broadcasts and public notices in 2008, ahead of the Beijing Olympics, whereby residents in the capital and other co-host cities were exhorted to queue in an orderly manner in shops and on public transport and not to spit in public areas.

China's Tourism Law in brief

The 112 articles of the Tourism Law – the stated objective of which is to "protect the legitimate rights and interests of the tourists and tourism operators [and] regulate the order of the tourism market" – are broad-ranging and address strategic issues related to inbound, domestic and outbound travel.

With regard to outbound travel, a new regulatory framework tightened licensing procedures for tour operators and online travel agencies, clearly stated the operational rules for tour agencies and tour guides, improved the transparency of travel agency marketing and promotions, and imposed certification requirements for outbound tour guides.

Clauses were included regarding tour operators' liabilities towards their clients, a mechanism was created for dispute mediation and litigation, and a scale of fines was introduced for travel agencies and tour operators that transgress the law. To support the new regulations, a liability insurance system was announced for travel agencies, accommodation and tourism transport service providers and the operators of high-risk tourism activities, officially defined as "those conducted high up in the sky, at a high speed, or on the water, diving, adventure, etc."

In addition, the Tourism Law shifted a degree of personal responsibility onto Chinese travelers. Contractual agreements between travel agencies and tourists, stipulating the rights and responsibilities of both parties, were clarified, and the law stipulated that Chinese travelers should purchase their own travel insurance rather than rely on a travel agency to buy it on their behalf.

The three articles garnering most attention were numbers 9, 13 and 35.

- Article 13 was essentially a statement on international behavior. "Tourists shall observe public order and respect social morality in tourism activities, respect local customs, cultural traditions and religious beliefs, care for tourism resources, protect the ecological environment, and abide by the norms of civilized tourist behaviors." This was a clear response to the embarrassment felt by the Chinese government at the tide of coverage highlighting uncivilized behavior by Chinese travelers. A 48-page booklet defining tourism responsibilities supported a public education program.
- Article 9 states that "Tourists shall be entitled to select tourism products and services independently and refuse coercive trade behaviors of tourism operators." It notes that the products and services provided by a travel agency and/or tour operator must be clearly stated in a contract, and that the travel provider must not undertake "hidden" activities that are designed to glean more revenue from travelers.
- Article 35 reiterates this fact, stating that "Travel agencies are prohibited from organizing tourism activities and luring tourists with unreasonably low prices, or getting illegitimate gains such as rebates by arranging shopping or providing tourism services that require additional payment. When organizing and receiving tourists, travel agencies shall not designate specific shopping places, or provide tourism services that require additional payment."

Chinese package tour travelers had increasingly complained – most notably in shopping tourism destinations like Hong Kong, but also within China – of being coerced into spending large amounts of money at shopping outlets selected by unscrupulous tour operators who received generous commissions for delivering tour groups to shop there.

This practice had become widespread, and was a vociferously discussed *bête noir* of the Chinese media during 2011 and 2012. It also provided a conundrum for the government, as Chinese tourists had become accustomed to cheap package tours. It was decided that the only viable option for rebalancing the relationship between tour providers and consumers was to outlaw the practice. Greater transparency would result in raised prices for packaged tour trips, but the trade-off was that tour agencies would be compelled to improve the quality of tourism products and services being offered.

In recognition that curtailing the practice of shopping excursions that do not appear on travel itineraries would be tricky in the short term, the Tourism Law stated that tourists who felt their travel operator had violated their legal rights would have a 30-day post-trip period to "require the travel agency to return their purchases and pay the price of the returned purchases on behalf in advance, or refund the payment made for tourism services that require additional payment."

After the new law

The immediate result of the new law was a decline in the volume of package travelers, as tour operators raised prices to recoup the shortfall from shopping center commissions. Media reports noted that popular destinations for Chinese group travelers, such as South Korea, Taiwan and Thailand, experienced a notable decrease in Chinese arrivals during the 2013 October Golden Week compared to the previous year. Bangkok's Don Mueang Airport, which offers numerous low-cost flight connections with Chinese cities, reportedly experienced a 30 percent drop in Chinese visitors in October. Macao received 526,600 mainland Chinese package tourists in October 2013, 10.6 percent fewer than in the same 2012 period.

As Chinese group tourists reconsidered the value of packaged tour products, the price differentiation between group travel and self-planned free independent travel (FIT) was reduced. The government's long-term objective was to recalibrate China's travel infrastructure, not just influence ambassadorial behavior. The legislation sought to drive the tourism industry to become more market-focused, efficient and transparent, so that consumers have a clear choice when deciding the pricing, booking process, travel format and itinerary of their trip.

Viewed from the outside, Chinese government regulation of travel and tourism may appear overly prescriptive. Consumers in most parts of the global travel economy have become accustomed to the deregulation of airlines, a varying level of "open skies" agreements, the diminution of the "flag" carrier concept, the emergence of privately funded low-cost carriers and relatively open markets for travel agencies and tour operators. The core precept of tourism – enhanced by the Internet – is the personal freedom to explore and experience new destinations, landscapes and cultures.

But, as this chapter has discussed, outbound tourism is an infant industry in China – a country in which economic matters are controlled, to greater or lesser degree, from the center, with the provincial capitals incentivized to manage policies and regulations. Lest we forget, China still manages its economy around five-year national plans.

Consequently, patterns of travel are still settling into place. Indeed, the rising volume of consumers empowered to travel may mean that China's outbound market will remain highly fragmented for several years. Trend watchers and researchers are now monitoring spending patterns in New Urban China to discern how the much-discussed shift from purchasing products to buying travel experiences will be realized. The expectation is that the greater the proportion of future travelers heralding from beyond Beijing, Chengdu, Guangzhou, Shanghai, and Shenzhen – which powered the tourism industry's formative growth – the higher the potential for further fragmentation and the emergence of newer niche travel segments.

Issues that harm Chinese tourism

As China's fragmented tourism sector continues to grow, a new narrative thread has emerged that illustrates the surging value of Chinese spending to international destinations, governments and their national economies. Here are a few recent examples of "issues that harm Chinese tourism":

- Diplomatic relations and economic ties between China and Norway took a nosedive in 2010 when Chinese activist Lu Xiaobo

was awarded the Nobel Peace Prize, which is administered via a parliamentary committee in Oslo. China argued that it represented foreign interference in its internal affairs.
- Airbus saw aircraft orders disrupted in 2012 following a strengthening of the EU's proposed Emissions Trading Scheme, which sought to charge airlines for carbon emissions. China was not alone in its anger – many non-EU nations, including Russia and the US, were similarly displeased.
- In Japan, strained relations between Japan and China over the disputed Diaoyu/Senkaku Islands were blamed in the Japanese media for a 27 percent shortfall of Chinese visitors in the first half of 2013.
- In the Philippines, media reports suggested Chinese visitation was reduced by as much as 70 percent during certain months of 2013 following heightened political tensions between the two countries.
- In 2013, Chinese media took exception to a decision by Canada to cancel two initiatives – the Immigrant Investor Programme and the Federal Entrepreneur Programme – that awarded visas to foreign investors who met minimum net-worth and investment criteria.
- In early 2014, Chinese media reported that political turmoil in Thailand had caused Chinese airlines to cancel flights before and after the Spring Festival holiday.
- In the UK in June 2014, the government bowed to lobbying pressure from tourism groups, retailers and Chinese investors who argued that the restrictive visa policy prevented more Chinese tourists from visiting and was damaging the economy.
- In 2014, Malaysia witnessed an inbound decline following criticism in China of its handling of the disappearance of Malaysia Airlines flight MH370, and the kidnapping of Chinese nationals in Sabah.
- Also in 2014, violent anti-China protests in Vietnam resulted in the Chinese government issuing a travel warning about potential security concerns.
- In China itself, high levels of air pollution were cited as a reason for the 2013 decrease of both domestic and international visitation to the capital, Beijing.

Chapter 2
Going Global: China's New Travel Class Spreads Its Wings

A short discussion of the emerging "travel class"

One liberally peppered phrase dominates the discussion about China's travel revolution: "the expanding middle class." It's rare to read anything on the subject, either in China or elsewhere, without this frequently undefined social categorization, about which estimates and projections differ greatly.

Defining the Chinese middle class – which the government hopes will help elevate the economy into an exalted sphere of domestic consumption, and reduce the reliance on export manufacturing and state capital investment – is open to broad interpretation. Even trying to classify a "travel class," loosely comprised of Chinese Dreamers with the disposable income to experience overseas travel is maddeningly elusive, as in Chinese official calculations this encompasses a vast spectrum, from cross-border shoppers on day trips to Hong Kong or Macao to luxury mavens spending in the lavish manner of Hollywood movie star in the Maldives.

When discussing tourism potential, population size is, of course, a useful factor. Yet, China is an inordinately complex country, whose physical proportions are continental and whose population accounts for around one-fifth of humanity. The margin between "potential" and "reality" – especially in a nation where the pace of economic development varies notably from province to province, and city to city – can be considerable. The last official measure of China's population was the 2010 census, at which time the world's most-populous country counted 1,339.72 million people. Four years later, it is estimated to have topped 1.4 billion.

Even if we accept the premise that urban populations drive outbound tourism, we still have to take a few leaps of faith. Research by McKinsey & Company (*Meet the 2020 Chinese Consumer*, March 2012) suggests 57 percent of urban households in China will earn more than USD 16,000 per year by 2020, up from eight percent in 2010. The geographic dispersion of wealth is likely to spread, however. The McKinsey report notes that around 85 percent of mainstream Chinese consumers currently live in the top 100 wealthiest cities. "Another 10 percent of mainstream consumers live in the next 300 cities today, but this percentage will swell to nearly 30 percent by 2020."

JLL, which specializes in commercial real estate services and investment management, notes in its report *China 50: Fifty Real Estate Markets That Matter* (March 2012), that in addition to the four tier-one cities of Beijing, Guangzhou, Shanghai, and Shenzhen, nine other cities had decoupled themselves in economic development terms from the chasing pack. JLL defines these nine – Chengdu, Chongqing, Dalian, Hangzhou, Nanjing, Shenyang, Suzhou, Tianjin and Wuhan – as transitional tier-1.5 cities. Urbanites in these cities are now coveted by hoteliers, airlines and tourism boards, and are considered driving forces of outbound growth. They are not alone, however.

The Organization for Economic Cooperation and Development (OECD) noted in its report *The People's Republic of China – Avoiding The Middle-Income Trap: Policies For Sustained And Inclusive Growth* (September 2013), that by 2012, three Chinese municipalities had already transitioned from the middle- to high-income level (defined as having GDP per capita of USD$12,500 at 2011 prices). Furthermore, the OECD argues, if China's targeted growth rates are achieved, 260 million people will be living in high-income provinces by 2015. If the same growth rate is maintained until 2020, one billion people will be living in high-income areas.

The OECD's figure may seem optimistic, but as long-time China analyst Matthew Crabbe writes in his excellent book, *Myth-Busting China's Numbers*, the varying estimates promulgated for China's middle class population are not necessarily wrong, rather that "the situation is changing so fast that it is hard to be accurate."

Similarly, being defined as middle class in China does not necessarily equate to a uniformity of behavior, or even spending power. Crabbe notes with reference to the expansion of consumer products companies into China's lower-tier cities, that the main problem for understanding purchasing power and patterns is sheer diversity. "China is not one market, but a collection of regional markets, each with very distinct characteristics," Crabbe says. This analysis is equally relevant for tourism planners.

Significant wealth resides beyond the obvious locations. Forbes Asia's 2013 China's 100 Richest List, for instance, revealed that 51 percent of the nation's wealthiest individuals lived in the "first tier" mainland cities of Beijing, Shanghai, Guangzhou and Shenzhen, plus Hong Kong. The remaining 49 percent of China's super wealthy lived across 34 cities, ranging from Urumqi in the far west to Wenzhou on the east coast, and Shijiazhuang in Hebei province to Zhuhai in the southern industrial heartlands.

While the purpose of the Forbes survey is to put names and faces to China's commercial and financial elite, the subtext is intriguing. Entrepreneurs, real estate developers and industrialists – who comprise the majority of the Rich List – are, by definition, job creators, and their businesses are contributing to rising urban affluence across China, which, in turn, provides the cash to travel.

When do the Chinese travel?

This is an increasingly difficult question to answer. Since 1999, the Chinese government has mandated the annual holiday entitlement for all workers. The public holiday schedule, which is based around two (formerly three) "Golden Week" vacations, was implemented to ensure that workers actually receive days off, and to stimulate domestic consumer spending. It later became the framework around which overseas travel has been built.

Modified annually, China's public holiday policy is complicated, and requires a large element of give and take. Chinese workers must make up for the extended Golden Week holidays – which are the busiest periods for both the domestic and outbound tourism markets – by working during the weekends before and afterwards. The figures, though, are eye-watering: Chinese tourists made around 428 million domestic and international trips during the October 2013 Golden Week.

- The dates of China's 2014 public holidays were announced in December 2013. The schedule featured two seven-day Golden Week holidays – Spring Festival, from 31 January to 6 February, and China National Day, from 1 to 7 October. The third Golden Week, for the May Day holiday, was scrapped in 2008, and those days off were distributed to create more shorter holidays throughout the year.
- Beyond the main weeks, other holidays include New Year on 1 January, Tomb Sweeping Day, Labour Day, Mid-Autumn Festival and the Dragon Boat Festival.
- In 2014, extra flexibility was built in to enable long-weekend holidays; for example, if a public holiday falls on a Tuesday, the previous Monday becomes a day off, likewise, if the holiday falls on a Thursday, the Friday is also incorporated.
- For the first time in a Golden Week, Chinese international travelers during the 2014 Spring Festival exceeded the number visiting Hong Kong, Macao and Taiwan, according to the China Tourism Academy. Some 39.3 percent of outbound mainlanders headed abroad compared to 35.4 percent who visited Hong Kong, Macao and Taiwan.

Ongoing diversification in Chinese travel means that important segments not adhering to official public holidays – such as students and new graduates, retirees, affluent entrepreneurs and business owners, the super wealthy, including heirs and heiresses to large fortunes (the infamous, much-discussed Little Emperors), and the rapidly expanding travel media – are traveling all year round. Christmas and New Year, too, are gaining traction with younger travelers, while new drivers such as weddings and honeymoon travel, medical tourism, visiting family and friends living or studying overseas, and travel niches determined by seasonal factors, such as winter sports, island vacations and sailing, increasingly influence the time of travel. Employees of foreign companies and Chinese multinationals usually receive a holiday allowance in addition to state mandated vacations.

Corporate travel patterns are also changing. Hoteliers and airlines in China and worldwide have long noted that business travel slows dramatically in the weeks before and immediately after the Golden Weeks. Some business travelers are now extending overseas trips to add leisure vacation time with family and friends.

China's Golden Week-based vacation system has become a victim of its own success. Implemented at a time when the government wanted to encourage more Chinese to travel and spend, the officially sanctioned rest periods served a distinct purpose. Limiting such spending to two periods per year has since generated frictions. Rising incomes have raised the propensity and desire to travel, and as a result, airports, roads, train stations, hotels and tourism sites are overloaded before, during and after each Golden Week, and prices for flight tickets and travel packages inflate considerably.

Indeed, when the 2014 Spring Festival travel migration kicked off during the second week of January 2014, state media published photos of be-suited staff at China's official train ticket booking website kicking a punch-bag in the company canteen to relieve stress. Train bookers had flooded telephone lines to complain after the website repeatedly stalled due to oversubscribed demand. In addition, newspapers reported on ticket scalpers selling overpriced and counterfeit tickets to passengers desperate to get home to spend the holidays with their families.

Some analysts argue that the growing unpopularity of official holidays is creating a sense of "travel turn-off," and that a more evenly distributed annual leave entitlement would result in greater economic value. Freed from the time and capacity constraints, high prices and long queues that hallmark each Golden Week, Chinese travelers would likely travel more frequently and spend more tourism RMB throughout the year. This argument is possibly true for domestic travel, but the travel crush is likely to push rather than curtail outbound travel during the major holidays, and staggered travel times are increasingly evident.

The Chinese public covets a more flexible annual leave system, and this is being reflected in media coverage. An online survey by the China National Tourism Administration (CNTA) in 2013 revealed that 60 percent of interviewees wanted the National Day Golden Week to be abolished. The government recognizes that a new policy approach is needed. In February 2013, the State Council indicated that China would establish a form of paid annual leave system by 2020.

As in most nations, the Chinese school summer holidays are also popular for travel, particularly to destinations close to home, such as Hong Kong, Hainan Island, Macao and Taiwan. Chinese visits to South Korea increased 52.5 percent year on year in 2013, to 4.32 million – or 35.5 percent of Korea's total inbound arrivals.

A likely trend in the coming years is greater overseas travel during the Spring Festival, which is traditionally a holiday spent with family. A record 4.5 million Chinese are estimated to have traveled outbound during the 2014 Spring Festival, a rise of 12.5 percent from 2013, according to the CNTA. Two key factors could boost travel during this time; firstly, the "splitting" of the Golden Week into two parts so that the Chinese New Year is spent with family and the remainder is used for overseas travel; and secondly, a predicted increase in family travel, whereby more extended families may spend the holidays together outside of China.

And consider this; official figures from the CNTA claim 231 million tourists – roughly equivalent to the combined populations of Belgium, France, Germany, the Netherlands, Portugal and Spain – traveled domestically in China during the 2014 Spring Festival. If just five percent of that total decided to travel overseas during the 2015 Spring

Festival, that would mean an extra 11.5 million Chinese holidaymakers – about the same as the population of Greece – traversing the globe for a week in mid-February.

Another trend to watch is intra-Asian long-weekend travel. New flight connections to resort destinations are providing extra options for time-restricted Chinese travelers. Bali could be a likely beneficiary: "The recently launched direct flights will definitely make Bali more accessible, and perhaps Bali will evolve to become more of a weekend destination for our Chinese guests," says Doris Goh, Vice President, Sales and Marketing of Alila Hotels and Resorts.

What do Chinese travelers like to eat?

This is another tricky question. Chinese travelers span a sprawling constituency, and the image of Chinese tour groups eating all meals in local Chinese restaurants is outdated. That's not to say the Chinese do not share a predilection for the cuisines of their home country. They do. But misconceptions exist about "Chinese food," since it is not a singular concept. China's continental landscape and diverse climactic conditions mean that food preparation and consumption differ greatly not just between regions or provinces, but also within cities.

As a basic definition, there are eight recognized schools of Chinese cuisine, ranging from the peppery hotpots and spicy stews of Sichuan province to the double-boiled soups and seafood dishes of Cantonese cooking. The other six schools are loosely comprised of the culinary traditions from Anhui, Fujian, Hunan, Jiangsu, Shandong and Zhejiang provinces.

Cantonese immigrants owned a large proportion of the Chinese restaurants that opened across Europe and North America in the 1980s, although the dishes served were heavily adapted to local tastes. Visitors from Chengdu, Shenyang and Guiyang would find the food served totally alien, while visitors from Guangzhou would shake their head at the globalization of a cuisine revered in China as the finest of its creed.

Chinese diners have also become accustomed to a transformed culinary landscape, particularly in the major cities. Global brands and foreign restaurateurs are evident on major streets and in shopping malls. The fast-food chains, such as KFC, Pizza Hut and McDonald's, led the charge, followed by coffee-and-muffin purveyors, like Starbucks and Costa Coffee, which wants expand its store total in China to 700 by 2017. Having saturated the major cities, these brands are now growing their presence in second-, third- and fourth-tier cities. In Shanghai, small foreign-owned chains, such as Wagas and Element Fresh, serving coffees, salads, pastas and juices have grown and expanded to Beijing, Guangzhou and Nanjing. Quick-meal chains created by Chinese and Taiwanese companies, including Little Sheep, Dicos, Yonghe King and Kung Fu, have enlarged their market shares.

Further up the chain, M on the Bund became a touchstone for sophisticated international dining when it opened in a grand mansion beside the Shanghai riverfront in 1999, and in 2008 opened a sibling restaurant overlooking Beijing's Tiananmen Square. As China's palate began to crave fancier fare, vaunted chef-restaurateurs, like Daniel Boulud and Nobu (both in Beijing) and Jean Georges Vongerichten and Jason Atherton (both in Shanghai) opened restaurants, while Umberto Bombana, who earned three Michelin stars in Hong Kong (at the end of 2013, no Michelin restaurant guide had been published in mainland China) expanded to Shanghai and Beijing.

Further evidence of the qualitative shift in international dining in China was provided by the 2014 Asia's 50 Best Restaurants poll of industry experts. Nine restaurants from Hong Kong, one from Macao, five from Shanghai and one in Hangzhou made the list. The highest placed China restaurant (ranked eighth) was Paul Pairet's Ultraviolet in Shanghai, which serves a 20-course set menu – including a foie gras cigarillo dipped in cabbage ash – accompanied by kaleidoscopic wall projections, scent diffusions and surround sounds to evoke the ingredients and flavors.

Expansion overseas is also on the menu. In 2013, Hong Kong's Bo Innovation (ranked 15th on the 2014 Asia's 50 Best Restaurants list), which serves what its Michelin-starred chef Alvin Leung describes as

"X-treme Chinese" cooking – including creations such as cured mackerel, compressed cucumber, black sesame, "chin kiang" vinegar and rose mist – opened a branch in London.

Discerning diners worldwide enjoy pairing fine dining with good wines, and China is no exception. Figures from Vinexpo, the international wine and spirits exhibition, revealed China is now the world's largest consumer of red wine. Some 3,388 Chinese wine professionals attended the 2013 Vinexpo show, more than any other nation except France. Vinexpo has launched satellite editions in Hong Kong, Beijing and Tokyo. Myriad wine-pairing dinners are also hosted by the world's top wineries at China's leading restaurants. In 2014, Robert Parker's Wine Advocate dinners visited three venues in Beijing and Shanghai, with upscale catering for each event provided by Beijing-based Brian McKenna @ The Courtyard.

As would be expected in any major international city, diners in Shanghai, Beijing, Guangzhou or Shenzhen can now choose from Thai, Indian, Italian, French, Spanish, Japanese, Korean, Mexican, American Steakhouse and Middle Eastern cuisines, plus restaurants serving local dishes from across China. Beyond the first-tier trendsetters, the dining scenes in fast-developing cities like Chengdu, Hangzhou, Nanjing, Suzhou, Tianjin and Xiamen are also diversifying at a frantic clip.

Restaurant owners and chefs are paying heed to the influence of Chinese online and mobile dining review website Dianping.com which counts upwards of 75 million active users. Founded in 2003 in Shanghai, Dianping has been coveted by all of China's major online conglomerates, and in 2013 sold a stake to Tencent, owner of social media network WeChat. This highlighted the importance of social media as another crucial marketing platform for restaurants in China, given the preference by local diners for posting real-time photos of dishes particularly in new restaurants. The widening geographical spread of Chinese travel will further influence the flavors and dining trends travelers seek upon returning from vacation.

"About 85 percent of our clientele is Chinese. This has grown much faster than we anticipated, and we now have a lot of repeat Chinese visitors," says Belgian-born Ignace Lecleir, who managed restaurants in New York and Beijing for Michelin-starred French chef and restaurateur Daniel

Boulud before founding Temple Restaurant Beijing (TRB) in 2011. Located in an ancient temple complex in a *hutong* district northeast of the Forbidden City, TRB's frequently evolving international brasserie menu – with dishes including suckling pig, pumpkin puree, brussel sprouts, bacon and maple shallot glace – excellent wine list and sleek, minimalist interiors have made it a darling of the Beijing dining scene.

"Chinese diners are very curious, and willing to try new dishes," says Lecleir. "I think they also like that this is a sophisticated dining venue, but not too upscale. Couples or business groups can linger over dinner and enjoy the wines but it is also semi-casual dining. This relaxed approach to good food has been a growing trend in cities like New York and London, and it has proved successful also here in Beijing."

Innovative homegrown restaurant Hai Di Lao from Sichuan was founded in 1994 and serves classic Sichuan-style hotpot, whereby diners gather around a shared pot of spicy broth and cook their chosen raw ingredients. There are 73 branches in China and Singapore and long queues for tables, but instead of this being a turn-off, it has become its own attraction. A large section at each colorful restaurant is set aside as a waiting area, where patrons can play backgammon, surf the Internet with free Wi-Fi, have their shoes polished and get a manicure – all on the house. Complimentary snacks and drinks are also served in an ambience akin to a fairground. Service is excellent throughout the meal, too. You even get iPhone-sized ziplock bags with screen cleaners provided at the table, so your phone won't get spattered during the meal.

Online shopping is helping to internationalize dining in China. Alibaba's Tmall e-commerce platform worked with the US Department of Agriculture to offer prized Alaskan seafood to Chinese netizens. The menu has since expanded, with seasonal promotions including Chilean blueberries, New Zealand lamb and lobsters from Canada. Tmall says one of the reasons for its success is that it provides a platform for global food producers to reach millions of consumers in second- and third-tier Chinese cities that do not have high-end supermarkets selling imported foods.

Beyond the homeland, Chinese travelers are eager to discover more about the world's gourmet dining and wine cultures. Bespoke tour operators and upscale hotels are beginning to offer gastronomy-themed tours and activities for Chinese guests, with opportunities to meet celebrated local chefs, gourmet food producers, organic farmers and vineyard owners. Cooking schools in France, Italy and northern Spain and wineries in Burgundy, Bordeaux, Champagne and Tuscany are welcoming ever more Chinese visitors, as are those in "New World" destinations like Australia, New Zealand, Argentina and Chile, and Michelin-starred restaurants worldwide.

Overseas cooking shows are popular on Chinese TV. In early 2014, *Taste South East Asia* featuring the different cuisines from ten countries of ASEAN ran for 30 episodes across two seasons on CCTV 9. A press release from ASEAN Tourism claimed each episode "had a TV audience of about 100 million per episode."

Where do Chinese travelers want to go?

Patsy Yang, Shanghai-based fashion journalist and luxury brand consultant

"My first trip was to Hong Kong when I was in university. After that, in my early 20s, I explored Southeast Asia, initially visiting Singapore, Thailand and Indonesia."

Since then, she has traveled extensively for work and pleasure, with Rajasthan in India, Myanmar and Italy being favorite places. "Chinese people tend to be hesitant about India due to hygiene concerns and the travel preparations required. I loved it. The service is good in high-end hotels and restaurants, but the people are the best part. They are genuinely welcoming and smiling. Rajasthan is colorful and traditional and you can take beautiful pictures. The architecture is amazing and well protected in an organic way. You can touch and live amongst history in the palaces."

Favorite Myanmar experiences included the ancient ruins at Bagan, "much more mesmerizing than Angkor Wat, which is too commercial and crowded," and the beaches – "We ate a full table of crab, lobster and fresh seafood for about RMB100 each. I almost fell off my chair when

I saw the prices." As for Italy: "The people are beautiful, everything is beautiful. It's a small country but very diverse and the food is fantastic. I really like the seaside at Puglia. Not many Asians go there yet, so you can relax and travel more like a local."

Travel plans usually emanate from "an idea in my mind, then I'll research the specifics online or through friends' recommendations. It's very spontaneous. Most of all, I want to experience the lifestyle like a local and try the most authentic foods and traditions. I don't like to sightsee like a tourist. I avoid the "must-go" landmarks. For example, I didn't see the Taj Mahal."

As for a dream destination: "Tanzania, because I love animals and grand landscapes. Africa is far away and more difficult to organize, and I have to find the right person to go with me."

Johnny Chang, CEO and Founder, Spa Solutions

"My first trip was to Perth in 1986. I later lived in Australia for six years. I travel regularly for work and pleasure, and took around 20 trips in 2013, including Hong Kong, Cambodia, Malaysia, Bali and Australia."

Australia retains a strong affection. "I love its fresh air, blue skies, clean water and natural scenery. Like many Chinese, I'm a city person but I like to enjoy natural scenery. I don't want to swim in the ocean, but I love looking at it from the Versace Hotel on the Gold Coast."

Bali for "its beautiful hotels and service style, at prices that are much cheaper than China," and Hong Kong: "it's always amazing from the time you land to the time you depart. It's refreshing to get away from the mainland from time to time" are other favored destinations.

The key inspiration for traveling is to gain knowledge and develop new opinions. "These are enriching things that money cannot buy. I also love to swim but it's not pleasant to swim in China so I always choose a hotel with a nice swimming pool. I'm afraid to swim in the ocean, except in the protected waters at the northern tip of Borneo. Being in the spa industry, spa is an important activity for me. A really good spa can make guests stay at least an extra night by a factor of 40 percent."

A distinct change in service attitudes has been noticed. "Five years ago, I visited Uluwatu, Bali and was impressed by the quality of service at two of the best resorts there. Recently, I returned and found them overrun by Chinese travelers, and the service attitude was dismissive and abrupt. My partner and I had a spa treatment and then lunch in the resort restaurant. The first thing we were told as we arrived was "there's a minimum charge to eat here." This is not the type of service you would expect from this standard of resort, and these brands need to be careful as word travels fast and they'll quickly lose favour with high-end Chinese travelers."

Dream future destinations: "South America and Marrakech."

Vicky Wang Yanli, China Regional Manager for an educational institute

"My first overseas travel was in 2004 to Hanoi in Vietnam for a business trip. I traveled on four occasions in 2013. When traveling, I want to enjoy great nature, food, unique culture and history. Activity-wise, I like hiking or walking trips and in the past two years, I have also got into the habit of visiting an art museum in cities I visit."

Favorite destinations are Kyoto, Nice and Florence. "I visited Kyoto twice in 2012, and it is my favorite city since it felt like seeing and experiencing Tang Dynasty China right there around me. It is so elegant, and the scenery, history, culture and food are fabulous, I felt like could live there from the moment I arrived." Nice gets a thumbs-up for its "relaxed atmosphere, nice beach and great food," while Florence has "fascinating history, great architecture, great food and interesting local people."

The planning and research of overseas trips is mostly done online. "I use Qiongyou (穷游) a lot. I've booked hotels with booking.com many times, and once with Agoda. For flights, I often book through the airline's website."

When it comes to a dream destination, several places spring immediately to mind. "Right now, the top ones on my list are South Korea, for the food and because I love the language and watch a lot of Korean TV shows. Spain, for the culture and history, great scenery, and beaches. I took Salsa lessons and want to see a *flamenco* performance. Sweden and Denmark, for the lifestyle and general attitude to life. The company I've been working for more than 10 years is Swedish. I would also like to visit Nepal for a hiking trip, plus New Zealand, Greece, India and Madagascar."

Cotton Ding, Owner, Cotton's Bar, Shanghai

"My first overseas trip was in 2005 to visit my business partner in Switzerland. My first solo adventure was to Argentina for a month in 2010. I generally take one big trip lasting around two months during the winter, as the other times of the year are way too busy. In 2013, I went to Singapore, Indonesia and Malaysia.

The favorite trip so far is the one taken in 2014 to Colombia, Cuba and Paris. "I love the diversity of the landscapes, the culture, history and people. How they all blend together is just amazing."

Important vacation activities are related to specific locations. "I'll try pretty much everything. It depends on my destination, but I have enjoyed Inca trekking in Peru, tango dancing in Argentina, surfing in Malaysia, playing ping-pong in Cuba, paragliding in Colombia, horseback riding whenever I can find a horse."

Planning for a trip and setting a budget are important aspects of traveling. "I book my flight tickets and first four days' hotel accommodation, and the rest I will just go with the flow. I find TripAdvisor really helpful. I like to stay in bed & breakfasts, as it gives me a feeling of home and nice contacts with local life wherever I travel.

And a dream destination: "Istanbul, Barcelona and Italy. I've heard so much about them, and every day I have not been there they become more and more enchanting."

Students of the world

Studying overseas has contributed significantly to Chinese outbound tourism, both by the students themselves and from visiting families and friends. Here are four of the leading destinations for Chinese overseas study:

Australia

In 2011, 97,423 Chinese enrollments were noted by the IIE, up from 56,603 in 2008. In 2012, 149,758 (or 26.4 percent) of the 515,853 enrolments by fee-paying international students in Australia were from China, according to the Australian Government – more than double the second ranked country, India.

Canada

The number of Chinese students in Canada jumped from 20,371 in 2001 to 80,627 in 2012, an increase of 296 percent increase, according to the Canadian Bureau for International Education.

UK

China is the leading sender of overseas students to the UK, with 78,715 enrollments – or 26 percent out of all non-EU students – in 2011/12 (up from 67,325 in 2010/11), according to the UK Council for International Student Affairs.

US

In the 2012/13 academic year, 235,597 Chinese students contributed US$22 billion in tuition and living expenses, according to the Institute of International Education (IIE). This almost quadrupled the 62,582 Chinese students enrolling in 2004/05. Since 2009/10, China has been the leading source of overseas students in the US.

Adapting for the Chinese luxury traveler

EXPERT INSIGHT: LINDY ANDREWS, CEO, LUXPERIENCE

Lindy Andrews is CEO of Luxperience, Australia's only bespoke luxury travel showcase. Founded in 2012, the three-day event "connects the world's most exclusive travel providers dealing in luxury and experiential travel." Before joining Luxperience, Andrews was director of LCA Communications for 18 years.

How important is China to the luxury travel market?

It's fair to say that China is extremely important to the luxury travel market, and it represents a huge opportunity for the industry. In terms of luxury travel, there used to be the "big three" nations – Germany, the US and the UK. However, China and Russia are now big contenders. China saw a 26 percent rise in outbound trips in 2013 and is now number one for total spending, number two for the volume of trips and number four for the quantity of overnight stays. Chinese outbound travel was expected to further increase in 2014 and beyond. This surge in international travel reinforces China's leadership of Asian outbound travel.

This increase is underlined by the rapid growth in the number of Chinese consumers with higher disposable incomes and a passion for high-end experiences. Whilst incomes across China remain low, there is a small contingent of well-off Chinese consumers already spending lots on property, luxury items, Western branded goods, plus luxury travel. Given the young profile of these consumers, this trend is definitely set to stay.

I'm from Sydney and tourism in Australia performed sluggishly in 2012, but 2013 saw China save Australia's inbound tourism market. It occurred so quickly that

Australia's travel and tourism operators had to rapidly adapt their offerings to cater to arrivals from a country that now spends more in Australia than arrivals from any other country.

What are the key attributes of the Chinese luxury traveler? Is the travel industry attuned to the emerging patterns of experience seeking in China?

China is experiencing a "modern capitalist" phase of growth. Experiential travel and luxury goods are symbols of wealth, and demand for these luxury experiences is expected to grow as the market matures. Shopping makes up the largest part of a Chinese traveler's budget, and other important criteria for the travel experience are staying in a hotel with five or more stars and traveling business class.

However, they are not just looking to shop. The Chinese luxury traveler wants the immersive "out-there" experience, like VIP tickets to an F1 Grand Prix. They want exclusivity. They no longer want to be surrounded by other Chinese tourists. Ultimately, they are the kind of traveler for whom money is no object. Companies will have to learn how to offer these travelers individual and exclusive experiences.

It's also important to remember that whilst Chinese travelers desire luxury, not every single aspect of their holiday will be about luxury. They may choose to save on some aspects, like food or travel, to ensure they can afford luxury when it comes to shopping or their hotel or experience.

What were some of the noted trends from Chinese buyers at the 2013 Luxperience show?

Chinese buyers are looking for individual, bespoke, tailored and immersive experiences. The "new Chinese traveler" is young, affluent and better educated. Whilst they are still looking for the traditional experience of visiting famous places worldwide, many steer away from tour groups and seek quality individual experiences. They want to explore and discover. This is a trend we are continuing to see from most buyers. Consumers worldwide are seeking that immersive experience.

Europe remains the most popular destination for the Chinese traveler. This is due to its diversity, natural attractions and good shopping. Australia, particularly Sydney, is also a must-see destination. France is first choice for shopping, followed by Hong Kong, Italy and the US. The Maldives, Hawaii and Bali are three favorite island destinations.

You planned a series of pop-up events, including one in Beijing. What was the purpose of those shows?

It's interesting – we always have our ear to the ground and ensure that we are aware of all the different trends in the travel industry. China is booming – over the past decade it has become the fastest-growing tourism source market in the world. Luxperience took this into account, and decided to launch a pop-up event there. We underestimated the preparedness of companies promoting themselves to the China market, so we postponed the Beijing event, This is down to how rapidly the market is evolving and changing. We expect that in the coming years, it will be different.

Chapter 3

Magnetized by Macao: Creating a Global Tourism Phenomenon

Casino tourism with Chinese characteristics

David Beckham, Roger Federer, LeBron James and Manny Pacquiao may not be names that spring to mind in a discussion about Chinese tourism. But the rules are different in Macao (also spelt as Macau). All bets are considered – and some seem less likely to fail than others. And certain celebrity names carry an irresistible cachet to those gambling on Macao's future.

First and foremost, Macao is the only place in China where gaming is legal, although horserace betting has long been officially sanctioned and hugely popular in Hong Kong. Strictly controlled horseracing has also returned to selected locations in China, although the system of backing a horse is rather confusing and nothing like the bookmaker system used worldwide – or, indeed, previously adopted in large Chinese cities like Shanghai, where the racecourse that galvanized high society in the late nineteenth century was later paved over to become People's Square.

Macao has been administered by Beijing under the "one country, two systems" principle as a "special autonomous region" (or SAR) since the 1999 handover of sovereignty by Portugal. Allowing for considerable land reclamation from the sea that has roughly doubled its landmass from the 15.5 square kilometers in 1984, Macao is a sliver of space on China's south coast with a population of around 600,000. Yet, over the past decade, Macao has redefined the consumption of tourism for a generation of Chinese travelers. "Casino tourism with Chinese characteristics" is a twenty-first century phenomenon the ramifications of which are rippling across Asia and heading for Europe, the Americas and Australasia. Gaming and tourism are what Macao does more successfully than anyone, including its US forebear, Las Vegas.

At the end of 2013, Macao was home to 35 casinos, which earned a record MOP 360 billion (or around USD 45.2 billion), an increase of 18.6 percent from the not inconsiderable MOP 304 billion garnered in 2012 – and triple the 2009 figure of MOP 119 billion (USD 14.9 billion), when gaming taxes accounted for more than 70 percent of Macao's total fiscal revenue. A decade ago, in 2004, Macao's gaming revenues amounted to a relatively derisory MOP 47 billion (USD 5.8 billion).

As the Gaming Inspection and Coordination Board candidly acknowledges on its website: "Gaming is now the pillar industry of Macao." The board posits three main reasons for the gaming revolution: policy support by the governments of China and Macao, robust entrepreneurial investment and "the preference in gaming by the Chinese."

The surge in visits from China to the casino tables of Macao is one of this decade's most astonishing tourism tales. Around 800,000 tourists from China visited Macao in 1999, a number that was almost equaled during the 2013 National Day Golden Week alone, when 720,000 visitors crossed the border. In 2013, Macao received more than 18 million Chinese tourists.

Table 3.1 Macao inbound arrivals from mainland China, 2003–2013

Year	Total China arrivals	% of Total arrivals	Total tourism arrivals
2013	18,632,207	63.5	29,324,822
2012	16,902,499	60.2	28,082,292
2011	16,162,747	57.7	28,002,279
2010	13,229,057	53.0	24,965,411
2009	10,989,533	50.5	21,752,751
2008	11,613,171	50.6	22,933,185

(continued)

Table 3.1 Continued

Year	Total China arrivals	% of Total arrivals	Total tourism arrivals
2007	14,866,391	55.1	26,992,995
2006	11,985,617	54.5	21,998,122
2005	10,462,966	55.9	18,711,187
2004	9,529,739	N/A	16,672,556
2003	5,742,036	N/A	11,514,589

Source: Data from Macao Government Tourism Office.

Deities, dockers and diamonds

The Macao peninsula derives its name from an ancient fable of a young girl named A-Ma, who sailed with a poor fisherman in his decrepit boat. A storm descended on the sea, sinking all other boats but sparing the fisherman's vessel after A-Ma stood and ordered the storms to subside. Stepping ashore, she climbed to the top of Barra Hill and ascended as a goddess to heaven in a flash of light. The still-standing A-Ma temple was built in her honor overlooking the bay, and is believed to protect fishermen in its waters. The bay became known as A-Ma Gau (Bay of A-Ma), and this name later evolved into Macao.

Macao's southern coastal location saw it develop as an important shipping port. The Portuguese secured Macao as a self-ruling colony in 1557, integrating it into an Asian network of trading posts spanning from India to Japan. Portugal continued to call the shots for 442 years until finally handing back Macao to Chinese rule on 17 December 1999 (two years after the termination of 156 years of British rule in neighboring Hong Kong) in a ceremony presided over by then Presidents Jorge Sampaio of Portugal and Jiang Zemin of China.

Gambling in Macao is claimed to date from the sixteenth century, when Chinese off-duty laborers and dockworkers began frequenting gambling stalls set up by local bankers. When Hong Kong was ceded by China to the British in 1842, it usurped Macao as a strategic trading port. To meet the revenue shortfall, Macao's Portuguese government legalized gaming in 1847, and by the late nineteenth century, gaming tax had become the main source of government revenue.

By the late 1930s, the forerunner to today's "integrated casino resorts" had emerged. Macao's casinos were monopoly owned by the Tai Heng company, and were refurbished to offer newer forms of gaming, such as Baccarat – which remains popular today – plus Chinese opera shows, free snacks and cigarettes. Elsewhere, horse racing and greyhound racing offered extra gambling diversity.

In 1961, local Macanese businessman Stanley Ho's Sociedade de Turismo e Diversões de Macao (STDM) won a bid to operate Macanese casinos as a monopoly. The city's flagship Lisboa Hotel opened in 1970. After the 1999 handover, the Macao SAR government commissioned studies to determine the most profitable way to boost tourism revenues. The casinos were underperforming and stale, with gloomy facilities and downbeat, intimidating interiors. An auspicious new era beckoned to position gaming at the heart of Macao's twenty-first century tourism-driven economy.

Progress was swift. On 8 February 2002, concessions to build new casino resorts were awarded to Stanley Ho's STDM, Galaxy Casino and Wynn Resorts. Later, the Sands organization, Wynn, MGM Grand and Melco PBL were brought into the fray. In May 2004, the Sands casino resort – the first officially sanctioned gaming development by an American company in Asia – opened to chaotic scenes as long queues of Chinese gamblers rushed to become the first to enter this gilded new palace of financial opportunity.

In the same year, Galaxy's Casino Waldo opened, while Wynn opened its first Macao casino and hotel in 2006. More casino resorts followed. In 2006, Galaxy Entertainment opened the StarWorld Macau. In January 2014, Lui Che-Woo, founder of the Galaxy Entertainment Group, which owns the Galaxy Macau resort, was named as Asia's second-richest person.

Design razzmatazz is a critical component. One of the city's tourism landmarks, Stanley Ho's Hotel Lisboa, reopened after a top-to-toe revamp, including a restaurant by celebrity chef Joël Robuchon (four of its restaurants have since earned Michelin stars), and was joined by its sibling Grand Lisboa, a 58-floor, high-kitsch casino resort also featuring a Robuchon eaterie, plus a 218-carat cushion-shaped diamond, called "The Star of Stanley Ho" in the lobby. It is a peerless emblem of the aspirational ostentation that fuels Macao's fortunes.

Four mega-stars and a mega-resort

In March 2007, I donned a construction helmet and embarked on a guided tour through the bowels of The Venetian Macao resort as it underwent the internal fit-out process. Such "hardhat tours" are instructive, providing startling visual insights into the meticulous transformation of a basic building shell into a resort capable of operating at optimum standards of luxury.

As I exited the grimy workers' elevator, the suffocating humidity and acrid dust illustrated the size of the task being attempted. Sheldon Adelson's Las Vegas Sands Corp had invested USD 2.4 billion to create what was being grandiosely marketed as "Asia's first Las Vegas-style integrated mega-Resort." Once completed, it would feature 3,000 hotel suites, 1.2 million square feet of convention and exhibition facilities, 30 restaurants, 300 retail outlets set around replicas of Venice's canals and St. Mark's Square, a spa and a 1,800-seat theatre. The pre-opening spiel had positioned The Venetian Macao as a game changer for twenty-first century tourism in Asia. With just five months until the grand opening, it appeared a rather big ask.

The empty vastness of the interior was striking. My guide told me it was the second-largest building in the world. Cavernous gaming halls were unadorned and resembled warehouses rather than "the future of tourism development in Asia." We picked our way across floors strewn with construction debris, giant rolls of cabling and stacks of delivery crates. The exact locations for each of the 870 gaming tables were marked in black pen on the wooden floor. The only indication of decorative largesse was the Italianate frescoes cast across Rococo-style ceilings. These extravagant renderings of Renaissance Italy were completed save for the gold etchings being diligently inked by immigrant workers clasping large paint pots.

Aside from its own grand ambitions, The Venetian Macao marked the completion of the first phase of the Cotai Strip – a stretch of reclaimed land connecting the offshore islands of Coloane and Taipa set aside to create a city of modern man-made leisure for Chinese travelers. Its casino gaming resorts, hotels, retail malls, theme parks, entertainment venues and conference facilities are hugely ambitious in both scale and design. Still under development, the strip was conceived as Asia's elaboration of the Las Vegas Strip – a branded destination of lavish leisure and business travel and entertainment, rather than a network of individual casino resorts.

The Cotai Strip – home to the world's largest Conrad, Sheraton, and Holiday Inn hotels, plus the forthcoming Lisboa Palace resort, which will feature a Versace Hotel designed by Karl Lagerfeld, and Sands Cotai Central, a highlight of which will be *Monkey King, a Mythical Theatre Show*, a multimedia stage adaptation by film director Li Qiankuan of the Chinese fable *Journey to the West* – is central to Macao's self-enshrinement as a world center of tourism and leisure.

Which brings us back to Messrs Beckham, Federer, James and Pacquiao. My final stop on the hardhat tour was the Cotai Arena, a 15,000-seat venue created for box-office sports events, concerts and musical shows. The arena was already preparing for its launch event: an exhibition tennis match between the then world number one Roger Federer and former champion Pete Sampras.

Federer was an apposite choice to kick-start Macao's strategy of attracting major sports events – and large crowds of Chinese spectators to watch them. The Swiss player is a huge star in China. The Chinese love winners, and Federer's trophy cabinet is crammed with prestigious trophies. He was also part of the first generation of tennis players to compete regularly in China. The season-ending ATP Tennis Masters Cup – in which the world's top eight male players across the season compete for the final title of the year – was hosted in Shanghai between 2005 and 2008. Federer won the tournament in 2006 and 2007.

Basketball is the favored sport of Chinese male teens, and the US National Basketball Association (NBA) is its Holy Grail. A few Chinese players, most notably Yao Ming, have made it to the NBA, garnering great riches and deified status back home. The modern American mega-hero is LeBron James, who played an exhibition match for the Cleveland Cavaliers in 2007 at the Cotai Arena. James makes regular trips to China in a promotional capacity for Nike and "Brand LeBron" and thousands of fans descend on the stores, arenas and hotels where he is scheduled to appear, play or stay. Macao is no exception. James and Team USA stars such as Carmelo Anthony and Dwayne Wade stayed here while preparing for the 2008 Beijing Olympics.

The third member of our quartet is Filipino boxer Manny Pacquiao, the only man in history to win world titles across eight weight divisions. Arriving in Macao in late October 2013, I picked up a copy of the bilingual *Macau Tatler* magazine, which describes itself as "the guide to luxury living." The cover featured a photo of a be-suited Pacquiao, and inside was a six-page interview feature promoting the "Clash in Cotai" – Pacquiao's world welter-weight title fight with American Brandon Rios.

The fight, which took place on 24 November 2013, was promoted as the official launch of Macao as a stage for big-ticket fights, which, given the global TV coverage the Pacquiao–Rios fight was shown on HBO pay-per-view in the US and on CCTV5 in China – high ticket prices and celebrity-magnet status are huge money spinners. As Pacquiao succinctly surmised at a pre-fight press conference: "It is important to give the people of Asia a chance to see me fight. It will encourage people to love boxing in the Philippines, Thailand, China and everywhere."

Professional boxing was banned for several decades in China until being reinstated in 1986. Its popularity has been boosted since 2012 when former miner Xiong Chaozhong became the first Chinese fighter to win a major world title by lifting the WBC straw-weight belt. The pre-Pacquiao–Rios fight card featured China's two-time Olympic gold medalist and three-time amateur world champion, Zou Shiming. The attention of the sold-out crowd at the Cotai Arena, plus two live-feed screening venues at The Venetian Macao, was elsewhere, however. Celebrities sitting ringside included Paris Hilton, Stephen Baldwin, Daniel Wu and David Beckham.

And so to England's most famous footballing export. David Beckham is more than a sporting idol; he is a walking business opportunity. His football career, the undoubted business acumen of his advisors and, of course, his movie star looks have earned him a considerable fortune, and *Forbes* named him the world's eighth-highest earning sports star in 2013. Beckham is a global ambassador for the Chinese Football Association and is idolized in China – a status confirmed back in 2003, when four love-struck nurses rushed onto the pitch in Beijing bearing gifts before a pre-season friendly match when he played for Real Madrid.

In November 2013, Beckham's appearance at the Pacquiao–Rios fight gained added significance. His Beckham Ventures company announced a partnership with Las Vegas Sands "based around the development of dining, retail and leisure concepts" at Sands' properties in Macao and Singapore. Macao and China can rest assured they will be seeing plenty more of "Golden Boots" in the coming years.

Living the high life at the City of Dreams

At the start of November 2013, I boarded the Macao Ferry in Hong Kong. The one-hour journey is relatively smooth, save for a few minor bouts of pushing and jostling by suitcase-wielding tourists. Being a Friday afternoon, the ferry was packed with weekend casino travelers. Groups of middle-aged Chinese men steeled themselves for sustained sessions at the baccarat tables, couples dreamt of a quick flutter and a romantic meal at a Michelin-starred restaurant, while young families hoped the kids didn't get seasick.

The air-conditioned ferry ride is pleasingly devoid of sharp wave movements, and as we pulled into the Macao terminal my mobile phone beeped incessantly. A slew of text messages from telecoms providers in both English and Chinese informed me about roaming rates, Wi-Fi download charges and online gaming options.

Emerging from the ferry terminal, where signage is written in Portuguese and in Chinese characters, fleets of brightly painted coaches designed in the liveries of casino resorts offer complementary transfers. My destination was the 791-room Grand Hyatt Macau, which that evening hosted a lavish poolside party for 1,200 invited guests to celebrate its fourth anniversary. The evening epitomized the elevated levels of hospitality to which upscale Chinese travelers are now accustomed.

Guests gathered at sunset on 12 elevated dining podiums flanking the pool to sip Perrier-Jouet champagne, while open bars served 50 different labels of free-flow wine, beer, whisky and sake, plus Davidoff cigars. The 40-metre pool terrace was lined with 30 tonnes of ice blocks bearing silver platters of shucked oysters, lobsters and a two 35kg blue-fin tuna. Other culinary offerings included foie gras and roasted quail, kebabs and steak sandwiches and tandoori chicken. Distinctive touches included a dim sum and hand-pulled noodle station, a selection of Chinese spirits and a popular counter serving pu'er and longjing teas in porcelain cups.

The party didn't end after the banquet. Guests sashayed into a large marquee transformed into a nightclub. The interior was decorated with velvet and leopard skin prints and featured a central bar and lounge sofas. Giant vases were filled with flowers and peacock feathers, a live DJ provided a pulsing soundtrack and female performers attired in hot-pants danced suggestively on the stairways.

These kinds of parties are held frequently in Macao, but they are not easy to execute. The scale of the hotel's investment in the party and the meticulous attention to detail dedicated to the dining, drinking and entertainment were hugely impressive. All evening, guests waved mobile phone cameras, and self-images and photos of the elaborate cuisines and pavilions zipped across Chinese social media. This was a party that was enjoyed by those at the venue and vicariously in real time by friends and family with access to the Internet or a 3G connection.

The Lion City stakes its future on integrated resorts

When a successful idea becomes a phenomenon, the chances of its adaptation, replication and imitation are heightened. The Macao tourism model, based around the Chinese penchant for gambling and high-value resort entertainment, shopping and dining on which to spend winnings or commiserate losses, has created significant wealth. Unsurprisingly, the earning power of Macao's major casino operators gleaned covetous governmental eyes.

After Macao, the casino tourism model ventured next to Singapore. Widely recognized to be a forward-thinking destination, its history of Chinese immigration plus diverse tourism attractions, plentiful upscale shopping and its status as an affluent twenty-first century Asian city have made it popular with Chinese travelers. Singapore was also quickest to spot the cresting wave of casino tourism.

In 2006, Singapore enacted the Casino Control Act (which was revised in October 2007, and later amended in 2012) which removed Singapore's constitutional ban on gambling and paved the way for the opening, in 2010, of the country's first two "integrated resorts": Marina Bay Sands, by Sheldon Adelson's US-based Sands organization, which also operates The Venetian Macao, at Marina Bay, and Resorts World Sentosa, by Malaysia-based casino resort specialist Genting, on the Singaporean island of Sentosa.

Both resorts offer large, lavishly designed casinos, in addition to deluxe hotels, fine dining and entertainment. Among the attractions at Resorts World Sentosa are Universal Studios Singapore, the world's largest aquarium and *Lake of Dreams*, a fire, light and water show designed by Emmy award-winner Jeremy Railton. The architecturally arresting Marina Bay Sands features a luxury shopping plaza, a 57th floor pool terrace with views across Singapore, and restaurants by celebrity chefs including Guy Savoy, Daniel Boulud and Tetsuya Wakuda.

Although controversial among local Singaporeans – who are required to pay an entrance fee that is not enforced for foreign visitors – the two licensed casinos quickly joined the global big league, generating receipts comparable to the Las Vegas Strip. In 2013, Singapore's casinos earned around USD 6 billion in gaming revenues.

The positioning of Singapore's integrated resorts was a marketing masterstroke. Although gambling is the main cash generator, the casinos are rarely mentioned in the promotion of either resort. Instead, both Marina Bay Sands and Resorts World Sentosa seek to appeal to a broad spectrum of leisure and business travelers. The casino dollars enabled the two operators to continue investing in their amenities, entertainment and dining options, and to secure international hospitality talent. As a result, Singapore garnered global respect for the diversity of its two resorts, which helped the city-state reinvent itself as a bona fide destination of choice, rather than a layover city for air passengers en route to somewhere else.

Sri Lanka: the Macao of South Asia?

Macao and Singapore released the genie from the Asian bottle. Although Las Vegas set the benchmark for casino-based tourism and entertainment from the 1970s onwards – long before Macao and Singapore sat at the table – two of Asia's smallest destinations reframed the model in a distinctively localized context. In both cases, annual revenues were generated to challenge Las Vegas, and to elevate gaming-based leisure as a powerful factor in tourism development worldwide. But after Macao and Singapore, where next?

A heated debate about the future of tourism is underway in the South Asian island of Sri Lanka, which has targeted 2.5 million annual visitors by 2016 (up from 660,000 in 2010 and 1.27 million in 2013). China is now the nation's third-largest tourism market, and the Sri Lanka Tourism Promotion Bureau (SLTPB) is aggressively marketing the country in China. You can probably see already where the debate is headed.

The SLTPB's campaign efforts have featured billboards at subway stations in Beijing, a radio ad campaign in Shanghai, branding 300 buses in Beijing, Shanghai, Chengdu and Guangzhou, and inviting journalists and tour operators to Sri Lanka. Air connectivity is being broached. "China is a main focus in Sri Lankan Airlines' marketing plans, as the future of the travel industry is in this region," said Nishantha Wickremasinghe, Chairman of Sri Lankan Airlines, in an official SLTPB statement.

In addition, in January 2014 the SLTPB facilitated a TV crew from The Travel Channel, which broadcast 2,500 ads and over 500 minutes of programing about Sri Lanka. The content was also distributed via social media to estimated 350 million people. Chinese visitation to Sri Lanka rose 137 percent year on year in the first half of 2014.

Proponents of "man-made" tourism development in Sri Lanka have pointed out that the nation has sought to increase tourist arrivals within a restricted paradigm of promoting beaches, wildlife reserves and ancient ruins. While appealing to traditional source markets, this version of tourism might not generate the coveted tourism revenues – and much-needed job creation – from "new generation" Asian tourists. From this viewpoint, encouraging longer stays, and greater accumulated spending, by tourists from China, India and elsewhere in Asia has led developers to propose the integrated resort concept in four Sri Lankan locations.

The Sri Lankan government bought into the idea as it prioritizes tourism as a key revenue-generating sector to rebuild an economy still devastated from nearly three decades of civil war, which ended in 2009. The "pro-casino tourism" argument is couched in terms of the region's intensifying competition for tourists. Countries such as Singapore, Macao, Malaysia and Vietnam all operate in the same marketplace and are using casino and entertainment-related options to attract affluent Asian travelers. Sri Lanka's model proposes an adaptation of the integrated resort concept combining "man-made" and "nature-based" tourism – with restaurants, shopping malls, theatres, theme parks and casinos alongside horse racing, polo, golf, sailing, water sports, biking, climbing and hiking.

The first three casino resorts to receive approval are all in the capital, Colombo. The marquee project is a USD 400m joint venture between Rank Holdings and Australia's Crown Group to create Crown Sri Lanka, a 36-storey resort featuring a 450-room hotel, a casino, dining and entertainment, conference facilities, a retail mall and a specially designed water feature. The development will "redefine luxury tourism in Sri Lanka," Crown's Chairman James Packer said in a stock exchange filing, adding, "Sri Lanka is a beautiful and unique country with huge tourism potential."

Alongside the Crown project, Sri Lanka's largest company by revenue, John Keels Holdings, will develop a USD 700m casino-based resort complex adjacent to Crown Sri Lanka, and Colombo's third integrated resort, Queensbury, is the brainchild of a local businessman and politician called Dhammika Perera.

The Macao model spans Asia

Since 2013, a stream of announcements surfaced regarding expansions of the Macao-style "integrated" casino-resort model. Tokyo has emerged as a high-profile target for cashed-up developers and casino operators since it won the bid to host the 2020 Olympics. Several casino-tourism players are knocking at Tokyo's door in the hope that the Japanese government would decide to issue licenses. Fitch Ratings estimates two integrated resorts in Tokyo and Osaka could generate USD 7 billion in annual gross gaming receipts.

While Tokyo waits, large casino resorts are being master-planned at metronomic speed, and the Philippines is emerging as a regional heavyweight. Developed by Japan's Universal Entertainment Corporation, the Manila Bay Resort is scheduled to open in 2015. The 1.13 million square-meter resort promises a now familiar mix of brand boutique shopping, dining, entertainment and gaming, in addition to budget and deluxe accommodation. Significantly, in November 2013, the founder of Universal Entertainment, Kazuo Okada, chose Xinhua, China's state-run media agency, to publicly elaborate on the details of the project.

Okada said he chose the Philippines for its proven high levels of hospitality and customer service, and its easily accessible location for outbound travelers from China and South East Asia. Just as Sri Lanka, the Philippines, which is an archipelago of more than 7,000 islands, will promote to casino tourists its diverse natural beauty and myriad marine-based activities – setting down a clear differentiator that Macao and Singapore cannot match.

The Manila Bay Resort is not the only game in town. Resorts World Manila at Newport Bay comprises hotels, a mall, a performing arts theatre and several cinemas. In addition, a subsidiary of Macao's Melco Crown Entertainment, planned to open Melco Crown Philippines in 2014. Conforming to the twenty-first century Asian model, it will offer a casino; hotels, including the first Nobu Hotel in Asia; retail; restaurants; a live performance venue; and a nightclub situated in a dome-shaped structure called the Fortune Egg. It's the second casino complex to open at the 120-hectare Entertainment City, which is being shaped as the Philippines' version of the Cotai Strip.

Courtesy of the successful Resorts World Genting tourism center at Genting Highlands, Malaysia – which is a short drive from the capital, Kuala Lumpur – had asserted itself as South East Asia's casino-tourism base, albeit by deploying a rapidly dating format. Despite its popularity with Chinese travelers, the success of Singapore's integrated resorts pushed Malaysia to refresh refresh its tourism offering. In December 2013, Malaysia's Prime Minister, Najib Razak, unveiled the Genting Integrated Tourism Plan.

The RM 5 billion (USD 1.54 billion) overhaul of Genting Highlands resort served notice of Malaysia's intention to compete for affluent Chinese and Asian tourists. Once reopened in 2016, the revamped resort will feature the world's first Twentieth Century Fox theme park, with rides and other attractions based on movie blockbusters, such as *Ice Age*, *Alien* and *Night at the Museum*. It will replace an existing outdoor theme park, which ceased operations in September 2013 to make way for the new development. The masterplan also promises new hotels, a show arena, resort entertainment and an outlet shopping center, plus – of course – a revitalized casino.

Geographically closer to China, Jeju Island, a holiday destination off the south coast of South Korea, has become popular with Chinese visitors who enjoy visa-free entry, plus windswept beaches, hills and coastal villages used as filming locations for syrupy Korean soap operas that are adored by young people in China. About 78 percent of the 2.3 million foreign visitors to Jeju in 2013 were from China. Casino gaming in Jeju is illegal for Korean nationals, but is permitted for foreign visitors. The Shilla Jeju and Paradise Casino Jeju Grand are among the venues offering casino gaming, and a swathe of new gaming-based resorts is planned in the coming years.

In February 2014, Genting Singapore announced a joint venture with Chinese developer Landing International Development to build the USD 2.2 billion Resorts World Jeju, based on the successful Resorts World Sentosa integrated resort – largely to target gaming tourists from China's eastern and northern cities. Chinese state-owned developer Greenland Holding Group – which has stated its objective to become a Fortune 200 company by 2015 – announced plans to invest RMB 6 billion (USD 0.96 billion) to build two 218-metre high towers offering serviced residences, a hotel, duty-free shopping outlets, entertainment venues and a casino on Jeju Island.

In March 2014, South Korea's Ministry of Culture, Sports and Tourism gave initial approval to the country's first foreign-owned casino resort. Located in Incheon, the joint venture between Las Vegas-based Caesars Entertainment, Hong Kong property developer Lippo and Singapore-based OUE will feature a casino, hotels and retail and convention centers. The consortium hopes to open the integrated resort in time for the 2018 Winter Olympics in Pyeongchang.

Gaming tourism goes global

After Asia, the world awaits. The US – with Las Vegas as its casino-tourism "heartland" – is relatively well serviced, although Asian investors are actively looking to building resorts in US coastal destinations.

Australia is one of the world's smartest casino-tourism players. Its highest-profile integrated resort is Crown Resorts Melbourne, which features a casino, hotel, luxury retail, event spaces, theatres, spas, and several smart eateries, including five Chinese restaurants. Crown, which has a 33.6 percent holding in Melco Crown Entertainment, owner of the Cotai Strip's City of Dreams – refurbished its Melbourne resort in

2011 to entice more high-rolling gamers from China and other Asian markets.

But the company, which also operates casinos in Perth and London, has set its sights even higher. Crown Sydney is lavishly described as "a once in 200-year opportunity to create a vibrant new place to live, work and visit" on the Sydney waterfront at Barangaroo. The controversial 275-metre tower with a 60-degree twist on its axis is being designed by British architects Wilkinson Eyre and will offer a 350-room hotel, VIP gaming facilities, conference venues residential apartments, a luxury spa, signature restaurants, and brand shopping.

Despite sparking popular protests, Crown Sydney has been supported by the tourism industry, not least because it will refresh Sydney's somewhat outdated offering for high-net worth Asian travelers. The unremitting showmanship of James Packer, Chairman of Crown, has forced the project towards public acceptance, as has his insistence that Sydney must build man-made tourism attractions that meet the increasingly gilded expectations of Asian travelers who are hugely indulged with signature landmark projects across the region. The ever-quotable Packer says, on the company's website, that Crown Sydney has set a goal to become "the best hotel in the world at Barangaroo."

Further north, Chinese investors, including billionaire Tony Fung, are seeking to develop casino resorts in North Queensland. The proposed AUD 4.2 billion Aquis Great Barrier Reef Resort is claimed by its backers to be the largest investment in tourism infrastructure in Australia's history. Conceived as "a fully integrated resort that leverages the stunning beauty of the Great Barrier Reef" it aims to "take advantage of the substantial near-term growth expected in outbound Chinese tourism and to position North Queensland as a tourism leader within the region" according to a company statement. Planned to open in 2018, the resort promises nine luxury hotels, 130 villas, an 18-hole golf course, luxury retail, a 25,000-seat stadium, a convention center and two theatres.

The ubiquitously invested Genting company – which, as previously mentioned, operates Resorts World Sentosa in Singapore, plus Resorts World Manila and has expanded into the Bahamas in addition to purchasing a casino in Las Vegas – now has its eyes on Europe. The company's sponsorship of Birmingham-based Aston Villa Football Club is linked to its upcoming integrated resort project. Resorts World Birmingham, which is expected to open in 2015, will deliver a casino, hotel, retail mall, cinema, and a banqueting and conference center, and has targeted Chinese tourists as a primary market. In March 2014, Birmingham Airport announced it would become the first UK airport outside of London to receive direct charter flights from Beijing operated by China Southern Airlines.

The Caribbean has also joined the integrated resort gold rush. In January 2014, Bermuda outlined plans to open casinos at integrated resorts to "enhance tourism infrastructure." Tourism Minister Shawn Crockwell told a press conference that Bermuda's approach to casino gaming would be "similar to the Aruban and Singaporean casino models." Proposed legislation to legalize gaming followed a review of the island's tourism economy and the publication of a National Tourism Master Plan in 2012.

In the Bahamas, China State Construction Engineering hired thousands of Chinese laborers to build the Baha Mar resort at Cable Beach. Planned to open in late 2014, the beachfront Baha Mar development, which markets itself as The Bahamian Riviera, comprises hotels operated by Grand Hyatt, Mondrian and Rosewood (which was acquired in 2011 by Hong Kong-based New World Hospitality), a convention center, an 18-hole Jack Nicklaus-designed golf course, spas and luxury retail. The centerpiece is Baha Mar Casino & Hotel, home to the Caribbean's largest casino, a 9,000 square meter gaming palace, including "private high-limit rooms, state-of-the-art machines, and every popular table game in the world." Also in the Bahamas is the 3,414-room Atlantis resort on Paradise Island, created by Kerzner International, which will open a third Atlantis resort on China's Hainan Island.

For both resorts, it should not go unnoticed that the Bahamas and China have been working on the so-called Two Center Tourism Program, enabling Chinese tourists to Canada or the US to visit the Bahamas as part of the same travel package.

Chapter 4

The Purchasing Prerogative: Hong Kong and Shopping Tourism

China's favorite shopping destination

It is mid-afternoon at Hong Kong International Airport on the last Saturday of January 2014. The restaurants and fast-food outlets are crammed with travelers awaiting flights, and the boarding gates are alive with expectation. Luggage carts are stacked with gifts for family members and airport retailers are offering last-minute discounts and promotions for Chinese credit cardholders. A scan of the flight departures screen reveals that between midday and 4pm, 25 flights are scheduled to leave for destinations in mainland China.

Between shopping and waiting to board, most people seem oblivious to the bilingual public announcements warning about H7N9 avian flu ("Please don't touch poultry or live birds while traveling"), recent cases of which had been confirmed in Shanghai and Beijing. Instead, the mood is festive. The Chinese are heading home for the principal holiday of the calendar: Spring Festival, which marks the beginning of the Chinese New Year.

Amid the melee, airport management and staff know the annual exodus of homeward-bound Chinese holidaymakers is a temporary phenomenon. They will soon return – most likely, in even greater numbers. In 2013, Hong Kong welcomed 54.3 million visitors, with

40.7 million (or more than five times the population of Hong Kong) arriving from mainland China. A Hong Kong government report released in January 2014 predicts 70 million arrivals in 2017 and 100 million arrivals by 2023, with the majority expected to emanate from the mainland. A tourism logjam is impending.

To emphasize China's dominance as Hong Kong's major provider of tourists, the second-largest source market in 2013 was Taiwan, with 2.09 million arrivals. Visitors to Hong Kong from traditional source markets of the US (1.1 million), Australia (609,000) and the UK (513,000) all recorded an annual decrease compared to 2012.

The primary motivation for Chinese visitors to Hong Kong is consumption. For the past ten years, Hong Kong has been China's preferred shopping destination, its plethora of glitzy malls and brand boutiques made further appealing by a low sales tax rate and a strengthened renminbi versus the Hong Kong Dollar that render the prices of prized branded goods much cheaper than back home. Consequently, inbound tourism from China is crucial to Hong Kong's economy. Official statistics show that from 1999 to 2012, tourism spending in Hong Kong increased by 693 percent, with the share of spending by Chinese visitors leaping from 33 percent to 57.9 percent during that period.

From its formative Hong Kong base, the impact of China's outbound consumer revolution is radiating across the globe. Overseas spending by affluent Chinese has been widely credited for most of the 41 percent expansion in the global luxury-goods sector between 2009 and 2012. Demand from China increased 135 percent over this period, boosting their share of the market from 19 percent in 2009 to 31 percent in 2012. A report by Hong Kong-based brokerage CLSA expects this proportion to increase to 50 percent by 2020, as China's consumer class wields its credit cards with increased geographical reach.

Hong Kong was perfectly positioned to benefit from the initial wave of Chinese outbound spending, and proudly promotes itself as a Premier League purchasing destination. "The devotion Hong Kong applies to shopping is a sight in its own right," is the Hong Kong Tourism Board's deft appraisal of its purchasing appeal. It begins upon arrival. Hong

Kong International Airport's bilingual promotional literature hails the flight center as a "shopping and dining paradise," offering more than 280 shops and 80 restaurants. Such is the dedication to consumer spending, that duty-free stores are positioned for newly landed visitors to browse before joining the airport's immigration lines to confirm their entry into Hong Kong.

Chinese visitors's glee at spending in Hong Kong has sparked a headlong rush by global brands to establish flagship stores in prime city locations. This strategy is twin-edged, seeking to tap into the purchasing demand of Chinese visitors, and to use the flagship Hong Kong boutiques as launch pads for expanding into, and diversifying across, China.

International fashion stores, luxury brand boutiques and high-technology gadget retailers compete to pay top-dollar rentals for prestigious sites at the Pacific Place, Harbor City, The Landmark and ifc malls, plus the coveted street-fronts of Queen's Road Central and Canton Road in Tsimshatsui. High demand for retail space and scorching rents have resulted in several brands moving into "overspill" areas, such as Johnston Street in Wanchai, Wellington Street in Central and Peking Road in Tsimshatsui, that were not previously recognized as high-end retail locations.

During the run-up to Chinese New Year, these locations enter a competitive season of discount sales and free-gift promotions. Levi's, Juicy Couture, Shanghai Tang and Cerruti 1881 were among the brands at Hong Kong Airport offering ten percent discounts throughout January 2014 to China UnionPay cardholders who were Chinese residents on purchases that met or exceeded a minimum spend threshold. Meanwhile, fresh spring and summer fashion collections started hitting shelves, forcing retailers to heavily mark down leftover stock from the previous season. And no one values a bargain higher than the Chinese holiday shopper.

Asia's World City

Over the last decade, Hong Kong has emerged as the primary training ground for the waves of urban vacationers now departing China to explore cities across Asia and worldwide. In the early years of Chinese outbound travel it also served as a connective nexus for mainlanders – offering a far greater choice of international flight connections than airports in Beijing, Shanghai or Guangzhou.

For many years, Hong Kong was inaccessible to mainlanders unless traveling on business, on an approved tour group or attending university in the city. Since the Chinese government began permitting private travel to Hong Kong in 2003, it has been a coveted destination that often serves as the first experience beyond the homeland for millions of Chinese travelers.

It's a dynamic place in which to cut your tourism teeth. Promoted as "Asia's World City," Hong Kong lives up to its billing as a thrilling urban destination. Whether observed from Hong Kong Island or Kowloon, the photogenic landscape of Victoria Harbor flanked by soaring skyscrapers by star-name architects, gently curving hills and the outlying islands beyond entice visitors from across the globe.

Gazing upwards at the glassy skyline from the iconic Star Ferry, it's hard to imagine that more than 40 per cent of Hong Kong's islands are protected green areas, and that hiking and hill walking are popular weekend and holiday pastimes. More affluent visitors jump in a helicopter from atop The Peninsula Hong Kong hotel to view one of Asia's most unique cityscapes from above.

Look beyond the showy façade, however, and Hong Kong is a city defined by its formative history, as much as its neon-blazed futurism. Hong Kong's strategic location at the southern tip of China made it an important trading port. In 1842, following the first Sino–British Opium War, Hong Kong, known as "the barren rock," was ceded by China to British rule. As a British colony, it developed its own education, government and justice systems, although its wealth and prosperity were tied closely to the sea, and its impressive port capacity. Its unique appeal resided in the curious overlapping of British and Chinese cultures, cuisines and customs.

Hong Kong was returned by Britain to Chinese rule in 1997, amid strong fears among its people about whether China would uphold the commercial freedoms they had latterly enjoyed. No-one quite imagined, as the grandiose harbor-side handover ceremony was completed, that one of the major effects on Hong Kong over the next two decades would be the developmental scale of its China-fuelled tourism sector.

The attention-grabbing "Asia's World City" slogan was adopted by the Hong Kong Tourism Board – a statutory body whose activities are primarily funded by the Hong Kong government – after the board's establishment in 2001. The new positioning sought to elevate Hong Kong as the region's most cosmopolitan and vibrant city and to confront competition for tourists from other Asian cities, such as Singapore, Bangkok and, in the years that would follow, Macao. The new branding also demonstrated Hong Kong's aspiration to be considered alongside global cities like London, Paris and New York as a "bucket list" destination for discerning global travelers.

One of Hong Kong's first promotional opportunities under the new branding came in late September 2004, when the harbor-front Hong Kong Convention Centre – which had been constructed for the 1997 handover ceremony and was the centerpiece for promoting Hong Kong as a city capable of hosting international conventions – hosted the annual World Travel Congress of the American Society of Travel Agents (ASTA), one of the world's largest tourism industry associations.

Hosting the ASTA Congress targeted two key goals. The Hong Kong Tourism Board rolled out a red carpet welcome to influential American travel agents and tour operators in the hope they would encourage more US tourists – who were proving reluctant travelers following the 9/11 terrorism attacks in New York – to visit and spend in Hong Kong. In addition, Hong Kong was repairing the damage to its reputation following the Severe Acute Respiratory Syndrome (SARS) epidemic that emanated in late 2002 from southern China's Guangdong Province, which borders Hong Kong.

Viewed a decade later, hosting the ASTA Congress seems like a strategic play from a different era. At the time, Hong Kong commanded the largest share of US outbound travel of any destination in Asia. The following year, in 2005, The US contributed 1.14 million visitor arrivals

Table 4.1 Hong Kong arrivals from mainland China, 2002–2013

Year	Total inbound arrivals (m)	Total arrivals from mainland China (m)
2013	54.30	40.7
2012	48.60	34.91
2011	41.92	28.10
2010	36.03	22.68
2009	29.59	17.96
2008	29.50	16.86
2007	28.20	15.49
2006	25.30	13.59
2005	23.35	12.54
2004	21.81	12.25
2003	15.54	8.47
2002	16.56	6.83

Source: Data from Hong Kong Tourism Board.

compared to 12.54 from China. The subsequent surge of Chinese visitors to Hong Kong has ensured its primacy as a source market, with visitors from China in 2013 outstripping those from the US by a ratio of 34:1 (see Table 4.1).

Unleashing the dragon

As Hong Kong prepared for the ASTA Congress in 2004, projecting tourism flows over the next decade was an ambiguous occupation, particularly in the wake of the Asian Financial Crisis, the effects of which were still rippling through the region, the SARS outbreak, the impact of 9/11 and widespread fears of more terrorism attacks in the US and in its ally nations that had supported the wars in Iraq and Afghanistan. Opacity regarding China's mid-term policy towards Hong Kong exacerbated the doubts.

The Chinese government spotted an opportunity. There was official recognition that economic growth was encouraging the Chinese to travel more frequently within their country, and interest was peaking to experience new destinations beyond the nation's watertight borders. With Macao still a few years away from completing its first wave of new casino resorts, Hong Kong fitted the bill as a short-haul destination that held historic and cultural intrigue and aspirational appeal for Chinese vacationers.

Since the 1997 handover of sovereignty from the UK to China, Hong Kong has – like Macao – been governed as a Special Administrative Region (SAR) under China's "one country, two systems" precept. While strong influence from Beijing is increasingly prevalent, Hong Kong retains its own Chief Executive and its people hope to achieve universal suffrage in 2017. Back in 2003, though, Hong Kong's economy needed boosting, and China was able to provide the consistently large flow of ready-to-spend tourists Hong Kong craved.

Hitherto, visitation to Hong Kong from China had been administered under the Hong Kong Tour Group Scheme, a quota-based program that enabled leisure travel only as part of a registered tour group. Viewed as outdated and unable to facilitate the volume of tourists that China wished to send and Hong Kong wanted to receive, the scheme was abolished in January 2002.

From 28 July 2003, a new tourism administration program was implemented between China and Hong Kong, the Individual Visit Scheme (IVS). Announced, as policies in China often are, on a pilot basis, it permitted residents of four cities – Dongguan, Foshan, Jiangmen, and Zhongshan – all in neighboring Guangdong Province, to apply to visit Hong Kong as individual travelers without joining a group tour. The scheme was extended to cover Guangzhou, Shenzhen, Zhuhai, and Huizhou in August 2003; and to Beijing and Shanghai on 1 September 2003.

The IVS Scheme was later extended to cover 49 Chinese cities (with a total population of around 270 million), including all 21 cities in Guangdong Province, Shanghai, Beijing, Chongqing, Tianjin, Chengdu, Dalian, Shenyang, Jinan, Nanchang, Changsha, Nanning, Haikou, Guiyang, Kunming, Shijiazhuang, Zhengzhou, Changchun, Hefei, Wuhan, Fuzhou, Xiamen, Quanzhou, Nanjing, Suzhou, Wuxi, Hangzhou, Ningbo, and

Taizhou. The dragon had been unleashed, and Hong Kong's shopping-tourism industry was set to cash in.

The tourist-shopper hybrid

The backstreets of Hong Kong's densely populated downtown areas – interspersed between the glamorous hotels, elevated cocktail lounges and private clubs – are where its southern Chinese traditions remain intact. Cantonese noodle shops and roast goose diners vie for space alongside narrow markets and dried seafood stores. These blend with Hong Kong's easily consumed sightseeing backdrops. Photo opportunities are readily consumed on the Peak Tram, atop the Peak observatory overlooking Hong Kong and while riding the iconic Star Ferry across the harbor.

But it's the brand name stores along the central thoroughfares and in the air-conditioned malls that are the best place to find an answer to the oft-asked question of why the Chinese have, over the past decade, preferred group travel to independent travel. Hong Kong has become China's most popular package tour destination, largely because the cost savings of group travel have enabled travelers to spend more disposable cash on their number one pastime: shopping.

Since the opening of mass Chinese tourism in Hong Kong, group tourists have swarmed to Hong Kong's best shopping spots. As previously mentioned, this is largely credited to the value of products and shopping services offered, but it also mirrors the approach to mass tourism in China over the past two decades. The domestic tourism model has long treated the Chinese traveler as a walking cashcard.

Massive captive audiences at signature spots, such as the Great Wall of China, the Forbidden City in Beijing, the Chinese gardens of Suzhou, the terracotta warriors of Xi'an, the temples of Lijiang and West Lake in Hangzhou, resulted in the respective city authorities adding significant retail and consumer components to the sightseeing experience. This occurs worldwide, of course, but the intensity of consumerism in China is intriguing. Overseas visitors to those aforementioned tourism sights often remark on the expansive mix of souvenir stores, cafes, produce markets and hawker stalls clustered around the entrances and exits – and the volumes of local tourists frequenting them.

Shopping and sightseeing are inseparable in China, and while independent, white-collar Chinese travelers are now seeking more experiential-based holidays, most will tell you that wherever they travel time will be set aside for shopping. Meanwhile, given China's huge population base, large volumes of less-affluent group trippers from lower-tier cities are expected to continue enjoying the purchasing prerogative.

Brands that are researching Chinese consumer patterns beyond the major cities know this, and are adapting accordingly. In October 2013, DFS, the world's leading luxury travel retailer, which is majority owned by the luxury brands conglomerate LVMH group, hosted a lavish media reception to showcase the T Galleria rebranding of its three DFS Galleria stores in Hong Kong – the company's founding city and home to its global headquarters. The event followed the first T Galleria rebranding in Hawaii, and preceded the conversions of two Galleria stores in Macao before the end of 2013, and a global rollout during 2014.

The timing was impeccable to maintain the DFS profile in the minds of Chinese travelers. One month earlier, DFS signed a global partnership deal with a subsidiary of China UnionPay, China's largest payment system, enabling cardholders to enjoy customized offers at DFS stores worldwide. "We are continuing to accelerate the global development of UnionPay International," said Su Ning, Chairman of China UnionPay, at the agreement signing. "With numerous stores around the world, DFS Group is the world's leading luxury travel retailer and preferred destination for UnionPay cardholders during their travels abroad."

Can a destination have too many tourists?

Despite their unquestioned economic value, Chinese visitors have not been universally popular in Hong Kong. Overcrowded malls and theme parks during national holidays, pushing and shoving on the subway system and loud behavior in hotels and restaurants have irked local sensibilities. Another issue to cause concern has been the smuggling of infant milk formula back over the border into China.

This has been a constant issue since the 2008 baby formula milk scandal in China, when supplies of dairy products were found to contain melamine. Several children died as a result of being poisoned, and China's dairy industry lapsed into meltdown. Officials of the companies involved were imprisoned and Chinese consumers cleared the shelves in Hong Kong of foreign branded milk formulas. Hong Kong Customs & Excise responded by imposing a limit of two tins totaling 1.8kg of baby milk formula to combat shortages.

These issues have heightened fears that access to Hong Kong has become too easy, and that the city cannot cope with the influx from China. Mainlanders have two primary transportation options: train or plane. Analysis published by the South China Morning Post ("*Is the MTR Too Much of a Tight Squeeze*," 24 January 2014), revealed that around half of the 40.7 million Chinese visitors to Hong Kong in 2013 arrived via two overland railway points – Lo Wu and Lok Ma Chao – which are both operated by Hong Kong's Mass Transit Railway (MTR). Meanwhile, Hong Kong Airport is expanding to handle an extra ten million passengers – from China and the thriving outbound travel markets of countries across Asia Pacific – by the end of 2015, and is building a third runway planned for completion by 2023.

For Chinese travelers, two new transport options will soon enhance Hong Kong's accessibility. The cross-border Guangzhou–Shenzhen–Hong Kong Express Rail Link, which began operations in 2011, will be upgraded to connect Hong Kong to China's high-speed rail network in 2015, making it easier for consumers in central China to visit both Shenzhen and Hong Kong. In addition, the Hong Kong–Zhuhai–Macao road bridge will enhance mobility for millions more high-spending visitors from southern China when it opens in 2016.

To cope with the inflow, Hong Kong's infrastructure planners are seeking new ways to relieve the pressure on its groaning transport system, particularly the MTR subway network. One idea being promulgated is to build new shopping malls closer to the Chinese border. Implementing a cap on tourist permits in Hong Kong has also been discussed, with suggestions that residents of the border city of Shenzhen should no longer be allowed to make unlimited day trips in and out of Hong Kong.

Exporting and re-importing "shopping tourism"

China's obsession with shopping tourism may have developed in Hong Kong, but it is now a global phenomenon. Chinese consumers bought 47 percent of luxury goods sold worldwide last year, according to the Fortune Character Institute research consultancy. Chinese visitors account for more than 20 percent of all sales at McArthurGlen's 21 luxury retail outlets in Austria, Belgium, France, Germany, Greece, Italy, Netherlands, and the UK, with Chinese spending rising 270 percent across those venues in 2012 and 2013.

This penchant for purchasing is inspiring new phrases. Song Rui, Director of the Tourist Research Center of the Chinese Academy of Social Sciences, noted that the Chinese are increasingly referred to as "Walking Wallets," while Londoners joked about the "Peking Pound" as Chinese visitors embarked on a buying spree during the 2012 Olympics.

The economic allure of high-spending shopping tourists from China was evident in the decision in June 2014 by the UK government to amend its visa policy for Chinese visitors. The government had experienced sustained lobbying pressure from retailers because, put simply, it was becoming obvious that the British economy was turning away large volumes of cash via its strict visa entry rules – particularly during a period of austerity among British consumers.

Around the same time representatives from the London Luxury Quarter, a collection of 42 streets in Mayfair, Piccadilly and St. James that are home to select luxury retailers, completed a promotional visit to China. During a showcase in Beijing, London mayor Boris Johnson launched a series of initiatives to encourage high-net worth individuals (HNWIs) to visit the UK and shop in the district.

London-based Value Retail, whose Bicester Village outlet shopping center in Oxfordshire claims to have the highest sales densities of any shopping center in the world, has also refined its concept for China. It boasts a collection of nine Chic Outlet Shopping Villages in Europe, including Paris, Milan, Munich, Madrid, Barcelona, Frankfurt and Dublin, with Chinese visitors representing the number one non-European nationality across all the Villages.

Bicester Village provides Chinese-speaking service staff, store maps denoting which outlets accept China UnionPay credit cards, and VIP discount cards distributed through Chinese tour operators. It receives such a high volume of Chinese tourists that when UK Prime Minister David Cameron asked the Chinese Ambassador what the nation's visitors would like to see more of, the reply is said to have been "Bicester Villages."

Value Retail is now exporting its "luxury tourism shopping" concept to China. Its first project, Suzhou Village, is modelled on Bicester Village and defined by "international luxury, fashion and lifestyle brands and an authentic European shopping experience," according to a company statement. A second China shopping center, Shanghai Village, will open in 2015 at the Shanghai International Tourism and Resorts Zone – adjacent to the Shanghai Disney Resort. Once completed, it will feature 50,000 square meters of outlet retail and restaurant space, and is predicted by the company to become "one of the most important retail destinations in the world."

Chapter 5
Sun, Sea, and Shopping: China Goes to the Beach

Hawaiian shirts and happy shoppers

At 11 a.m. on a Wednesday in late May 2011, I stood outside the China Duty Free store in Sanya. The place is alive with consumer excitement. Scores of China's hybrid tourist-shoppers dressed in Hawaiian shirts and floppy sun hats take photographs beside fountains and palm trees with luxury brand logos as a backdrop. The sun is fiercely hot.

This is no ordinary duty-free store, of course. In fact, duty-free store is a misnomer. It is a stadium-sized retail mall on a tropical island crammed with stores by the world's most recognizable brands. Floor-to-ceiling entrance windows are emblazoned with Cartier, Tag Heuer, Piaget, Omega and Shiseido banners. Once inside, the aromas of expensive perfumes and cosmetics welcome you to the world of tax-free shopping – Chinese holiday style.

A sizeable queue had formed to enter the Gucci store, and Police sunglasses and Tiffany keys drew sizeable crowds. Amid this carnival of consumerism, harried sales assistants tending the multi-brand cosmetics section are fending off customer complaints. Rows of shelving bearing the names L'Occitane, Yves Saint Laurent, Calvin Klein and Bulgari stand embarrassingly empty. A throng of unlucky shoppers is protesting the right to buy. "We put the products out early in the morning, but some sell out very quickly," says a tearful assistant who admits this cosmetic catastrophe had been a frequent occurrence.

My visit occurred one month after the opening, in April 2011, of the Sanya Duty Free Center. Already it had achieved bona fide tourist destination status. I was seeing for the first time the new reality of tourism in Hainan Island – China's tropical island getaway, where sun, sea and sand are combined with prolific shopping.

The previous evening, the General Manager of one of Sanya's internationally branded resorts had rather curtly told me, as we sat on a beachfront terrace overlooking the South China Sea, that duty-free shoppers did not represent his target market. Shoppers flocking to the island, he told me, were unlikely to stay in resorts commanding premium room rates. In fairness, he was trying to stay on-message and expound the brand's stated objective of attracting affluent travelers. But a quick scan around the breakfast restaurant the following morning confirmed that a large constituency of his guests were indeed preparing to visit the China Duty Free mall, which is located in downtown Sanya, a 20-minute taxi ride from the beach resorts clustered along Yalong Bay. Upscale hotels have since embraced the trend, and some provide free early morning shuttle buses to the duty-free center.

Sanya's first government-sanctioned China Duty Free (CDF) mall was a carefully calculated "man-made" tourism attraction designed to appeal to the multitudes of Chinese travelers taking short holidays and long weekend breaks on sun-drenched Hainan Island. Billed as the nation's only tropical resort destination, Hainan was, at the time, being marketed as "China's Hawaii" – a play on the similar latitude and landscapes of the two islands that spawned a craze among male Chinese visitors for wearing tropically patterned shirt-and-shorts combos.

A disconnect between the promotional promise and the tourism reality was developing, however. As mainland interest in Hainan gathered pace, and travel agencies began selling large numbers of short-break packages, Chinese tourists enjoyed the shiny resorts built for them and took excursions to Hainan's natural attractions and sites of historic interest. They did not, though, enjoy the expansive beaches. Cultivating a suntan is mostly frowned upon in a nation long convinced of the purity of porcelain skin, and where most skincare products contain skin-whitening chemicals.

Shunning the beach created periods of boredom for travelers, as Hainan simply didn't offer enough to do. As visitors passed more time in their resorts, media reports surfaced criticizing the pricing of dining and leisure services. Hainan's deluxe resorts are packed closely together along the coastlines, and as such no beach or street culture has developed around them. Unlike, say, Phuket or Bali, the organic infrastructure integral to the beach holiday experience is missing. You cannot take a stroll along the beach to find a bar or a local restaurant, because they do not exist.

Confronted by growing complaints that Hainan was over-pricing and short-changing visitors, officials struck upon a classic "win-win" solution. Duty-free shopping would enable Chinese tourists to partake in their favored leisure pursuit and yield eye-popping tourism-related revenues. A third factor was also important. The initiative appeased the world's luxury brands which were investing in flashy China flagship stores and advertising campaigns for only-for-China product lines – but whose sales growth was sluggish due to the high duties on upscale goods sold in Chinese malls.

Duty-free shopping in Hainan proved an instant success. Some 140,000 people passed through the doors of the Sanya duty-free center in the first week. At the time of opening, visitors aged 16 years and above were permitted a duty-free allowance of up to RMB 5,000 (USD 804). This figure proved inadequate, and was increased in 2012 to RMB 8,000 (USD 1,286).

Startling statistics flowed through the cash tills. From the opening of Hainan Island's first duty-free mall in April 2011 until the end of December 2013, Customs figures reveal the two duty free centers – in addition to Sanya, a second was opened in Haikou, the island's provincial capital – garnered 2.51 million visitors, who spent a total of RMB 6.3 billion (USD 1.01 billion), RMB 3.3 billion (USD 0.53 billion) of which was spent in 2013 alone. During the 2014 Spring Festival Golden

Week, the two duty free centers attracted 56,000 shoppers who spent RMB 226 million, representing annual increases of 30 and 33 percent, respectively.

Those big numbers fuelled escalating ambition – and more shopping developments. In the north of the island, Mission Hills Haikou opened in 2010 as a sibling golf and leisure resort to Mission Hills Shenzhen, the world's largest golf club. It counts ten 18-hole courses, a five-star hotel and spa, thermal hot springs, a sports center and an aquatic theme park. Nearby, Hainan Provincial Duty Free has launched what it calls a "duty free shopping paradise," in partnership with DFS, at the Mission Hills Tourism Town Center.

Meanwhile, the CDF Group says it is building the "world's largest duty free complex" in Haitang Bay, which will be completed in "two to three years." The company estimates Hainan's duty free shopping boom has opened up "a potential market of USD 425 million annually" – roughly the equivalent to the turnover of Chelsea Football Club in the 12-month period to 30 June 2013.

As always with Chinese tourism trends, the inevitable head-scratching questions accompany such pronouncements. How did visitor volumes expand so quickly? Is shopping tourism really so profitable? And what is the link between Hainan Island and China's expanding class of resort vacationers now securing high-priced suites in Bali, Maldives and Seychelles? So, firstly, let's take a step back.

Build big resorts and they will come

At the turn of the millennium, Hainan Island – which is roughly the size of Belgium, and sits off the southern coast between China and Vietnam – hardly registered on the radar of Chinese travelers, let alone global tourists. Chinese domestic and outbound travel was in its infancy, and inbound tourism was mostly focused on Shanghai, Beijing and Xi'an. Despite its splendid tropical beaches, forested highlands and hot springs, Hainan Island – which is China's smallest province – was a barren backwater.

This perception was influenced by historical factors. During the Tang and Song dynasties, Hainan Island was considered to be the End of the World, a place where disgraced government officials and criminals were exiled offshore to live in squalor and penury. The Li ethnic minority people inhabit large swathes of the interior, and the Han Chinese often shunned their cultural traditions – although they are now being revived and promoted in some of the swankier resorts.

The first I heard about Hainan Island was in 2003, while watching a TV documentary about veteran British entertainer Bruce Forsyth, who was filmed playing golf on the island while accompanying his wife on a business trip. Lady Wilnelia Forsyth, a former winner of the Miss World beauty pageant, was visiting Hainan to design swimwear for the contest. The hosting of the 2003 Miss World event at the Sheraton Sanya Resort in Yalong Bay attracted voluble media interest. Hoteliers regularly cite the pageant as placing Hainan onto the tourism map. The Miss World competition has since returned on four occasions, in 2004, 2005, 2007 (the first time the pageant was won by a Chinese contestant) and 2010.

Eight years later, in 2011, Sanya welcomed a contrasting group of VIPs. Presidents Dilma Rousseff (Brazil), Dmitry Medvedev (Russia), Hu Jintao (China) and Jacob Zuma (South Africa), and Prime Minister Manmohan Singh (India) flew in to attend the 2011 BRICS Leaders Summit (Brazil, Russia, India, China, South Africa). In less than a decade, Hainan Island had graduated from courting Miss World to hosting a high-level economic conference of global leaders.

At the same time, the Hainan Tourism Development Commission was working with the World Travel and Tourism Council (WTTC) to produce a forecast for its development potential over the next ten years. In its report, the WTTC noted that the earmarking of Hainan as an "international resort island" by China's State Council was attracting "growing interest among tourism and hospitality investors and management companies." According to the Hainan Government, the island had "embarked on a plan to compete with regional top draws like Bali, Phuket and Boracay by 2020."

But despite signing up the world's leading resort operators, Hainan is not really an international destination. Its limited tourism infrastructure beyond the resorts, lack of international flights and the relatively high cost compared to other Asian destinations stymied tourism interest beyond the Chinese mainland. Hainan received 36.73 million visitors in 2013 (up from 10.1 million in 2010), but only 756,400 were from overseas.

Hainan did successfully attract Russian charter packages during the icy northern European winter – and many hotels still have their menus printed in Russian, in addition to Chinese and English – but volumes dropped from 227,557 in 2011 to 113,092 in 2013. Attempts by a British tour operator to launch charter packages to Hainan were predictably short lived, and despite a marketing push in Malaysia and Singapore, the overwhelming majority of visitors to Hainan hail from mainland China.

As a result, hotel operators are struggling year round to fill the rooms and suites in cavernous resorts constructed at high cost. Even with total overnight visitors to the island increasing from 22.5 million in 2009 to 36.73 million in 2013, a significant increase in room inventories weighs upon the shoulders of general managers, as does the fierce competition for staff to service resorts that often count upwards of 500 rooms, plus several restaurants, a deluxe spa, landscaped tropical gardens, water sports activities, kids' clubs and conference and weddings facilities.

Among the solutions being favored is to integrate private villas into the new beach resorts. A few years ago, the general manager of a luxury Sanya resort gave me a tour of his new property. He dutifully answered my questions about target markets, food and beverage sales and the strategy for grabbing a chunk of the island's high-end meetings, incentives, conferences, and exhibitions (MICE) market. Then, he pointed to a path that clipped between slim palms and tropical bushes at the far end of the resort. It led to a collection of private villas. With hindsight, he admitted, the resort planners should have allocated more space for villas.

Private villas are increasingly an integral aspect of resort development in China. These multi-level luxury homes afford premium amenities ranging from private saunas, jacuzzis and gyms to banqueting suites with private chefs, personal butlers and access to private yachts. In addition, they provide a rare, potent combination for the jetset who made their fortunes in China's crowded cities: exclusive sea views and total privacy. The general manager told me that wealthy mainland businessmen booked the villas for extended periods then flew in and out as they wished by private jet. Managing the villas resembled overseeing private safe-deposit boxes in a Swiss bank.

Changing locational trends have also impacted the finances of Hainan's resorts. At the end of 2008, 55 percent of Hainan's five-star hotels were located in Yalong Bay – which developed as China's first beach resort destination. It features beachside resorts by Marriott, The Ritz-Carlton, Hilton, Sheraton and Crowne Plaza. These were joined in 2012 by MGM Grand Sanya, which opened its first non-casino resort. Further along the beach, Starwood's St. Regis brand operates a deluxe resort, while in nearby Sunny Bay a long-delayed Park Hyatt resort is taking shape.

But these developments on the curving white sands of Yalong Bay, which are credited with encouraging beach holidays as a new form of tourism in China, are the first phase of a more extensive plan. A few coastal Chinese cities, such as Beihai, Dalian, Qingdao, Qinhuangdao, and Xiamen, offer beaches, but their restricted facilities no longer appeal to China's self-consciously aspirational travelers who desire more experiential excitement for their RMB.

Hainan was the "next big thing," offering design-led lodgings, palm-fringed spas and swimming pools, seaside sunsets and year-round sunny weather. The necessity of taking a flight to reach it elevated its exotic appeal, as did the fact that Chinese travelers do not require a visa to access their own piece of paradise. Once the momentum was created, Hainan became an increasingly easy sell to mainland tourists with money to spend and a desire to escape the daily grind. During school summer holidays and the two Golden Week vacations, it's almost impossible to find a hotel room.

Hainan's initial success in attracting Chinese tourists encouraged property developers to build more resorts. Another driving force was the emerging trend among both international companies operating in

China and Chinese multinationals for hosting regional sales meetings and seminars, incentives trips and staff teambuilding programs beside the sea. From the outset, sizeable conference, meeting and banqueting facilities were a signature feature of Hainan's resorts.

With constructive capacity saturated at Yalong Bay, developers persuaded global hotel companies to sign up for new projects across southern Hainan. The next swathe of openings included Mandarin Oriental at Coral Bay and Le Meridien Shimei Bay, on a remote stretch of coastline a 90-minute drive north from Sanya, where impressive waves during October and November have made it one of China's few surf destinations.

At the same time, attention was turning to the 20 kilometers of beachfront at Haitang Bay, west of Yalong Bay. Here, a planned mini city of up to 25 resorts includes Conrad, The Westin, Renaissance, Sheraton, Kempinski and InterContinental. Rosewood and Shangri-La are also preparing to open. Perhaps the highest profile new abode will be Kerzner International's joint venture with China's Fosun to develop the USD 1.6 billion Atlantis Sanya. Scheduled to open in 2016, the 62-hectare Atlantis Sanya will follow a similar aquatic theme to the two existing Atlantis Resorts, in the Bahamas and Dubai.

More than just beach malls

Resort construction alone does not a destination make. The inauguration of the Mission Hills Haikou golf club and resort and the expansion of duty free shopping was a tacit admission that greater diversity was needed in Hainan's tourism offering – particularly as swanky developments targeting the consumer class are springing up in Macao, across mainland China and in emerging destinations like Hengqin.

Hainan's beach resorts hold considerable appeal for first- and second-time Chinese travelers to the island, but once tourists have gained a liking for tropical beach destinations they often choose to further their horizons in Thailand, Philippines, Malaysia and, increasingly, Bali. The jet-set villa crowd, meanwhile, has averted its gaze to the white sands of Mauritius, Maldives and Seychelles, with the Caribbean emerging into view.

But for every Chinese traveler who passes through and beyond Hainan, long lines of replacements prepare to board flights for their first tropical vacation. The government doesn't want such first-timers to jump a phase and head overseas before spending time and money in the tropical tourism training ground of Hainan.

In April 2013, President Xi Jinping chose the 2013 Boao Forum for Asia, which is held annually in Hainan, for his announcement that in the next five years China will probably send over 400 million tourists overseas. This was not a coincidence. Hainan occupies a pivotal position in the government's plan for tourism to be a pillar sector of China's future economic growth.

This fact was highlighted by Hainan's hosting of the 2014 World Travel and Tourism Council Global Summit, during which Shao Qiwei, CNTA Chairman, said China is planning a "national leisure strategy." Before the event, Chinese media referred to the nation's "increasing affinity for traveling and shopping" – a trend that Hainan has so assiduously encouraged. He Xiqing, Deputy Head of Hainan province, was quoted as saying that the island provides China with a testing ground to improve its tourism industry.

Signs of tourism diversification are emerging. In 2014, Hainan hosted the International Association of Golf Tour Operators' third annual Asia Golf Tourism Convention, at Mission Hills Haikou. The event, which attracted golf tour operators from 32 countries, presented Hainan and China as flourishing golf destinations, and provided a platform for Asian golfing locations to tap the region's fastest growing outbound golf market.

Another potential money-spinner is medical tourism. In April 2013, Hainan published a plan to build the first medical tourism zone in China. Already the Sanya Traditional Chinese Medicine (TCM) Hospital, which offers TCM therapies like acupuncture, massage and cupping has attracted patients from Russia and Central Asia. The hospital has established its own travel agency to expand its business.

Promoting the luxury lifestyle

Hainan Island is also the founding location for China's most coveted luxury travel and lifestyle showcase. China Rendezvous was launched in 2010 (under its original name, Hainan Rendezvous), and is a high-profile annual meeting place for super-rich Chinese, plus the world's leading yacht, private aircraft and lifestyle brands. Held at the Sanya Visun Royal Yacht Club, China Rendezvous describes itself as "a leader in promoting luxury lifestyles in China." The show is divided into four main sections: yachts, private jets, luxury cars, jewelry and lifestyle brands, and art.

The fifth edition of the show, held at the end of March 2014, was timely. In late 2013, China's aviation regulator relaxed rules for obtaining a private pilot's license and for the operation of small jets in China. Although numerous obstacles exist, notably the number of airports able to handle executive jets, the rule changes were an attempt to spur growth in the civil aviation sector. New rules on low-level aviation enabled Hainan Sanya Jubilee General Aviation to launch sightseeing helicopter flights from Haikou.

In 2014, the China Rendezvous show was rebranded So Rendezvous, Now a touring showcase, the debut event in July 2014 was held in the northeastern port city of Dalian – chosen because "Dalian is already the destination of choice for China's northern elite," according to a press statement. So Rendezvous showcases are also planned in Hainan, Cannes and Hong Kong.

The move to Dalian was not coincidental. Yacht ownership, which is still in its infancy in China, received a fillip in 2013 when the Dalian Wanda Group purchased UK-based Sunseeker yachts and agricultural machinery manufacturer Shandong Heavy Industry Group bought a controlling stake in Italian yachtmaker Ferretti SpA. In addition, Sundiro Holdings purchased a stake in Italian shipyard Sanlorenzo, and is establishing a joint venture to building medium-sized yachts in Hainan.

Showing a canny sense of PR savvy, the show's organizers held a press conference and investor showcase at the Monaco Yacht Show in September 2013. During the media event, the founder of China Rendezvous, Wang Dafu, told the media that the show's mission was to "lead the high-quality lifestyle and redefine the high-end lifestyle in China."

China Rendezvous has coincided with a succession of ocean-focused tourism trends in China, such as the proliferation of yacht marinas, increased use of yacht charters and cruise vacations. Each one is predicted to grow significantly. Another important development occurred in early 2014, when Hainan – taking its cue from island destinations like the Maldives, Hawaii and Australia's Great Barrier Reef – introduced China's first seaplane trips. The Cessna planes are operated by Sanya-based Meiya Air, and take tourists on flights around Hainan Island and the offshore Xisha Islands.

Around 180 nautical miles southeast of Hainan, the Xisha islands (also called the Paracel Islands) comprise a cluster of islets boasting a tropical ecosystem, sandbanks and coral reefs. Hainan is targeting three of the island groups, Xisha, Zhongsha and Nansha, for tourism development. A small number of 20-hour round-trip cruises aboard the 200-person Coconut Princess to Yongxing Island in the Xinsha archipelago have been offered since April 2013 from Haikou, and a second ship was due to begin sailing in late 2014. Infrastructure development – including a port, hospital, power station and seawater purification plant – is slated for Sansha, which was only founded as a city in 2012.

China's beach mavens join the jetset

The critical success of Hainan Island has been the way it has encouraged the Chinese to enjoy a beach-centered holiday with family and friends, a type of vacation previously off limits. As the founding venue of Chinese coastal tourism, Hainan has nurtured an expanding class of resort vacationers that now join the global jet set beside beaches and infinity pools from Bondi to Hawaii and Boracay to Florida – a development that seemed fanciful a decade ago.

Located southeast of China – directly north of Indonesia and east of the Indochine Peninsula – the Philippines is a collection of 7,107 islands spread across 300,000 square miles of land in the western Pacific Ocean. In 2013 it received 426,352 arrivals from China, up 69.9 percent from 250,883 in 2012. China accounted for 9.1 percent of total visitors, making it the fourth-largest source market after South Korea, US and Japan.

The Indonesian beach playground of Bali is also brushing up on its Mandarin and Cantonese language skills. China was Bali's second-largest tourism source market (after Australia) in 2013, delivering 387,533 visitors (more than the combined total from the UK, France and the US). This figure amounted to 11.8 percent of Bali's total arrivals despite no direct flights being available between China and Bali. This situation was remedied in early 2014, when Hainan Airlines introduced three weekly flights between Beijing and Denpasar. Strong demand for trips to Bali is expected to drive more new flight services.

'Aloha' is another word being added to the Chinese travel lexicon. Visitors from China to the eight Pacific islands of Hawaii more than tripled from 41,900 in 2009 to 132,634 in 2013, according to Hawaii's Department of Business, Economic Development and Tourism. Some 85.2 percent of Chinese visitors in 2013, who stayed an average length of 6.24 days, were first-time visitors. It's not just the stunning beaches and surfing that attract Chinese travelers, of course; shopping for gemstones and branded goods in Honolulu, touring volcanoes, whale watching, seaside dining and even purchasing real estate are cited as additional motivations.

Air connectivity was a major hindrance – until recently, flights from China to Hawaii were routed via Seoul and Tokyo. China Eastern launched direct flights between Shanghai and Honolulu in 2011, and Air China added flights from Beijing to Honolulu in early 2014 – its fifth US destination after New York, Los Angeles, San Francisco and Houston. Hawaiian Airlines launched three weekly flights to/from Beijing in April 2014, and plans to expand to other Chinese cities.

Resort brands are accordingly positioning themselves in China. Alila Hotels & Resorts is a leading Asian boutique hotelier, with properties in

India and Indonesia, and new resort openings in 2014 including Oman, Bali and Bishangarh, India. Alila will also open its first Chinese resort Alila Anji, in Zhejiang province, followed by three more properties, at Tianxi Lake, Yangshuo and Hainan Island, over the next two years. The expansion of the brand's "understated luxury" resorts concept into China is aimed at enhancing the Alila portfolio and growing its Chinese clientele base.

"Alila Villas Uluwatu and Alila Ubud are the popular choices for Chinese guests," says Frederic Simon, Chief Executive Officer of Alila Hotels and Resorts. "It happened organically for us by being promoted through word of mouth by discerning Chinese travelers. Through a growing network of Alila fans in China, we were accorded the 2013 CTW Gold Award for Service Quality presented by the China Outbound Tourism Research Institute."

Design innovation, lifestyle options and environmental sustainability are aspects of the Alila brand that play well with Chinese guests, says Simon. Tailored services are also provided. "We ensure that Chinese-speaking team members are available to enhance the overall experience, and we launched our Alila Chinese website last year," Simon adds. The Chinese media is also an important connecting mechanism. "Their stories help educate and enlighten the growing segment of Chinese travelers that are pursuing authentic cultural and eco-intellectual tourism," says Simon.

The Maldives is also a coveted destination. China accounted for 29.5 percent of all tourist arrivals in 2013. The 331,719 Chinese visitors (staying an average 6.3 days) represented a 44.5 percent increase from 2012.

"China is without doubt the year-round feeder market for the Maldives. During China's main holidays business increases, however, there has been a steady number of Chinese visitors throughout the last couple of years," says Haydee Cruz, Director of Sales and Marketing for Sun Siyam Resorts. "Chinese guests tend to stay for shorter periods due to fewer vacation days. There are a lot of honeymooners, but not many repeat visitors to the destination. The cultural differences are remarkable, and we have adapted to the demands. To promote the resort, we [are] working closely with regional luxury travel and destination specialists."

Chinese tourism and national development in Seychelles

Receiving 7,745 Chinese visitors during 2013 may not seem a big deal, particularly when they represent a small proportion of the 230,272 arrivals to Seychelles in 2013. But 7,745 represents a more than seven-fold increase in Chinese visitors compared to 2010, and in the context of the mid-term development of a Small Island Developing State (SID), optimism is being channeled into action.

A relatively young democracy, independent since 1976, the Republic of Seychelles comprises 115 islands in the Western Indian Ocean. Isolated and under-developed, Seychelles is turning to tourism – described as "the key sector of our economy," by Minister for Finance Pierre Laporte in his 2012 budget address – to fund its goals of eradicating poverty and disease and improving social provision. *The Millennium Development Goals Status Report*, published in 2013 in partnership with the United Nations Development Programme (UNDP), provides a road map for economic development in a nation the ageing population of which is predicted to reach 100,000 by 2020.

The tourism industry dominates recent economic performance and future development. The Seychelles tourism board describes the country as "one of the world's very last frontiers." In addition to picture-postcard beaches, golf, glass-bottom boat trips and water sports are popular activities, as are guided eco tours through its forest river valleys. In 2012, 92 percent of visitors arrived on holiday, with just two percent visiting for business.

According to the Seychelles Investment Board, tourism accounts for around 60 percent of total foreign exchange receipts. Included among the investment opportunities advertised on its website, are yacht marinas, eco tourism villas, intra-island mini cruises, niche hotels, and integrated tourism projects.

Expanding tourism revenues requires a new vision. The Millennium Development report notes "the country has attempted to diversify its tourist markets given the persistent difficult external environments in traditional source markets which have been affected by the Eurozone crisis." Instead, its attentions turned to buoyant outbound markets, including China.

On 31 January 2014, Chinese Year's Day, the culmination of three days of Seychelles–China Day celebrations, featuring lion dancers, the Liaoning Ballet, Shanghai Jinshan Art group, Shenyang Acrobatic Troupe and Chinese banquets, took place at a luxury resort. The festival, which is expected to become an annual event, was designed to showcase Chinese culture, and enable the people of Seychelles – especially those with Chinese ancestry – to learn more about a nation from which immigrants began arriving in the 1880s.

Most importantly, it formed part of the Seychelles Tourism Board's outreach strategy to Chinese tourists. In 2013, Seychelles established tourism offices in Beijing, Shanghai and Hong Kong, and Air Seychelles, which is 40 percent owned by Abu Dhabi's Etihad Airways, launched a flight service to/from Hong Kong. The promotional push brought some initial gains. Of the 16,521 tourists who landed in Seychelles during January 2014 (during which the Chinese Spring Festival began), 2,086 were from China – the month's third-largest source market, after Russia and France.

Cruising the high seas

Cruise travel is being hyped as a "coming force" in Chinese tourism, and big-name operators, including Costa Cruises, P&O Cruises, Princess Cruises and Royal Caribbean, are bringing sizeable ships and sales forces to China. The main ports for passenger cruising are Shanghai, Tianjin, Dalian, Qingdao, Xiamen and Sanya. In 2012, those six cities received 285 cruise vessels (up from just 24 in 2006), according to the China Cruise & Yacht Industry Association.

During its decadent 1930s "Pearl of the Orient" era, Shanghai received the world's leading cruise lines, which sailed along the Huangpu River and docked on the Bund. Despite its cruise dream being curtailed by the pre-war Japanese invasion and Mao's subsequent Communist Revolution, Shanghai is back in the frame as a cruise destination. The RMB 870 million (USD 139.8 million) seashell-shaped Shanghai Wusongkou International Cruise Port at Baoshan was expected to receive 239 cruise ships and around 1.55 million passengers in 2014, a huge increase on the 357,000 cruise passengers handled in Shanghai in 2012.

Asian cruising, as a whole, is only starting to develop, accounting for 3.4 percent of the global cruise capacity market in 2013, with a predicted rise to 4.4 percent in 2014, according to the US-based Cruise Lines International Association (CLIA). Hong Kong and Singapore are the two primary ports for boarding and departure.

Chinese cruisers have thus far proved to be of the "party" variety, mostly taking short four- or five-day trips to South Korea and Japan. To meet customer demand, ships docking in China are regularly custom-fitted with Chinese restaurants, karaoke lounges, casinos and even shopping arcades. More expansive voyages to South East Asia, taking in Vietnam, Malaysia and Thailand, are now being offered, while in 2014 the Costa Atlantica – operated by Carnival's Costa Cruises brand, the first international cruise line to run homeport cruises from Shanghai in 2006 – was scheduled to launch an 83-day round-the-world cruise departing from Shanghai, and stopping at 23 destinations in 16 countries, including Sri Lanka, Maldives, Italy, Spain, Miami and the Hawaiian Islands.

"China's first around-the-world cruise is the lynchpin of our Asia strategy over the next couple of years. It heralds a new milestone in China's cruise industry," said Pier Luigi Foschi, Chairman and CEO of Carnival Asia, in a company statement.

Meanwhile, in October 2013 the Dubai-based owner of the QE2 cruise liner – which has hosted kings, queens, presidents, prime ministers and celebrities throughout its legendary 40-year history – appointed the COSCO Shipyard Group in Zhoushan, Zhejiang province, to refurbish the ship into an all-suites luxury cruise hotel.

Chapter 6

Lights, Camera, Action: Chinese Tourism on TV and Film

On your marks, get set ... shoot!

In late February 2014, my email inbox was jammed with press releases global tourism boards congratulating themselves on a successful start to the year. January, the texts read, witnessed high double-digit year-on-year increases for visitor arrivals from China. This data was extrapolated to predict another China-inspired record-breaking tourism year.

Such has become the addiction to Chinese outbound spending that travel marketers are resorting to trickery of the above kind. Great statistics make for great marketing copy, but these had a little added spin. Casting aside the issue of whether record volumes of Chinese will head overseas in 2014, there is a simple reason why foreign destinations witnessed the much-hyped January spike. In late January 2014, Chinese vacationers began traveling for the Spring Festival Golden Week holiday. The previous year, in 2013, the Spring Festival – which is based on the lunisolar calendar – did not begin until the second week of February.

Chinese travelers have issued an open invitation to "Catch us if you can," and the response underscores the degree to which travel marketing has evolved. For the past half-decade, it has no longer been about promoting and selling hotel rooms, airline seats and tour products. Instead, all sectors of the travel industry are now compelled to present image-rich narratives and tempt travelers with overlapping experiences and activities that previously may have seemed unattainable. If there is one buzzword that defines today's travel zeitgeist, it is "experiential." We are no longer considered to be mere travelers or tourists, but consumers of travel-based services and experiences.

In China, a country that is embracing consumerism with gleeful relish, these changes have occurred within a compressed time scale. The travel and tourism industry has jumped several phases in much less than a decade, moving from marketing activities focused on educating the public about overseas destinations and hotel brands to delivering travel service strategies that are credible, authentic and engaging for a knowledgeable travel class that is bombarded with consumer advertising at every turn of daily life.

A second challenge is the proliferation of platforms. Long gone are the days when tourism boards, hotel chains, airlines and tour providers earmarked a large chunk of their annual budget to shoot expensive "Welcome to Our Country" TV commercials and attend travel trade shows to show them to travel agents, who were the middle men between destinations and consumers. The Internet intervention transformed the destination–consumer dynamic, creating a direct, interactive relationship.

Another interesting factor in the Chinese experience has been the role of state-run television. Chinese major TV stations now send crews to shoot their own travel documentaries – often in partnership with overseas tourism boards. These programs are often broadcast as a series and are closely framed to what Chinese travelers wish to watch and the travel activities to which they aspire.

This reactivation of tourism promotion uses multimedia technology to better connect the different aspects of the media mix. Where once the travel trade was the number one platform, tourism marketers now utilize social media, database marketing, HD TV screens and the near-24/7 use of smartphones and mobile devices to distribute bespoke messaging, imagery and information. In this way, tourism providers are the producers and directors of their own content, and can package, publish and distribute it across myriad platforms. Such smart content management adds more interactive and easily monitored verticality to their marketing strategies.

Video marketing is a particularly effective tool that is being deployed more frequently by destination marketers in China. This works for a number of reasons:

- Total control is gained over the visual messaging for a targeted market segment or niche – because, unlike a TV advert for which payment is required on a per-minute basis, there are no set limits on duration or scope.
- The content can be re-edited and reused on several platforms to capture different captive markets, for example, on a destination website, on screens in elevators, shopping malls, city centers and airports, on Chinese video sites like youku.com, in-flight TV screens, and for distribution through Chinese social media.
- It appeals to the voracious appetite for engaging visual content, particularly by Chinese commuters on the way to and from work, who regularly download and watch TV shows and movies on smartphones while waiting for and riding the city metro networks (NB, often to the detriment of subway platform advertising).
- Video content has the propensity to "go viral" at high speed, through being viewed and shared by users of social media sites.
- Very importantly, it enables marketers to contexualize their destination for Chinese consumers, particularly by featuring Chinese travelers and activities that appeal to Chinese consumers in each video package.

Destination marketing in the movies

Governments and tourism promoters working to attract more Chinese visitors might wish to consider inviting a Chinese moviemaker to shoot a film on their shores. The experience of Thailand suggests that the flourishing Chinese cinema business offers rich marketing rewards.

In late 2012, first-time Chinese director Xu Zheng released a comedy film set in Thailand with little expectation of success. Within one month of hitting Chinese cinemas, 38 million moviegoers had seen *Lost in Thailand*, making it the year's highest grossing movie. It also sparked a tourism surge to the Land of Smiles.

The slapstick movie follows the exploits of two ham-fisted Chinese businessmen and a bleached-blond Chinese tourist in Thailand. Likened by *Hollywood Reporter* to "China's version of *The Hangover*," the film's release in December 2012 was propitiously timed. Chinese travel agencies spotted an opportunity to create tours to locations featured in the movie, including Chiang Mai, for the upcoming Spring Festival holiday in February 2013. Chinese travelers signed up in droves.

The Thai Tourism Board notes that more than 1.12 million Chinese travelers visited Thailand in the first quarter of 2013 – the first time any source market had exceeded the one million mark in a single quarter. Some 2.7 million Chinese travelers visited Thailand in 2012, which jumped to 4.7 million in 2013. Director Xu Zheng was even invited to a private meeting with Thai Prime Minister Yingluck Shinawatra as a personal thank you for helping promote Thai tourism in China, albeit inadvertently.

Thailand is not the only country backing movie-based travel. Tourism New Zealand heavily marketed its Middle Earth tourism program in China, as *The Hobbit* was one of only 34 foreign films released in China during in 2013. It held private screenings in Shanghai and Beijing for travel agents and media, and launched the 100 percent Middle Earth, 100 percent Pure New Zealand consumer campaign. Coverage of New Zealand Brand Ambassador Yao Chen's red carpet appearance at the movie's global premiere in Wellington generated across-the-board social media coverage.

Seattle also plotted to attract more Chinese visitors by being cast in a blockbuster movie. *Beijing Meets Seattle* (also called *Finding Mr Right*) was released in China in March 2013. The romantic comedy by writer-director Xue Xialou tells the story of a spoiled Chinese woman who is sent from Beijing to Seattle to escape a relationship with a criminal businessman, and who searches both for love and for US citizenship for her new baby in the northwestern US city of Seattle.

The Greek island of Santorini received money-can't-buy publicity as a wedding destination by starring in the hit movie *Beijing Love Story*. The Greek National Tourism Organisation's emblem and details were also featured in the movie credits. Directed by Chen Sicheng, the movie is the big-screen version of a popular Chinese TV series, and features movie superstars Tony Leung and Carina Lau.

Mauritius also utilized "destination placement" in a Chinese movie. Released in late 2013, the Chinese–Japanese co-production *Five Minutes in Mauritius* is a romantic mystery featuring Chinese ballerina-turned-actress Cecilia Liu in a lead role. During the shooting of the movie the Mauritius Tourism Promotion Authority and Minister of Tourism and Leisure, Michael Sik Yuen, hosted a press conference for Chinese, Japanese and South Korean media.

The Himalayan landscapes of Nepal are taking their big-screen bow. Released in China at the end of 2013, *Up in the Wind* is a romantic-comedy movie starring youth favorites Ni Ni and Jing Boran about two young Chinese who visit Nepal to explore their inner happiness. Around four-fifths of the movie was shot on location in Kathmandu, Pokhara and Chitwan. China's *Global Times* newspaper reported that after watching the movie, many young people had posted messages on social network sites saying they wished to visit Nepal in 2014.

The list of "movie marketers" continues to lengthen. In February 2014, Director Cao Dun began shooting *Love is Brave*, a 30-episode Chinese TV series to be broadcast nationwide. While some scenes starring Huang Haibo and Zhang Jingchu were shot in Beijing, around 100 actors and crew spent a month filming in Cambodia. The Cambodian Deputy Prime Minister approved the use of Angkor Wat and other locations for shooting the series to showcase the nation's tourism and culture to Chinese viewers. Cambodia received 463,000 Chinese visitors in 2013, and has targeted an increase to 800,000 in 2015 and up to two million in 2020. Air China operates regular flights between Beijing and

Siem Reap, while Cambodia Angkor Air connects with Shanghai and Guangzhou.

Celebrity match-ups made in tourism heaven

Take a stroll along the historic streets behind the Bund in Shanghai or among the grand European villas of its former French Concession, and young couples being photographed wearing western wedding gowns and morning suits are a common sight. Carefully staged "wedding photo shoots" against classic Shanghai backdrops have become a de rigueur element of the wedding planning process. The opportunity to export this faux-wedding photography to pristine beaches, country estates and man-made landmarks is a high-priority agenda for tourism marketers.

Wedding tourism is firmly established on the Chinese domestic travel landscape. Numerous online forums are devoted to wedding planning, and luxury hotels in major cities and in getaway destinations like Hainan Island maximize bookings by offering dedicated wedding planners, honeymoon packages and promotions, bespoke banquets and, not infrequently, an onsite wedding chapel.

For destinations wanting to send Chinese social media into overdrive, inviting Chinese celebrities to get married in an eye-catching destination is a no-brainer. Not only will it attract enormous interest from Chinese netizens, it can transform a beach, stately home or lakeside retreat into a coveted wedding destination for young Chinese couples. The following overseas weddings made big news in China:

- In 2008, actress Hu Jing wed Malaysian businessman Frank Choo in Kuala Lumpur.
- In 2008, celebrity couple Carina Lau and Tony Leung wed in Bhutan.
- In 2011, Hong Kong actress Sonija wed Chinese martial arts choreographer Zhu Shaojie in Guam.
- In 2012, actress Yao Chen wed photographer Cao Yu in Queenstown, New Zealand, which generated an estimated 7,000 media articles

and depicted Queenstown as a romantic destination for Chinese travelers.
- In 2014, TV and social media star Yang Mi wed Hong Kong actor Hawick Lau at the Bulgari Resort in Bali. Images of the nuptials set aflame social media, providing a marketing boost for the forthcoming Bulgari hotel opening in Shanghai.

The classic princess

Tourism marketers seeking China's hottest opinion-forming starlets for campaigns and promotions – and, be warned, they don't come cheap! – should scout the catwalks and front rows of the Paris, Milan, New York and London Fashion Weeks. The 2014 Mercedes-Benz Fashion Week in New York, for example, was abuzz with Chinese celebrities and a huge entourage of Chinese photographers. Among those taking center stage were actresses Zhang Lanxin, Jiang Xin and Wang Luodan, dancer Hou Honglan, fashion icon Zhang Xinyuan and models Ming Xi and Shu Pei.

Classical beauty is a pre-eminent current theme in the Chinese fashion media, and few celebrities define that more than Audrey Hepburn. Waiting for a flight at Shanghai's Pudong International Airport in early 2014, I noticed a black and white photo of Audrey Hepburn wearing a tiara and a diamond necklace and earrings framed in a giant backlit ad-box at the flight gate. I strolled along the departure hall and spotted several more of the same advert. A QR code and a URL address pointed me to the Chinese website for Princess Cruises.

Alluding to her "princess-like persona," the company's Chinese-language website (as its English-language counterpart) explains how Hepburn was one of the most admired celebrities of her era, and in 1989 became the "godmother" of the *Star Princess* cruise ship. Other female celebrities to have been named as godmothers of Princess ships include Diana, Princess of Wales, Sophia Loren and Martha Stewart. The Chinese website also featured text about Her Royal Highness, The Duchess of

Cambridge who, while not a ship godmother, is admired in China as the fashionable embodiment of a royal princess.

Using a timeless image of Audrey Hepburn to promote cruise trips in China struck me as an inventive strategy, especially for a brand that is relatively new to the market. Combining Hepburn's classic beauty with a modern British princess whose 2011 wedding sparked a rush for counterfeit versions of her dress in China was particularly deft – particularly as consumer brands have moved away from using international celebrities in preference for local movie stars, pop singers and models to connect with Chinese consumers.

In August 2013, the Carnival Corporation had announced it would bring its Princess Cruises brand to China in 2014, with Shanghai designated as the home port for the 2,670-passenger *Sapphire Princess* during a four-month season starting from May.

Princess Cruises released a press statement saying that China was "foremost in the company's deployment plans due to the market's burgeoning economy and increasingly discerning travelers seeking a premium cruise vacation."

Sales offices were opened in Beijing, Tianjin, Shanghai, Guangzhou and Chengdu to sell four different itineraries to South Korea and Jeju Island, ranging from three to seven days, which, according to the company's research, "is the ideal number of vacation days for the Chinese market."

Make mine a "selfie"

An undoubted challenge will be the ability of hotels, destinations and tourism attractions to provide new "experiential" photo opportunities. Chinese travelers love to take self-portraits, or "selfies," to share instantly via social media. Creating and offering unique, frequently changing photogenic backgrounds will appeal to Chinese tourists.

The Hong Kong Tourism Board showed ingenious adaptability when low-hanging smog enveloped the city and denied Chinese visitors the

Central skyline photos they desired. Local tourism officials quickly erected a giant canvas depicting a sunny image of the Hong Kong skyline on a clear day. Chinese visitors snapped themselves and each other in front of the canvas backdrop, using the artificial backdrop as a replacement selfie opportunity for the real thing. This "pop-up" photo opportunity was hugely appreciated, and garnered considerable media coverage.

Hotels can learn a few "photo opportunity" tricks from 1888 in Sydney, which claims to be "the world's first Instagram hotel." The 90-room heritage property was relaunched as a boutique hotel in 2013, and devised a collection of experiential design elements to encourage guests to shoot and share Instagram images. Instagram users with more than 10,000 followers can redeem a free night's stay at the hotel, which also offers a "Selfie space" in the lobby where guests can take pictures, which if tagged to the hotel will instantly appear on a screen near the reception. The hotel also teamed up with a fashion blogger to create an Insta-Walk: a 45-minute stroll around the hotel and Darling Harbour for taking photos. This is the kind of novel experience combining modern technology and savvy marketing that Chinese travelers seek to help gain a new perspective on their chosen destination.

10 things that savvy Chinese travelers know…

1. That they comprise the most coveted group of travelers on the planet – and tourism providers are designing products and services specifically for them.
2. That the RMB is one of the world's strongest currencies – and any tourism provider, retailer or hotel wanting their trade should accept Chinese payment cards.
3. That your wine list needs updating – as China is expected to become the second-largest consumer of wine by 2016.
4. That they know more about your popular culture, than you do about theirs – as TV shows including *Downton Abbey*, *House of Cards*, *Sherlock* and *Ellen* are licensed for online viewing in China

on Sohu.com and Youku.cn. China also has its own versions of *The Voice* and *American Idol*.
5. That city transport beyond the bounds of state-controlled pricing is expensive: In Beijing, the taxi flag fall is RMB 12 (USD 1.92), or RMB 14 (USD 2.25) in Shanghai, and the shortest metro journey costs RMB 2 (USD 0.32) in Beijing, or RMB 4 (USD 0.64) in Shanghai.
6. That URL and website marketing is so 2012 – it's all about QR codes and mobile app downloads now.
7. That smartphone taxi booking is easier than on-street hailing. China's two largest Internet companies Alibaba and Tencent (which, as previously noted, owns WeChat) have invested in the Kuaidi Dache and Didi Dache, respectively, smart cab-booking services similar to Hailo and others in the West.
8. That mobile travel planning and booking aren't developing trends – they are right here, right now.
9. That free Wi-Fi access in a hotel room, not just in the hotel's public areas, is an expected service, not a privilege.
10. That themed trips and itineraries with aspirational hooks, like gourmet dining, wine culture, artisan food products and distinctive regional brands, push their buttons.

Chapter 7

All Around the World: Tourism Marketers Target China

Part I: Grand China plans

ASEAN targets India and China

Regional tourism cooperation is a developing global trend, particularly in Europe and the Caribbean, where individual nations collaborate to improve tourism flows within a region by concentrating on fast-emerging source markets like China. In 2011, the ten members of the Association of South East Asian Nations (ASEAN) – Singapore, Malaysia, Thailand, Vietnam, Indonesia, Myanmar, Brunei Darussalam, the Philippines, Cambodia and Laos – published a five-year Tourism Marketing Strategy.

Spanning the period from 2011 until 2015, the plan coincided with the establishment of the ASEAN Economic Community (or AEC) in 2015. Regional economic integration has been a long-cherished goal in South East Asia, and its leaders believe a single market will help member nations to compete more effectively for investment against regional heavyweights China and India.

The ASEAN tourism strategy was agreed by all ten national tourism organizations to promote "a competitive and world-class tourism destination" under the "South East Asia: Feel the Warmth" regional brand. It was devised within a competitive global environment "where many regional groups are now working very effectively together and dedicating resources to position their products and experiences," ASEAN says.

The strategy document recognizes that the opening of new easily accessible source markets by Asian low-cost carriers has challenged the previous reliance on long-haul markets. Allied to this, the diversity of intra-Asian travel is boosting untapped segments like incentive travel, experiential adventure, culinary tours and senior tourism, plus "the growing trend in cities as attractions."

Unsurprisingly, the five-year plan focuses on "the Indian and Chinese mass-markets" as the most important sources of visitors to ASEAN countries. The report observes that "while it is true that there are growing segments of the China market that have identified North America and Europe as preferred destinations, for many first-time travelers, South East Asia is still seen as an important destination."

ASEAN's growing reliance on China and India is emphasized in its tourism arrival predictions. The ten nations received a total of 79.2 million visitors in 2011, a figure projected to reach 107.4 million by 2015. A heavy emphasis for delivering those figures is being placed on digital marketing in China and India.

Australia and New Zealand

Tourism Australia is among the most proactive foreign bodies to engage with Chinese travelers, and targeted marketing has reaped success. Australia received 709,000 visitors from China in 2013, a yearly increase of 14.5 percent. The *Tourism 2020 Strategy* (published in 2011) estimates that Chinese visitation could earn annual revenues of between AUD 7.4–9 billion by 2020.

Australia's approach to Chinese tourism is aided by strong historical links. The Chinese Museum in central Melbourne claims the city's Chinatown is one of the world's longest continuously inhabited Chinese settlements outside Asia. Its founders arrived, mostly from China's impoverished southern provinces, in the mid-1850s to work in the mines in Bendigo, Ballarat, Castlemaine and Ararat during Australia's gold rush. By 1858, the Chinese population had swelled to 40,000. More than 150 years later, the 2011 Census revealed that 866,000 Australians define their ethnic origin as Chinese.

The China 2020 Strategy identified five strategic pillars: (1) knowing the customer, (2) a dedicated geographic strategy, (3) delivering quality Australian tourism experiences, (4) a healthy aviation development environment, and (5) strong partnerships between government and industry. In addition, Tourism Australia commissioned external research into the long-haul travel behavior and preferences of Chinese leisure visitors to "improve understanding of what drives their travel decisions," and AUD 1 million was ring-fenced for translating tourism information into Chinese.

Tourism Australia increased marketing spending in China by 41 percent in 2012/13, after a doubling in 2011/12. Part of that was invested in an online drama, called *Discover Your Australia*, filmed in New South Wales, Victoria and Tasmania in March 2012. The five 10-minute episodes feature Taiwanese pop stars Show Lo and Rainie Yang, who Tourism Australia say have "a combined social media following of 25 million fans throughout China."

Visitors to New Zealand from China – the nation's second-largest tourism source market after Australia – exceeded the 200,000 threshold for the first time in the year ended March 2013, and reached 240,288 (179,184 of whom visited on holiday) in the year to January 2014. Funded by the Ministry of Business, Innovation and Employment and managed by Tourism New Zealand, the China Toolkit was launched in November 2013. Designed to improve tourism sector knowledge of the requirements of Chinese travelers, the online toolkit's stated objective is "to accelerate the ability of New Zealand businesses and destinations to raise their service levels for the Chinese visitor market."

The toolkit features market research and statistics, a primer on learning the Chinese language, and an infographic showing visitation by municipality and province in China, locations visited and the preferred activities of Chinese visitors to New Zealand. Also included are background information on Chinese foods and beverages, a Chinese-language video about self-drive vacations and information about a Chinese language campaign promoting the "Middle Earth" locations for shooting *The Hobbit* and *Lord of the Rings* movie trilogies.

Intriguingly, for a destination that is a 12.5-hour flight from Shanghai or 16 hours via Hong Kong from Beijing, the average length of stay for holidaymakers was just 7.5 days in the year ended June 2014. Purchasing power is strong, though, with Chinese holiday visitors spending an average of NZD 3,781 per day in the year ending March 2014.

China, Brand USA and 100 million visitors

"The United States has largely missed out on the global travel boom of the past few years… the nation's share of long-haul arrivals is still well below historic levels, having declined from 17 percent in 2000 to 12.4 percent in 2011." This clear-minded assessment featured in the Brand USA 2014 business plan. "International travel is growing more than three times as fast as U.S. GDP," it continues. "The travel and tourism industry is also hiring people at a much faster rate than other sectors of the US economy." The conclusion was clear: the US must up its tourism game.

Brand USA was established by the Travel Promotion Act, which became law in March 2010, as the first-ever national travel promotion program to attract international travelers to the US. The Act would, said Roger Dow, President and CEO of the US Travel Association, "support the power of travel to serve as an economic stimulant, job generator and diplomatic tool," in an official statement.

The economic value of inbound travel was not lost on the Obama Administration. Tourism accounted for 26 percent of all services exports in 2013. The government wants to improve this figure, not least because the US welcomed 2.4 million fewer overseas visitors in 2009 than in 2000, costing an estimated USD 509 billion in total spending.

The US ranks second to France for international arrivals, but it has lost ground to the competition from emerging economies like China, Hong Kong, Malaysia, and Thailand as it seeks to achieve 100 million visitors by the end of 2021. The problem, highlighted in the Brand USA report, is that America is perceived as a "middle-aged," tourism nation that is "neither as attractive as the timeless, historical destinations of Europe, nor as alluring as the newcomers of the East."

Brand USA was created to make America more relevant for dynamic global source markets, of which China is the choicest pick. In 2006, China ranked as the 17th-largest international inbound market, with over 320,000 Chinese visitors. In 2013, China ranked seventh, accounting for 1.81 million arrivals The US Department of Commerce predicts Chinese visitation to the US to rise 139 percent between 2013 and 2018, when it is likely to send 2.5 million annual visitors.

China was the sixth-highest spender in the US in 2013, splashing out USD 9.8 billion. It didn't even make the top ten spending rankings in 2008. Tourism spending by Chinese travelers rose by 47 percent in both 2010 and 2011; and in 2013, travel and tourism accounted for 29 percent of all US services exports to China. Brand USA research revealed that Hawaii ranked as the destination of most interest to Chinese visitors, followed by California, New York, Washington state and Alaska.

A taste for Europe

Pre-dating the European Economic Community and the European Union, the European Travel Commission (ETC) was established in 1948 to promote tourism as a tool to help rebuild Europe after World War II. Today, the ETC comprises national tourism authorities from 33 European countries – including five non-EU members: Monaco, Montenegro, Norway, San Marino, Serbia, Switzerland and Turkey – who collaborate to promote Europe as a tourist destination. Its operations are focused on four primary markets, China, US, Brazil and Canada.

The ETC has actively researched Chinese travel developments to better educate its members. In 2012, it published a report entitled *Understanding Chinese Travelers*, followed in 2013 by the *Chinese Outbound Market* study. The ETC also worked with the UNWTO to produce a "netnographic" study, entitled *Understanding Outbound Chinese Tourism – What the Blogosphere is Saying*. A VisitEurope app was under development in early 2014.

In 2012, the ETC and the European Commission jointly launched Destination Europe 2020, a long-term strategy to promote Europe in the four key long-haul source markets. The central precepts were pan-European tourism themes and utilizing online marketing to connect with potential and repeat travelers to Europe.

Taking European tourism into the Middle Kingdom saw the ETC team up, in October 2013, with the European Commission and the UNWTO to host A Taste of Europe. The event was promoted as a multi-destination and culinary showcase for 200 Chinese and European tour operators, travel agencies, national tourism organizations, airlines, media and travel bloggers. "We want to highlight the great importance that China has for Europe. The European public and private sectors are committed to work together with the Chinese tourism industry to develop products that meet the real needs and expectations of Chinese travelers," said Eduardo Santander, Executive Director of the ETC at the event launch.

Part II: Tourism promotion in action

A Canadian winter wonderland

In 2013, Canada received 334,000 Chinese visitors, and has witnessed 20–25 percent annual growth since being granted ADS in 2010. Apart from the US, which is by some distance Canada's largest tourism source market, China stands third behind the UK and France, although the Canadian Tourism Commission (CTC) expects it to leapfrog France in the next two years. In addition to the growth of independent Chinese travel in the past two years, Canada has benefited from the 1.2 million people of ethnic Chinese origin who live in the country and a large Chinese student population which have created strong travel demand for visiting family and friends.

Although Canada received ADS in 2010, the CTC had established an office in Beijing five years previously. While it was not permitted to promote Canada to Chinese consumers until ADS was confirmed, the CTC was able to arrange familiarization trips for Chinese tour operators, travel agents and media to educate the market and build interest.

With ADS secured, the CTC worked with Air Canada and Chinese airlines to amplify flight capacity between China and Canada. In 2014, Canada expected to add around eight percent of air capacity from China. "We now have two main gateways – Vancouver and Toronto – in Canada, but five gateways from China – Beijing, Shanghai, Guangzhou, Chengdu and Shenyang. China has the largest number of gateways for flights to Canada after the United States," says Derek Galpin, Managing Director, China, Canadian Tourism Commission.

Greater flight access enabled the CTC to prepare tailored winter holiday itineraries for Chinese travelers, which were sold via online travel agency Ctrip. The packages include polar bear safaris, skating along Ottawa's Rideau Canal and excursions to watch the Northern Lights, combined with shopping and dining in gateway cities like Vancouver. In 2012, the CTC launched the Canadian Explorers Competition, offering two Chinese residents the opportunity to travel across Alberta, British Columbia, Manitoba, Ontario and Quebec and star in the *Canadian Explorer* TV series on China's Travel Channel.

"In some of the winter packages, we included skiing and snowboarding as secondary components," says Galpin. Faster than expected, the CTC discovered a substantial interest among Chinese travelers for winter sports as part of their Canadian vacation. This inspired a campaign initiative. "In China, we worked with the Nanshan Ski Resort near Beijing and branded the café the Canada Ski Café. We also worked with tour operators in China to develop trips based around skiing and winter sports," says Galpin.

Promoting winter sports to independent travelers will comprise a large part of the CTC's efforts in China over the next two years, although commissioned research revealed that Chinese skiiers and snowboarders also seek other experiences. "Unlike skiing vacationers from the US or Europe, Chinese skiiers rarely ski for more than two or three days of their vacation," says Galpin. "They want to experience other activities, like ice fishing, dog sledding and snow mobiling, and will usually allocate at least a day for shopping in a gateway city before returning to China."

Ireland "greens" the Great Wall

Voted the Best Potential Destination at the 2014 Ctrip awards, Ireland sought to take prompt advantage of its elevated profile. In the lead-up to St Patrick's Day on 17 March, Tourism Ireland presented a series of cultural events including an Ireland Family Day at Huaihai Park, Shanghai to showcase Irish cuisine and a concert in Beijing by traditional Irish band Altan. At the same time, a crew from CCTV flew to Ireland to film a 1.5-hour documentary about the St Patrick's Day Parade in Dublin and celebrations across the country.

The visual highlight of the initiative was the illuminated "greening," on St Patrick's Day, of a section of the Great Wall of China and Shanghai's iconic Oriental Pearl Tower. "This was Tourism Ireland's latest 'greening' of a famous international landmark, which over the past five years has included Niagara Falls, Sydney Opera House, Table Mountain, and the London Eye," says a spokesperson for Tourism Ireland.

Ireland received an estimated 19,000 visitors from China in 2013, up from 17,000 in 2012, and concerted promotional activity is tasked with achieving a target of 50,000 Chinese tourists annually within five years. One hindrance is connectivity. No direct flight links were in operation at the end of 2013 between Ireland and China, although a twinning agreement signed between the Dublin Airport Authority and Beijing Capital International Airport led to discussions about a Chinese airline launching a direct service.

Ease of access was improved in 2011 with the introduction of the Visa Waiver program enabling travelers from 17 countries, including China, who enter the UK on a valid visa to also travel to Ireland without requiring a separate visa. Although this has helped Tourism Ireland promote the destination – and reduced the cost and bureaucracy for visitors – it has made quantifying Chinese arrivals more difficult. A solution has been worked on between the UK and Irish governments, with the expected launch of a Common Travel Area visa enabling visitors to apply for a single visa, through a joint visa application center, enabling travel in the UK and Ireland.

Tourism Ireland – which has offices in Beijing, Shanghai, Guangzhou, and Chengdu – launched a Chinese version of its Ireland.com website. It also organized its largest sales mission to China in 2013 to raise awareness of Ireland as a destination. Twenty Irish tourism companies networked with 450 leading travel agents and tour operators, plus influential travel and lifestyle media in Beijing, Shanghai and Guangzhou.

Back home, Tourism Ireland hosted a familiarization trip for revered travel blogger Fan Yibo, who spent a week in August 2013 touring Ireland and posting reports and images for his 360,000 fans on Weibo. Tourism Ireland's counterpart organization, Failte Ireland, organizes seminars for tourism-related businesses to present the latest information about Chinese outbound travel and provide advice on travel distribution networks and engagement with Chinese visitors.

Selling Ireland's charms in China also benefitted from VIP approval. President Xi Jinping was photographed at the Cliffs of Moher during a trade delegation visit in 2012 when he was Vice President. Those photos were widely viewed in China and many visitors now want to visit the same spot to take their own photographs.

Beyond those rugged coastal cliffs, shopping is a preferred activity. Brown Thomas department store in Dublin offers Mandarin-speaking sales staff to assist visitors. A modern take on Irish folk dancing has also yielded an unexpected tourism trump card. "Riverdance is very popular in China, and many Chinese visitors like to take in a performance while they are here," adds the Tourism Ireland spokesperson.

The future of tourism in the City of Angels

In early 2014, Los Angeles Mayor Eric Garcetti and Los Angeles Tourism & Convention Board (LATCB) President and CEO Ernest Wooden Jr announced that the second-largest city in the US had welcomed a record 6.2 million international visitors during 2013. China was the number one overseas source market for a second consecutive year, shipping 570,000 visitors to LA – a 21 percent increase from 2012.

In addition to marquee attractions such as Hollywood, Universal Studios and Disneyland, tourism in LA was boosted by *The Endeavour* space shuttle at the California Science Center, and the reopening in summer 2013 of Tom Bradley International Terminal at Los Angeles International Airport. Revamped at a cost of USD 1.7 billion, the new terminal services six daily flights from China, and is integral to LA's goal of generating a high proportion of its targeted 50 million domestic and international visitors by 2020 from China and Asia.

The China tourism play is underpinned by economic reality. Official figures show that tourism spending supports one in nine jobs in LA – and as proven big spenders while visiting LA, the contribution from Chinese visitors is vital to the city's economic health.

Positioning LA as a vibrant destination for savvy 25–44 year old Chinese holidaymakers has necessitated new thinking. "The marketing of travel in China has developed in recent years. It used to be all about the travel trade, but now the focus is on the consumer," says Jamie Y. Lee, Director of China Services at the LATCB. "We looked at the models of outbound tourism development in Japan, Korea and Hong Kong, and in those places it took around 10 years for the market to move from group package tours to FIT. In China, it was around half that time."

Lee knows of what she speaks, having lived and worked in China for 16 years before moving back to LA in late 2013. In 2006, she established the LATCB's Beijing office, the first and only official city-level representative office to be licensed by the China National Tourism Administration, the Ministry of Foreign Affairs and the Ministry of Public Security.

An initial challenge was to bring in more direct flights from China. "That was a priority, because new flights don't just enhance connectivity, they improve the possibility of visitors making repeat trips for leisure and business," says Lee. Later, the LATCB opened a second office, in Shanghai, and is stepping up its destination marketing efforts to reach the large and growing market of independent travelers.

Turning the clock back eight years, Lee says although LA set up its Beijing office in 2006, China and the US did not sign a memorandum of understanding for the US to join the Approved Destination Status scheme until 2008.

"Those two years were important. We were on the ground in China hiring staff, researching the market and meeting officials and tourism agencies, so we were prepared for ADS when it was granted. I think Chinese officials were impressed about how serious we were to promote relations between the two countries," says Lee. That interim period also enabled her to build relationships with the Chinese media. "It was great timing. Today, the travel media in China can pick and choose where they want to go, but they were very receptive back in 2006. I often had journalists coming to my office craving information about LA."

Fast-forward to 2014, and the LATCB rolled out an integrated consumer marketing campaign for Chinese consumers. Lee notes, however, that despite the strong growth in arrivals, many Chinese visitors have commented on the lack of "China readiness" in different aspects of LA's tourism economy.

As a response, LA's "NiHao China" program was introduced in February 2014 to assist hotels, restaurants and tourism attractions to learn about the cultural and activity preferences of Chinese visitors. Described as "an innovative, multi-pronged marketing strategy to maximize Chinese tourist visitation to Los Angeles," it features a new Chinese language website, called "www.helloLA.cn" plus shopLA coupon books printed and designated Chinese tour guides program for Chinese tourists.

The custom tour guide education program offers a certification approved by the LATCB and the China National Tourism Office. "We found that Chinese travelers to LA were often bringing their own Chinese-speaking tour guides with them or hiring unqualified Chinese locals to take them around because local guides weren't meeting their expectations," says Lee. "Tour guides are ambassadors for our city and their recommendations are highly valued, so we want to help our guides improve their interactions with Chinese visitors."

Seafood and celebrities in Tasmania

The island of Tasmania, off the southern coast of Australia, receives less than three percent of international visitors to Australia, but it has ambitious plans to increase arrivals. China currently ranks fifth in Tasmania's international arrivals, with 13,000 arrivals for the year ending September 2013 – a 16 percent increase from 2012.

Tourism Tasmania has its Asian representation based in Hong Kong, and it set up an office in Shanghai three years ago. It seeks to expand the promotion of specialized tours and attractions that chime with Chinese tourists, including lavender farm visits, boating trips, Port Arthur and Cradle Mountain. The target market is educated, affluent Chinese couples in the 30–45 age bracket, who are comfortable communicating in English, have a sense of adventure and want an alternative option to add to their Australia itineraries.

"Chinese tourism to Australia is growing fast, but so far it has been focused on east coast destinations, like Sydney, Melbourne, Cairns and the Great Barrier Reef," says Lynn Wang, China Manager of Tourism Tasmania. "Tasmania is a heart-shaped island and we are positioning it as somewhere different for Chinese travelers; a place to enjoy beautiful nature and wildlife, breathe fresh air and sample unusual gourmet experiences."

Pennicott Wilderness Journeys, Tasmania's leading ecotourism operator, has created an in-demand tour product. Tasmania is the world's largest supplier of wild abalone, and abalone is highly prized in southern China. The Seafood Seduction cruise from Hobart to the Bruny Island coast attracts Chinese visitors who can gather oysters, mussels, sea urchin, crayfish and abalone from the pristine waters. "Chinese people love seafood, and this kind of experience takes them to the natural habitat of some of their favourite delicacies," says Wang.

Tourism Tasmania utilizes China's two primary social medial platforms, Weibo and WeChat, to develop word-of-mouth marketing and referrals, counting more than 200,000 followers on Weibo. The Chinese travel media is also engaged to broaden knowledge about Tasmania as a tourism destination, and Tourism Tasmania uses celebrity endorsements to help it spread the word.

Hong Kong megastar Eason Chan filmed a travel show on the island five years ago. "In 2013, we worked with Tourism Australia and Tourism Victoria for the production of *Heartbeat Love*, a movie starring Taiwanese heartthrob Lo Chih Hsiang (also known as Show Luo) and singer and actress Yang Cheng Lin. Parts of the film were shot in Tasmania," says Wang. In addition, Chinese A-listers Li Chen and Zhang Xin Yu (also known as Viann Zhang) visited to do a photo shoot for Beijing-based *Fashion Weekly* magazine. "Their visit generated huge interest for Tasmania in China," says Wang.

A window of opportunity in Kenya

Being voted the world's leading safari destination at the 2013 World Travel Awards is potential tourism gold for a destination pushing into new source markets. Kenya received Approved Destination Status from China in 2004, and the East African country has steadily grown its Chinese arrivals, welcoming around 41,000 Chinese tourists in 2012. Ambitions are high. Kenya is targeting one million Chinese visitors in less than a decade, and the Kenya Tourism Board (KTB) is looking to leverage its status as a safari destination. The KTB took a delegation of 11 companies on a roadshow tour of Beijing, Shanghai, Guangzhou, and Chengdu in Spring 2014.

Tourism is Kenya's third-largest foreign exchange earner after tea and horticulture, and accounts for around 13.7 percent of GDP. It has also been identified as one of six "pillar sectors" of the government's Vision 2030 economic development program. In 2013, the Kenyan government published a five-year national tourism strategy. It posits "a gradual paradigm shift from traditional source markets" towards four new focal points: 1) developing domestic tourism as the core market, 2) making East Africa the secondary market, 3) aggregating the emerging BRICs, Asian and Middle East countries as a combined tertiary market; and 4) the traditional tourism source nations of Europe and America are relegated to "defensive market" status.

Activating this strategy will require significant investment in infrastructure, people and marketing. "Kenya has all the pull factors, including wildlife safaris and bird watching tours, the Great Rift Valley, annual wildebeest migration and beautiful sandy beaches," says Kenyan-born tourism analyst Sandra Rwese. Turning those market advantages into real tourism numbers will require detailed planning.

Rwese has monitored Chinese tourism in Kenya for several years, and has advised companies on their engagement strategies. After attending a Mandarin course at a Confucius Institute in Nairobi, she launched Chinese Business Trainers, to teach corporate executives about Chinese business etiquette.

"My curriculum was poorly received in Kenya, but I launched my services using social media platforms and connected with think tanks in Germany, Denmark and Iceland." In 2008, Rwese moved away from China-based cultural training and into tourism planning and R&D. The company, renamed Gulu & Hirst, worked on strategy papers for hospitality companies seeking more Chinese arrivals, and consulted for a recruitment project to hire Chinese-speakers for a hotel chain in Kenya.

"Chinese dining preferences were sadly neglected," says Rwese. "So was the constant need for 24-hour connectivity to high-speed Wi-Fi. These may seem irrelevant, but to the Chinese visitors they are definite must-haves."

After planning a move to China for several years, Rwese jumped on a plane in September 2013, relocating from Nairobi to the Chinese coastal city of Xiamen. The aim, she says, was to further study Mandarin and to better understand the tourism and spending habits of Chinese travelers.

With regard to her homeland, Rwese believes that significant opportunities exist, but that tourism planners must identify particular market segments. In this way, Kenya would be better placed to strategically position its travel and hospitality services catering to travelers in each grouping. "Whether it's animal conservation tours, scenic movie shoots, thematic weddings, aerial helicopter tours or coastal marine excursions, cluster marketing is the way forward," says Rwese.

Securing more Chinese travelers is also predicated on improving brand equity. "This needs an urgent rethink. We are yet to brand our nation in people's hearts and minds. When I speak to Chinese colleagues about my country, all they know about are Kenyan marathon runners," says Rwese. "That's not sufficient to build a positive permanent impression that ultimately rakes in tourism foreign exchange. Conversely, when asked about Bali, South Korea and Vietnam, respectively, their immediate associations with those destinations are honeymoon vacations, medical tourism and magnificent culinary tours."

Rwese notes that to connect with savvy Chinese tourists, online communities boasting millions of daily users are core marketing beehives. "Interactive social media platforms like WeChat, QZone, Weibo, RenRen and Pengyou are used obsessively in China," she says. "Kenya should look to these platforms, rather than relying solely on traditional destination marketing strategies like attending trade shows and holding exhibitions."

Beyond Kenya, some African countries are performing better than others at branding their destinations in China. "South Africa and Egypt are notable in this respect, and some island nations are investing in outbound travel consultants with the aim of attracting Chinese travelers," says Rwese.

Interested parties in the tourism industry should consider that immigration policies in some African nations enable Chinese hoteliers to establish tourism outfits themselves. "These Chinese enterprises are heavily bankrolled. They organize end-to-end travel packages, right from sourcing travelers inside China to offering tour van services upon arrival, recommending Chinese-owned currency exchange bureaus, providing hotels and lodges outfitted with Chinese furnishings, plus Chinese chefs, liaison staff and gift stores within Chinese-owned enterprises across Africa," says Rwese.

The window of opportunity is closing fast, Rwese argues. "With recent waves of well-funded Chinese hoteliers pitching their tents right in the heartland of Africa's tourist attractions, the competition has suddenly taken a new twist."

From Beijing to St Moritz: Switzerland woos Chinese skiers

The flourishing appeal of winter sports among domestic Chinese travelers is catching international attention. In recent years, Switzerland has witnessed a yearly growth rate of tourists from China of between 25–35 percent, and it is eager to capture more. Swiss watches, chocolates and cheeses are highly regarded in China, and Switzerland aims to cash in on its alpine landscapes to make skiing as famous with Chinese travelers as its traditional consumer products.

In 2013/14, Switzerland Tourism created a campaign initiative around eight Chinese ski instructors who spent the ski season, from early December to late March, in Switzerland for a training and internship program. Together with Swiss Snowsports and a group of winter resorts and ski schools, it selected the eight instructors from 20 candidates during an evaluation process at the Beijing Qiaobo Ski Dome. The instructors were assigned to eight Swiss ski resorts – Davos, Engelberg, Grindelwald, Gstaad, St Moritz, Verbier, Villars, and Zermatt – which were chosen according to the number of Chinese winter guests they hosted during the previous winter season.

The initiative served as a marketing tool to communicate the appeal of Swiss winter holidays to Chinese travelers through the eyes of eight national ambassadors. In parallel, Switzerland Tourism teamed up with three Chinese tour operators – Utour Beijing, Caissa Beijing and Tonichi Hong Kong – to develop ski-focused travel products. The goal is to achieve a four-fold increase in the number of overnight stays by Chinese visitors in Swiss mountain resorts, from around 101,000 nights in winter 2012/13 to 400,000 in 2022.

"Our aim is to provide Chinese travelers with 'Swiss made' ski lessons in their own Chinese language. We recognized the need in Switzerland to sensitize the ski industry to the needs and behaviors of Chinese customers," says Batiste Pilet, Manager Central Projects & Partnerships for Switzerland Tourism in China. At the end of the initiative, plans were in place to leverage heightened interest in the chosen winter sports destinations. "After the 2013–14 season, we plan to publish a brochure in which the eight Chinese ski instructors give their tips about the eight different ski resorts. We shall also feature the instructors in online and offline activities."

China and the City of Dreaming Spires

On a damp winter afternoon in early 2014, I ducked out of the King's Arms pub on Oxford's Broad Street, and dodged the rain showers en route to the city's Visitor Information Center. The smart store offered numerous kinds of Oxford map, tour, history book, postcard and souvenir for overseas tourists – unless you happen to be Chinese. After perusing the shelves, I approached the sales counter to ask if they had any available information in Chinese. "I'm afraid we don't, except for the Pitkin guide book," the assistant told me. "It's a shame, as we are getting asked more often for Chinese maps and guides."

This seemed strange for two reasons. Firstly, I had just withdrawn money from a nearby bank ATM advertising free withdrawals for China UnionPay cardholders. Secondly, Oxford is my home city and I have witnessed a growing volume of Chinese tourists in the City of Dreaming Spires. Alongside its ornate university colleges, Oxford possesses some of the UK's finest historic architecture, including Christ Church College (whose Great Hall was replicated to create Hogwarts' Hall for the Harry Potter move series), the Palladian-style Radcliffe Camera, and the Ashmolean Museum, which, in 2013, acquired The Sullivan Collection, one of the world's greatest private collections of modern and contemporary Chinese art. A short drive away are John Vanbrugh's Blenheim Palace and one of the UK's top visitor attractions for Chinese: Bicester Village outlet shopping center.

"We do see a particular opportunity with the Chinese market," says Giles Ingram, Chief Executive of Experience Oxfordshire. "Oxford is well known with Chinese visitors to the UK, and some of our top hotels, such as Macdonald Randolph, Malmaison Oxford, and Four Pillars Hotel, are noticing increased numbers of Chinese guests. We also have the benefit of Blenheim Palace, which is a founding member of VisitBritain's China Welcome Program and was the launch venue in March 2014 for the 'Great China Welcome' initiative, and Bicester Village being nearby."

Funding and strategic planning have hampered Experience Oxfordshire – which is a young organization formed from a former city council department – and Ingram, who brings experience of dealing with the Chinese travel market from previous roles, is tasked with addressing new realities. Experience Oxfordshire underwent a major structural overhaul in early 2014, and has reappraised its tourism marketing strategy.

"We have to assess how we promote Oxford to our strong traditional markets, which bring the vast bulk of tourism, and maintain a keen eye on the long-term growth of emerging markets," Ingram says. "We are looking at maximizing tourism value, and attracting high-value Chinese visitors is certainly a part of our planning."

Oxford University is part of the tourism experience. "China provides the second-largest number of overseas students to the university colleges after the US, and Oxford Brookes University also has a large number of Chinese students," says Ingram. The collegiate system, comprising 38 colleges distributed across the city, offers myriad sightseeing opportunities. "One thing we need to look at is our guided city walking tours, which are very popular. To date, we haven't offered any tours in Mandarin, Cantonese, or even French. We need to become more commercial. If we have a growth opportunity like this, we must do something about it."

Taking on the China travel market challenge

In 2013, UK-based Jacada Travel began its push into the Chinese outbound market. Founded in London in 2008, Jacada creates personally tailored vacations for affluent travelers seeking authentic experiences in Latin America, Africa and South East Asia. Its itinerary options range from encountering Amazon tribes in Peru and archaeologist-guided tours of the Makgadikgadi Pans in Botswana to swimming with whale sharks off the coast of Mexico.

The timing of its decision to offer trips to China's new travel class was inspired by word-of-mouth demand. "We had Chinese clients reaching out to us, from articles written about Jacada in the press and our website," says Alex Malcolm, CEO of Jacada Travel.

Starting from scratch in China, Jacada created a Chinese company name (爵达旅程), engaged a PR company with proven experience in China to raise its profile with local media and consumers, and began setting up a sales office in Hong Kong.

The company targets high-end leisure travelers looking for "adventurous but very comfortable experiences" says Malcolm, who sees a widening window of opportunity in China. "People are limited in the time they have to travel, and seek to see and do a lot in the time that they have. Careful planning is required to ensure that whilst plenty is seen, travelers still have an enjoyable time and space to relax within their itinerary."

As part of its marketing plan, Jacada designed themed itineraries based around activities popular with Chinese tourists, such as the Gourmet Series, billed as "six once in lifetime guided food adventures," which garnered interest from the travel and lifestyle media and helped build awareness of the company's approach to travel.

Several months after entering the Chinese outbound market, two coveted options stood out. "Antarctica and Kenya have been the 'hottest' Chinese destinations for us so far," says Malcolm. "I think both destinations have attained an almost mythical status in China, which has fuelled their popularity. Kenya's tourist board has also been very active in engaging Chinese tourism."

Chapter 8

A Place to Stay: Checking-in with Chinese Travelers

From "China ready" to "China engaged"

Returning to my splendid Beijing hotel room on Chinese New Year 2014, I found a gold-wrapped chocolate coin placed on my pillow. Underneath was a *hongbao* packet designed in auspicious red and gold (it's no accident that these two colors comprise the Chinese flag) with a note explaining why the year of the horse is considered lucky in Chinese astrology.

My attention, though, was focused on the gold coin embossed with Chinese characters. It reminded me of the ones we as children used to hang on the tree at Christmas. It also made me think about the hotel staff that had just served me with food and drinks in the lounge. Smiling and courteous, their demeanor hid the sadness of being apart from their families on the most cherished evening of the year.

This, in turn, made me consider the complex dichotomy that the travel industry seeks to sell us. We live in a world of increasingly overlapping similarities, particularly in the consumer, transport and communications spheres; alongside the numerous obvious differences. Yet for all the exclusivities that are supposed to define and differentiate the product attributes and cultural relativism of the travel services we are offered, simple human touches are often all we need.

The issue of cultural relativity is pertinent to the hotel industry, which is frantically engaging its creative brains to devise promotions and packages appealing directly to Chinese travelers. These developmental strategies are often based on proven experience – international hotel brands, such as Kempinski, Hilton, Sheraton, Holiday Inn and Shangri-La, have been operating in China for between 20 and 30 years – plus a heady blend of considered ideas and offbeat hunches. The multitude of market analytics, focus group feedback and trend analyses collated over the years is deployed to plan further expansions across China, and to assist global hotel networks to better cater to business and leisure guests from China.

Having spent considerable time preparing formative "China Ready" strategies, global chains, upscale resort collections and emerging Chinese and Asian hoteliers are moving into the "China Engaged" phase. Standing apart from the cut-throat competition now means creating bespoke offerings that go beyond Chinese-speaking reception staff, packets of green tea in the guest room and Cantonese dim sum in the restaurant. The widescale reconfiguring of hotel layouts and amenities is based on certain market generalizations: for example, Chinese travelers tend to eat at least once per day in a hotel restaurant, but are unlikely to spend much time in the hotel bar, and prefer spa services with traditional Chinese medicine products.

As part of this process, hoteliers are looking beyond their own industry, particularly toward the luxury brands sector, which has proved adept at breaking down the shopping experience into distinctive components. In this way, high-end retailers have transformed the service provision for Chinese consumers during each carefully defined and tailored stage of the purchasing process.

To take forward their own China Engaged strategies, hotel executives are repeatedly asking themselves two probing questions: (1) "What do Chinese guests really want today, and what might they desire tomorrow?" and (2) "How well equipped are we for catering to the multiplying segments of the Chinese travel market?"

These questions are equally applicable to hotel general managers and F&B directors and guest relation officers in Chinese cities as they are in North and South America, Africa, Europe, and Australasia. A third question, perhaps even more pertinent, is: 3) "Where are the overlaps and where are the disconnects between the answers to questions one and two?"

The international chain race

The early years of the new millennium were inauspicious for China's hotel industry. The Asian Financial Crisis had sucked travel demand from the region, and the late-2002 SARS outbreak showed China's response mechanisms to be poorly prepared. Travel flows into the country slowed. It was an inopportune time to try and monetize previously growing interest in business and leisure travel to China, and a few hotel groups burned their fingers by opening lavishly designed and staffed properties in Shanghai and Beijing to percentage occupancy rates that struggled to strike double digits.

Fortunes began to turn in 2004, and the world's hotel operators have since signed management deals at a head-spinning pace. Beijing and Shanghai were initially most coveted, and both witnessed near saturation point of room supply at the top end of the hotel scale by 2010. Both cities continue to welcome luxury hotel openings. If you stand on Shanghai's famous Bund you can easily spot the Westin, Hotel Indigo, Waldorf Astoria, Fairmont, The Peninsula, Shangri-La, three Hyatts, Banyan Tree, Mandarin Oriental, Grand Kempinski and The Ritz-Carlton located on either bank of the Huangpu River.

Beyond these two first-mover metropolises, the commercially minded cities of Guangzhou and Shenzhen both attracted handfuls of international brands. Ambitious next-tier cities, like Chengdu, Tianjin and Hangzhou, followed by aspirants like Qingdao, Xiamen, Chongqing, Wuhan, Dalian, and Shenyang are expanding their hotel brand portfolios. As already discussed, Hainan Island is a story all of its own, having signed up almost every reputable resort operator worldwide.

Back in those post-SARS days, hotel companies in China talked almost exclusively about the inbound travel market. Leisure travelers from North America and Europe were targeted, as were business travelers and conventions groups from Hong Kong, Japan, and Singapore. The Chinese domestic market was underplayed. That changed as the 2008 Beijing Olympics and 2010 Shanghai World Expo came into view, and became "mission critical" when the long-haul travel market collapsed after the 2008 banking crisis. It was no longer just tourism boards that homed in on Chinese travelers – so did the global hotel chains, both inside China and across the planet.

In June 2011, US-based Starwood Hotels and Resorts, one of the world's largest hotel companies, relocated its senior leadership team for one month from White Plains, New York to Shanghai. During that time, President & CEO Frits van Paasschen and his team visited several of the group's hotels in China, signed new deals and held a board meeting. A key objective was to learn more about the preferences and expectations of Chinese travelers.

"As one of the world's fastest growing travel markets, China will play an outsized role in global travel within the next decade. The country continues to be the richest source of new loyal travelers for Starwood," van Paasschen told my business partner, Amy Fabris-Shi, during an interview for *TTG Asia* magazine.

Starwood traces its origins in China back to 1985, when the Sheraton Great Wall (although Sheraton was an independent company until Starwood acquired it in 1998) in Beijing became the first international branded hotel in the country. Starwood has sought to leverage this first-mover advantage – particularly by expanding the Sheraton marque – and China became its second-largest market, after the US. In November 2013, Starwood opened its 100th Sheraton hotel in Asia Pacific, and its 60th in China, in the city of Shantou.

In August 2013, the Starwood Preferred Guest (SPG) loyalty program introduced an app for Android in Chinese, and the company claims to register a new SPG member in China "every 20 seconds." It also created the Starwood Personalised Travel program, which was "designed to cater to the unique needs of the Chinese guest traveling abroad, at all hotels around the world." Launched in 2011 at 19 hotels in gateway cities including London, New York, Buenos Aires, Seoul, and Tokyo, it offers Chinese language and culture specialists to assist guests, translated hotel and sightseeing information and Chinese menu items.

After slow beginnings, Chinese traveler activation is now industry-wide. The Hilton Hotels & Resorts website lists hotels where its *Huanying* (Welcome) program of special Chinese amenities is offered, including 18 in Europe, 26 in Asia and 29 in North America. Launched in China in June 2012, Marriott's *Li Yu*, meaning "To Serve with Courtesy" program was rolled out to selected hotels in Asia later that year. In December 2013, Preferred Hotel Group – which counts 650 member hotels worldwide – launched its China Ready initiative, which requires participating hotels to meet a menu of certification standards, ranging from on-property services such as offering Chinese tea in guestrooms to having Mandarin-speaking reservations and a dedicated Weibo page.

UK-incorporated InterContinental Hotels Group (IHG) – which at the end of 2013 managed more than 4,600 hotels in nearly 100 countries and territories – has taken its China engagement strategy further. In March 2012, IHG launched Hualuxe Hotels and Resorts, which is claimed as "the first-ever upscale international brand designed specifically for Chinese guests." Being rolled out across China, Hualuxe had signed 22 Hualuxe management hotels across 20 Chinese cities, including Beijing, Shanghai, Chengdu, Kunming, Xi'an, Wuhan, and Tianjin, by the end of 2013.

French hotel giant Accor has re-defined its Grand Mercure brand specifically for China. Known in Chinese as *Mei Jue*, the brand is a "purpose-designed Chinese adaption of Grand Mercure" according to an official statement, and was launched in Shanghai in 2012. Accor says the services and amenities have been tailored for Chinese travelers based on observations of new consumption modes at its numerous branded properties nationwide.

Beyond the global hotel chains, niche resort operators are tailoring services to suit Chinese visitors. One & Only Resorts, a collection of deluxe resorts in destinations like Mauritius, Maldives, Bahamas, and Los Cabos, launched its *Huang Ying Ni* (Welcome to You) program to "make sure that Chinese guests feel welcomed and understood throughout their stay." The initiative was introduced in 2014, in advance of the opening of a One & Only resort at Tufu Bay, Hainan Island, the brand's debut property in China, and to recognize the "ever increasing importance" of Chinese guests across the resort portfolio, according to a company statement.

In addition to offering Chinese-speaking concierge, reception, spa, gift shop and restaurant staff, One & Only serves Chinese breakfast dishes including *baozi* (steamed buns) and *zhengjiao* (steamed dumplings), a selection of noodle dishes and offers chopsticks in all restaurants, while a restaurant at One & Only Le Saint Geran, displays its seafood live in tanks. Chinese magazines, newspapers and TV channels are also provided on request, and the UnionPay credit card system has been installed across its resort collection.

The Shangri-La experience

Based in Hong Kong, Shangri-La Hotels and Resorts opened its first hotel in 1971, in Singapore, and its first China property in 1984, in Hangzhou. At the beginning of 2014, the company counted 81 hotels across Asia Pacific and worldwide, including 37 in China. Nineteen more hotels are readying to open across China, from Diqing to Hefei, and Lhasa to Zhengzhou, in the next three years.

Internationally, Shangri-La – which, unlike most hotel management companies, invests in most of the mixed-use developments of which its hotels form a part – is continuing to expand. "There are still a lot of opportunities for global expansion, especially in new markets," says Kent Zhu, Chief Marketing Officer for Shangri-La Hotels and Resorts.

Chinese travelers will be a key part of this expansion. "The Shangri-La brand is very well known in China, and outbound volumes from China are going to continue to grow," says Zhu. Brand familiarity is an important part of the travel experience because Chinese travelers, whether for business or leisure, like to know what they can expect. They usually choose hotels that they think can understand their needs, and will deliver the kinds of services they want."

Shangri-La recently opened hotels in Paris, Istanbul, Doha, and at The Shard in London, and is studying options in the US. Among its forthcoming openings are Bali in 2016 and Yangon, Myanmar, in 2017. Those destinations are popular with Chinese travelers, and it is a frequently noted within the travel industry that a major constraint for Chinese outbound travel is air connectivity. "A lot of destinations could be very popular with Chinese travelers if airlines had the capacity," says Zhu.

One scheduled new location stands out for being adventurous: Accra, Ghana. "It will be our first hotel in Africa, and we believe there are huge opportunities across the African continent, which is progressing fast and there is a shortage of good hotels. The focus will very much be on business travellers, we think," says Zhu.

Utilizing technology is central to Shangri-La's strategy of engaging Chinese customers, and it was the first hotel company to offer free Wi-Fi across all its hotels worldwide. "Guests were beginning to expect it as a basic convenience," says Zhu. The marketing focus has since moved to mobile communications. "We began digital marketing in China in 2009, mostly using Weibo. At that time, outbound travel was really starting to accelerate, so we focused on promoting our international footprint to Chinese travelers by introducing our new properties and also providing information about popular destinations, such as Sydney, Canada and Istanbul. We also ran a "Stranger in Paris" promotion to coincide with the opening of our hotel there.

Since then, the digital marketing sphere in China has further evolved. "Weibo still remains, but now Weixin (WeChat) has been developed into a very powerful, interactive tool," says Zhu. "We use Weixin in three main ways; as a type of Twitter-style communications tool, although unlike Twitter it has no character limits; as a method of generating bookings and reservations; and as an interactive customer service option, enabling guests to order things directly, such as room service and special in-room amenities."

Blending history and modernity

The Peninsula Hotels, which is owned by the Hongkong and Shanghai Hotels Company, traces its history back to 1866 and promotes itself as

"China's first luxury hotel group and Asia's oldest hospitality brand." Its flagship hotel in Hong Kong is recognized as one of the world's foremost heritage hotels, and is hugely popular with Chinese travelers with an eye for heritage chic.

In August 2013, The Peninsula brand introduced the *Long Qing* (*Long* means dragon and by extension, the Chinese people, while *Qing* implies emotion and experience away from home) amenity program for Chinese travelers. Mandarin-speaking hotel staff and a Chinese breakfast (comprising dim sum, *congee* rice porridge, noodles and Chinese teas) are provided, plus Chinese-language newspapers and TV stations, and in-room materials and tourist publications translated into Simplified Chinese. All hotels are sensitive to cultural traditions by assigning rooms ending in "8" whenever possible (*ba* in Chinese resembles a word denoting fortune or prosperity), and avoiding room numbers with 4 (as *si* sounds like the word for death).

Individual hotels have also created their own programs. The Peninsula hotels in New York, Chicago and Beverly Hills offer The Very Best of America. The Peninsula Hong Kong's tablet technology enables an entire guestroom to be converted into Simplified Chinese (mostly used in mainland China) or Traditional Chinese (more widely used in Hong Kong and Taiwan) at the touch of a button.

In addition to the *Long Qing* program, The Peninsula Hotels and Industrial and Commercial Bank of China Limited (ICBC) launched a co-branded The Peninsula ICBC Elite Credit Card. The platinum and gold versions confer exclusive benefits and discounts at The Peninsula Hong Kong, The Peninsula Shanghai and The Peninsula Beijing. When launched in December 2012, it was the first strategic collaboration between a global hotel brand and a major Chinese bank.

From China to London's original "Grand Hotel"

Stately Victorian grandeur doesn't come much more exquisitely polished than at The Langham, London. Located on Portland Place, just off

Regent Street, this doyen of the UK's hotel scene was built as the capital's first "Grand Hotel" and celebrates its 150th anniversary in 2015. Its opening in 1865 was presided over by the Prince of Wales, and its stellar guest list includes Sir Arthur Conan Doyle, General Charles de Gaulle, and Diana, Princess of Wales.

Today, VIP attention is turning east. Visits by superstar pianist Lang Lang and movie starlet Fan Bingbing garnered notable attention in China – overlaying a sense of modern celebrity to the heritage London narrative that plays well with China's aspirational twenty-first century traveler.

Owned by Hong Kong-based Great Eagle Hotels, and managed by its Langham Hotels and Resorts subsidiary, The Langham, London has utilized its historic market position and regional connections to entice Chinese guests. In 2012, the hotel hired a dedicated China Sales Manager, who makes regular sales trips to China, and has also developed a guest services program tailored for Chinese visitors.

Competition is intense, however. "It has become very challenging among London hotels to compete for the China market," says Kate Xiong-Britton, Sales Manager for China at The Langham, London. "Two years ago, only a few hotels were proactively engaging with Chinese business and leisure travelers. Now, everyone is prioritizing China."

The hotel's appeal is easily sold in China. "We have this incredible history and this beautiful building. So for Chinese guests, they want to enjoy this very traditional British hotel in a way that is easier for them." Simple touches make a big difference. "Upon arrival, they like to see and speak with our Chinese-speaking front desk staff. This makes them feel immediately at ease," says Xiong-Britton. "Once in the room, they find a letter in Chinese welcoming them to the hotel, and explaining the bespoke amenities, including four Chinese TV stations and free Chinese newspapers. We also highlight the Chinese breakfast dishes offered."

Other tailored touches are based on experience. Themed activities include golf days and private trips to Bicester Village outlet center, near Oxford. Guest bookings at the hotel's Roux at the Landau restaurant –

helmed by high-profile father and son chef team Albert and Michel Roux Jr. – are usually accompanied by a bottle of champagne, but service adaptation is neatly honed. "Chinese people don't really drink champagne, so we can offer a good bottle of red wine instead," says Xiong-Britton. "The sommelier is attuned to different palates, and is on hand to suggest a red wine that can be paired with a dish that might usually be associated with white wine, such as Dover Sole. It's all about understanding what clients really prefer."

A Chinese national, Ms Xiong-Britton is well qualified for her role. She spent two years working at English-language magazine *That's Shanghai*, before becoming a PR executive at Three on the Bund – a high-end lifestyle emporium on Shanghai's fabled riverside Bund, which features restaurants by Jean-Georges Vongerichten. In 2006, Xiong-Britton relocated to the UK and initially managed hotel bookings for The Langham, London from its Hong Kong head office, and oversaw client relations with the Chinese Embassy, which is just along the street from the hotel.

Xiong-Britton takes two business trips per year to China, mostly to Shanghai and Beijing. In 2014, however, her visits took in Chengdu, following the launch by British Airways in 2013 of direct flights to London. She also met new and existing clients at the annual International Luxury Travel Mart show in Shanghai.

As competition intensifies between London hotels, clients are utilizing different booking methods. "Most booking used to come through agencies, now individual Chinese travelers are booking directly through different websites, and some of them just WeChat me to make a booking," says Xiong-Britton.

Mandarin Oriental introduces in-room shopping

Bringing bespoke shopping to the consumer is the idea behind Mandarin Oriental Pudong, Shanghai's in-room gift shopping service, which was launched in 2014 in partnership with chic lifestyle brand Shanghai Tang.

Founded with the opening of its flagship property, The Mandarin, in Hong Kong in 1963, Mandarin Oriental is renowned as a purveyor of twenty-first century luxury with Oriental aesthetics, sumptuous spas and several restaurants by celebrity chefs. The company counts 14 hotels in Asia, including three in its home base of Hong Kong, plus eight hotels in North America and a European footprint that includes London, Barcelona, Prague, Munich and Paris. Its development portfolio includes Beijing, Maldives, Taipei, Grand Cayman, Abu Dhabi, Milan, and Moscow.

Mandarin Oriental's logo is shaped like a Chinese fan, and its advertising campaigns have featured more than 25 celebrity "fans" ranging from Morgan Freeman, Dame Helen Mirren and Harry Connick Jr. to Hong Kong pop icon Karen Mok, Guangzhou-born architect IM Pei and Chinese-Mongolian singer Sa Dingding.

Guests at the brand's Shanghai hotel can browse a "Gifted Home" catalogue, which is exclusively printed for the hotel and available in all its 362 rooms and suites. The catalogue features more than 100 designer products from Shanghai Tang's Home and Accessories collections, including a Silk Road lacquer box, phoenix decorative plates and slippers embroidered with a dragon motif. The accessories and souvenirs can be ordered at the touch of a button 24 hours a day, 7 days a week, and a hotel Concierge delivers each order in an Art Deco styled Shanghai Tang gift box.

The hotel's sibling property Mandarin Oriental, Paris has also taken up the exclusive shopping theme, by offering the J'aime la MOde package, featuring VIP access – plus a VIP store card, personalized shopping and fashion advice, local delivery and shipping – to the city's prestigious Printemps Haussmann department store, which dates from 1865.

Chinese luxury hotels enter the arena

Almost a decade ago, I sat in the lobby lounge with the general manager of one of Shanghai's finest hotels. Over cups of green tea, he told me that the main advantage held by global hotel management companies such as his was that China would be "unlikely to create a luxury hotel brand of international quality in the near future." His reasoning was that Chinese hotel companies would concentrate on the budget end of the hotel spectrum, where lower costs, potentially high margins and fast growth through franchising were appealing. I pressed him for a definition of "near future" and he reluctantly replied, "not in the next decade, at least."

His prediction was only slightly mis-timed. Locally based budget hotels, such as Jinjiang Inn, Hanting Express, Green Tree Inns and Home Inn, have expanded speedily across urban China in the past ten years. The economy hotel market is now intensely competitive. Home Inn, for example, grew from having ten hotels in four cities in 2003 to 1,953 hotels by mid 2013 under three brands, including Motel 168, China's fifth-largest economy hotel chain, which it acquired for USD 470 million in 2011. Chinese mid-range and business hotels also mushroomed, but movement at the top end was slower. Now, hoteliers are starting to make an impact with themed architecture and designs that appeal to China's twenty-first century aesthetic.

On a singular hotel level, Fuchun and Longement are contrasting brands infused with Chinese styling. With a logo depicting a pavilion from the 660-year-old painting the *Dwelling in the Fuchun Mountains*, by Huang Gongwang, Fuchun Resort overlooks a calm lake framed by tea plantations and hills near Hangzhou. The 110-room resort was conceived as a stylistic update of the ancient Chinese landscape painting. Its grand polished teak lobby feels like a modern imperial palace with soaring wooden columns, grey brick walls and high, bracketed ceilings with glass lanterns. The lakeview suite rooms feature wooden lattice screens and Chinese objets d'art.

Back in the big city, Longemont Hotels is owned by a Shanghai-based property development company whose portfolio includes four- and five-star hotels managed by other companies. It established the Longement brand in 2008 when the company assumed management of The Regent Shanghai hotel – which occupied one of the buildings in its portfolio – and has stated plans to expand in China.

Shanghai will also be the launch pad for a highly anticipated new brand, J Hotel by China's largest hotel company, Jin Jiang Hotels (in collaboration with US-based Interstate Hotels), which counts over 1,400 hotels across 230 cities in China and owns several well-known properties managed by international hotel brands, including the Fairmont Peace Hotel in Shanghai and Waldorf Astoria Shanghai on the Bund. The global debut of the J Hotel brand will be unveiled in 2015 on the 84th-110th floors of the 632-metre high Shanghai Tower – thus usurping its near neighbor, Park Hyatt Shanghai, as the highest hotel in China. The 258-room hotel is described in an official release as "a luxury Chinese brand… [that] will also become one of the leading hotels of the world."

In the northeastern city of Tianjin, floor-to-ceiling glass windows of the upper floor rooms at the Tangla Tianjin Hotel overlook one of China's most dynamic skylines. From the bed or even the cubicle-free shower, Tianjin is presented in a perpendicular state of transformation. Elevated glassy constructs – occupied by hotels, offices, retail malls and serviced apartments – spear the hazy landscape, obscuring the River Hai around which the city was originally planned.

Nicknamed the "Shanghai of the North," Tianjin is 120 kilometers southeast of Beijing. Like Shanghai, its late nineteenth-century development was the result of foreign powers enforcing land concessions after the post-Sino–British Opium War treaties opened up China's largest ports. Tianjin was carved into more than half a dozen extra-territorial foreign concessions, more than any other Chinese city. Just as in Shanghai, the central feature is a meandering river with radiating streets flanked by handsome European mansions, neo-classical banks and granite-fronted municipal buildings.

Tianjin counts China's fourth-largest urban population, after Shanghai, Beijing and Guangzhou, but resided off the tourism radar until state funding spruced up the riverside and improved infrastructure ahead of the 2008 Beijing Olympics, for which it was co-host city. A 30-minute high-speed railway connected it with Beijing, while the Tianjin Economic Development Area is where Airbus built its first assembly line outside Europe. Since 2008, Tianjin has been the rotating co-host, alongside Dalian, of the World Economic Forum's Annual Meeting of the New Champions conference, nicknamed "Summer Davos."

The city also boasts a new name in Chinese hospitality. Tianjin Tangla Hotel, which was converted from a hotel originally managed by Raffles, is the flagship property of the Tangla brand – which has hotels in Beijing, Shenzhen and Hainan Island, and forthcoming in Shangri-La, Diqing, Yunnan Province. Tangla was created by HNA Hotels as the centerpiece for "an outstanding Chinese hospitality brand … The group also aims to collaborate with and contribute to the development of the tourism, real estate, hotel and airline sectors."

HNA is an abbreviation for Hainan Airlines International, and the hotel and hospitality management operation is a subsidiary of HNA Group, which owns Hainan Airlines, China's fourth largest carrier. In essence, HNA is emerging as a powerful travel and tourism conglomerate focusing on domestic Chinese and outbound travelers. It is building a portfolio of seven hotel brands, cascading from the "super luxurious" Tang Grand Palace marque, which is in development, to HNA Express Inn, a budget category first launched at Mount Emei in Sichuan Province and Danzhou in Hainan Province.

Some of China's most intriguing investment stories at present involve Dalian's Wanda Group (see World of Wanda, Chapter 14), which owns several hotels in China, including its tie-up with France-based Accor for the Sofitel Wanda luxury hospitality brand. In 2012, it founded Wanda Hotels & Resorts, with the lofty goal of becoming "China's preeminent global luxury hotel brand." The company, which is building a sizeable portfolio in China under the Wanda Reign, WandaVista and WandaRealm brands, before expanding internationally, opened its first luxury hotel in Wuhan in January 2014. Meanwhile, Wanda has announced its first European five-star hotel in London, as part of the One Nine Elms development on the South Bank.

A different northeastern coastal city, Qingdao, witnessed the birth of another upscale Chinese hotel concept in early 2014. Himalayas Qingdao Hotel is the debut property of Himalayas Hotels & Communities, which commissioned Hassell Studio Australia, the same firm behind the iconic designs of the Sydney Olympic Swimming Center and Chongqing Grand Theatre, to create its interiors.

The Himalayas brand is owned by the Zendai Group, which was founded in 1992 and operates in three major sectors: urban development, tourism development and financial services. Zendai owns five-star hotels in Shanghai and Qingdao managed by Jumeirah and Radisson. The Himalayas portfolio of deluxe hotels being opened across China includes Himalayas Nantong Hotel, Himalayas Watertown Shanghai Resort in Zhujiajiao and Himalayas Nanjing Hotel.

The golden promise

Also making hospitality waves is NUO (short for *Nuo Jin*, 诺金, meaning Golden Promise), which was launched at a lavish ceremony at Beijing's Temple of Heaven in September 2012. The 450-room debut NUO hotel will open in Beijing in 2015, and is designed to meet the Gold LEED accreditation for environmental sustainability. A second hotel is planned for Shanghai, and NUO is targeting landmark properties in Chinese first- and second-tier cities, plus major cities around the world.

The NUO brand is owned by the Beijing Tourism Group, and was developed in collaboration with Kempinski Hotels. The two companies have partnered on hotel projects in the Chinese capital for more than 20 years, and believe the growth of the Chinese tourism industry has increased the need for "an aspirational Chinese alternative" to the global luxury hotel chains to carve a market niche at home and abroad. A decade ago, such an approach would have been considered fantastical, but today it is an evident reality.

NUO does not lack ambition. It promises to "become a recognizable hotel brand that specifically understands and meets the needs of the Chinese traveler abroad," and be the "first truly authentic luxury Chinese hotel brand for foreign visitors to experience Chinese hospitality at its best," according to an official statement.

The vision for the brand, whose logo is a Chinese porcelain vase, centers on four pillars: (1) Chinese heritage, (2) luxury, (3) contemporary, and (4) green credentials. The design of the flagship Beijing hotel will be based on Ming Dynasty aesthetics, including giant white-and-blue porcelain vase sculptures, moon gates and outsized birdcages and oil paintings by contemporary artist Zeng Fanzhi – whose painting *The Last Supper* sold for USD 23.3 million at a Sotheby's in Hong Kong in October 2013. It will also offer round-trip transfers in a Red Flag (*Hongqi*) limousine, a tea pavilion, bamboo detailing in the elevators, and a "lifestyle manager" deployed on each guest room floor. The Shanghai hotel will be themed in Art Deco, the city's cherished architectural and design style from its 1930s "Pearl of the Orient" era.

In addition to premium hotel amenities, NUO's travel service company promises to arrange private jet travel or luxury sea charters aboard a super yacht. For guests who have seen and done it all, it can secure a berth on a 128-passenger capacity Russian nuclear-powered icebreaker in the Arctic, or a stay at an ice hotel at Inari, Finland, to watch the Northern Lights from the comfort of a private igloo.

"NUO will be the first luxury hotel brand with a truly Chinese DNA. It is proudly made in China and will be distinguished by Chinese style, service and etiquette," says Michael Henssler, President of Kempinski China and Managing Director of Key International Hotel Management Ltd, a joint venture between Kempinski and Beijing Tourism Group. "We are not taking a standardized approached so that every NUO hotel looks and feels the same. Instead, each one will be distinguished by a local adaptation of the four pillars on which the brand is founded."

Targeting mid-market urban travelers

China has witnessed strong competition at the upscale and budget poles of its hotel landscape, but the battle for customers is moving to the middle ground – and China's largest hotel group is setting a new standard. Having recognized a gap in China's mid-range hotel market, Jin Jiang Hotels unveiled its Metropolo (锦江都城酒店) brand in March 2014 with the official opening of a debut hotel on Shanghai's Yan'an Road.

Jin Jiang Metropolo resides in the center of the Chinese hospitality giant's portfolio, between the successful Jin Jiang Inn budget offering, which counts more than 900 properties across China, and its star-rated hotels. Five years ago, Jin Jiang trialed the mid-market Marvel brand, but it failed to ignite interest, and Metropolo – which is subdivided into two categories, Metropolo and the more upmarket Metropolo Classiq marque to be used for historic or boutique properties – is set for an aggressive rollout.

The name Metropolo is derived from the name of the Metropole hotel – a heritage hotel near the Shanghai Bund, which is closed for renovations and will reopen on 2015 as the brand's flagship property – and is also an allusion to thirteenth-century adventurer Marco Polo, whose travels in China are widely promoted nationwide.

"The target is to have 100 Jin Jiang Metropolo hotels in China within five years through a mixture of owned and managed hotels, acquisitions, renovations of existing hotels, leasing and franchising," says Christopher Sheldon, Executive Vice President, Shanghai Jin Jiang Metropolo Hotel Management. The Metropolo and Metropolo Classiq concepts were created for the Chinese urban market, but the possibility exists for taking it overseas in future, particularly as Jin Jiang has signed a licensing agreement to develop up to 30 Jin Jiang Inns in Indonesia, and is looking at a Metropolo resort brand.

Five of the group's Jin Jiang Inn economy hotels and star-rated properties are being upgraded to Metropolo hotels. Jin Jiang also purchased the Smartel hotel brand, and its 21 hotels in Fujian, Jiangsu, Anhui and Hebei provinces are being converted into Metropolo branded properties.

As part of the concept development for Metropolo, Jin Jiang Hotels commissioned Nielsen to undertake market research among educated 24–45 year olds in China who travel and are trend conscious. Some interesting findings were unveiled regarding desired amenities for the new mid-range hotel brand:

- Free Wi-Fi is considered a "must have."
- Room service isn't necessarily needed, but breakfast is very important – as is a café serving three meals per day. Guests like to know they can get an evening meal in the hotel.

- Bathtubs aren't desired, but a good-quality shower is.
- A hotel gym is viewed positively, although many guests suggested they may not actually use it.
- Branded beds and bed linens are highly coveted to ensure a good night's sleep.
- A 'very good cup of coffee' is a high priority.
- Demand for a full hotel bar was not high.
- Lobby space is very important to get out of the room and meet other people.

ESSENTIAL HOTEL AMENITIES

The most common requests made by Chinese guests in a survey of global hoteliers were:

Free Wi-Fi – 84 percent
Kettle for tea-making – 44 percent
Translated travel guides – 41 percent
Smoking rooms – 40 percent
Chinese TV programs – 33 percent
Translated hotel website – 31 percent
Translated welcome materials – 26 percent
In-house Mandarin speakers – 25 percent

Source: 2013 Chinese International Travel Monitor, by Hotels.com.

Chapter 9
Taking Flight: China's Aviation Revolution

Expansions and bottlenecks

There are several ways to better understand the dramatic changes in China's travel topography. Staying in one of its deluxe city hotels reveals the elevation of standards of service and amenities. The Peninsula Shanghai, for instance, was voted the World's Best Business Hotel in 2013 by Travel + Leisure magazine. Taking a high-speed train reminds visitors that rail networks can be central to a national transport strategy, while the proliferation of east coast cruise terminals presages a predicted boom in ocean cruising. But to best check the pulse of how China travel has, and hasn't, changed, head to one of its new airports and take a flight.

Statistically speaking, China's aviation sector is flying high. Domestic and outbound flight growth is increasing at rates not previously witnessed in air travel history. China's air passenger traffic climbed 11.7 percent in 2013 compared to 2012 (when 318.99 million air trips were made), the strongest rise for any global market, according to the International Air Travel Association (IATA). To support the demand surge, China has invested billions of dollars to expand its airport infrastructure and the growth aspirations of its major airlines.

China's Twelfth Five-Year Plan, announced in 2011, earmarked aerospace as a strategic industry, and set a target to increase the number of commercial airports from 175 to 220. Additionally, the CAAC expects Chinese airlines to order more than 2,000 aircraft during the period, resulting in a fleet surpassing 4,500 aircraft by the end of 2015. The CAAC predicts Chinese airports may handle 450 million passengers annually by 2015, and 1.5 billion by 2030. Statistical aggrandizement aside, the upshot is that China has posited itself at the forefront of the globalized evolution in demand for aviation services.

On New Year's Day 2014, commercial aviation celebrated its first century. One hundred years previously, the former mayor of St Petersburg, Florida, paid US$400 to become the world's first paying passenger on a scheduled commercial flight. The journey in a Benoist bi-wing airboat crossed Florida's Tampa Bay in 23 minutes.

During the latter half of the twentieth century, two primary markets – the US and Europe – dominated the world's skies, but the rising influence of travel in Asia Pacific and the Middle East, and the growth of air travel in Africa and South America, is effecting permanent change to the planet's flight map. In 2013, total air passengers worldwide surpassed the three billion mark for the first time. By 2050, IATA predicts that 16 billion annual passengers will zoom through the skies above us.

IATA says the recent shift eastward has been supported by strong passenger growth in China and India. Similar leaps have occurred in Brazil, Russia, and Mexico, while travelers from Indonesia, the Philippines, Vietnam, Iran, Turkey, Chile, and South Africa are starting to become more influential. "The result is a socially, culturally, and ethnically diverse pool of customers, with increasingly diverse demands ... that wish to visit an increasingly diverse range of destinations," says IATA. Airline and airport operators must deliver an equally diverse range of services to cater to new demands.

The expansion of international routes and flight frequencies in the past decade has afforded Chinese flyers similar options to passengers in established travel markets – the ability to choose a flight based on the time (rather than day) of departure and/or arrival, seat size and personal luggage allowance, and price – rather than configuring a route involving at least one connection.

In 2012, domestic air traffic accounted for 78 percent of China's total, with international travel comprising 20 percent, and the remaining two percent to Hong Kong, Macao, and Taiwan. Over the next 20 years, international travel is predicted to outpace domestic travel, increasing at an annual rate of 7.2 percent. IATA's Airline Industry Forecast 2013–2017 predicts airlines worldwide will see a 31 percent increase in passengers between 2012 and 2017. Routes within or connected to China are likely to be the single largest driver of growth, accounting for 24 percent of new passengers during the forecast period.

These upwardly curving statistics bring huge challenges. As more Chinese travelers desire to fly to more destinations more frequently, capacity issues are worryingly evident. Although China is building new airports and has improved the safety standards of its airlines, Chinese passengers have become accustomed to frequent flight delays and cancellations caused by over-crowded skies and strict military control of key parts of the airspace. Boarding a plane that subsequently sits motionless on the airport tarmac for two or three hours is not unusual, while many commuters rush to catch early flights knowing that delays are compounded in the afternoon and evening.

Clearing the runway

Despite the irritating bottlenecks, air travel in China has improved considerably. When I first arrived in Shanghai on a gloomy January day in 2004, flying in, around and out of the country was a vastly different experience.

At the front end of the process, purchasing a flight ticket involved visiting a travel agent or airline office, where the service could be brusque, especially if you were trying to change the date of a pre-purchased flight. Understanding the Byzantine system of flight discounting was akin to solving a Bitcoin algorithm with a hand-held calculator, and whatever the cost turned out to be (it never seemed to be the same price twice), cash payment was always required.

Global connectivity was another obstacle. In the early post-WTO accession years, China was still reluctant to sign high-volume access agreements with foreign carriers until ADS agreements were rolled out and its own national airlines were capable of competing against more experienced operators. Consequently, direct route services were underdeveloped. This often forced Chinese travelers to connect through Hong Kong, or Asian hubs such as Singapore or Bangkok, engendering a strong dislike for airport layovers. Ask any Chinese travel agent or check online booking statistics and you will find that point-to-point flight connections are now the overwhelming preference.

Upon entering an airport departure hall, check-in queues were long and cumbersome, as e-tickets, online check-in, and self-check terminals were still technologies of the future. The limited number of lines tended to be segmented for economy, business class and group tour passengers. An added burden was the payment of an airport service fee in cash at a kiosk before proceeding to customs.

As a foreigner, the lines and delays were, and remain, aggravating but tolerable. For Chinese travelers, the airport difficulties were just part of the rigors of leaving the country. Before getting near an airport, securing an entry visa for a destination was regularly problematic, while China's *hukou* registration system meant Chinese citizens living in a city different from that of their birth had to return home to have their itinerary approved. After checking-in at the airport, they reflected on the inevitably long passport line at their destination – and the likelihood of being asked several questions by customs officials about the purpose and length of their trip.

Chinese travelers who endured those tribulations during the early years of the nation's tourism development find it more than ironic that they are now the planet's most coveted travel demographic, when for many years – until the outbound volumes and sheer weight of spending power forcibly changed mindsets and procedural mechanisms – they felt at best neglected, and frequently unwanted.

The closed nature of China's commercial aviation market was another barrier to service enhancement. In 2005, I was asked by the Association of Corporate Travel Executives (ACTE) to give a seminar presentation in Beijing about the prospects in China for Asia's fast-growing low-cost carrier sector. It was a challenging assignment. "low-cost flying" was an infant concept for consumers who were just becoming comfortable with full-service air travel. Having accepted that flights involved a meal, drinks and a movie, it seemed unlikely that paying for ancillary privileges would appeal any time soon, especially as low-cost carriers had negligible penetration or brand cachet in China.

Furthermore, the issue of trust in airlines had resurfaced. A plane crash killing 55 people in November 2004 near Baotou in northern China's Inner Mongolia Autonomous Region had spooked the new generation of air travelers. China had developed a fairly good air safety record between a spate of accidents in the early 1990s and a fatal air crash near Dalian in 2002. Once again, the increased crowding of China's skies, the robustness of airline fleets, and pilot training all raised concerns. China's mainstream airlines were under pressure, and low-cost carriers faced a struggle for acceptance in a nascent air market with high regulatory barriers from government.

Ten years later, China's flight map is transformed, but it has been a tough journey to navigate. Gone are the days when the primary concern of international carriers was the inbound market to China. The volume of outbound passenger flows for business and leisure travel have forced open the airport gates. A new era of air travel is under construction.

The great airport infrastructure upgrade

The fulcrum of China's aviation industry is the capital, Beijing, which, as the political center, is where the nation's transport policy directives are stamped. It's also home to China's largest airport. Beijing Capital International Airport was ranked the world's second-busiest airport in 2013 by the Airports Council International (ACI) and is poised to overtake Atlanta Hartsfield-Jackson for the number one slot by 2015. Beijing did not even appear in the top 10 airport rankings until 2006, and in 2013 handled 83.7 million passengers.

Capacity is near stretching point at Beijing's three terminals – the third of which, designed by Foster and Partners, opened before the 2008 Beijing Olympics. Although Beijing has a small, rather obscure second airport, called Nanyuan, work has begun to build a second international airport at Daxing, 50 kilometers south of Beijing. Expected to open in 2018, the RMB 84 billion (USD 13.5 billion) new airport will be one of the world's largest aviation hubs.

Until completion of the Beijing mega-airport, Shanghai remains the only Chinese city with two international airports, Pudong International Airport, located on reclaimed land east of the city, and the older Hongqiao International Airport west of downtown, which was revamped and expanded in 2010. In 2013, Pudong unveiled plans to build the world's largest satellite airport terminal.

Beijing, Shanghai and Guangzhou airports account for around one-third of passenger movements in China, according to the CAAC. Although those three cities will continue to garner attention from international airlines, rapid growth is predicted across the country. China's vast geography and rising urban affluence mean demand for air travel is evermore dispersed. The government has therefore earmarked a network of airport hubs, which broadly follows the US model.

This network is headed by Beijing in the north, Dalian (which is building a 21-square kilometer island to site a new airport) in the northeast, Shanghai on the east coast, Guangzhou and Shenzhen (which opened a USD 1.4 billion third terminal in late 2013, including 13 "luxury travel retail" boutiques by names such as Versace, Coach and Hugo Boss) in the south, Chengdu (where passenger traffic grew from 5.5 million in 2000 to 32 million in 2012) and Chongqing in the west, Nanning and Kunming in the south east.

Travel distribution is also evolving to meet the expectations of tech-savvy travelers. IATA is working with technology companies worldwide to develop a new XML-based online ticketing system through its New Distribution Capability (NDC) program. Promising to offer "a modern shopping experience for airline travel products," it will give travel agents and customers a greater range of information – such as

Wi-Fi availability, extra legroom, or lounge access – when choosing a flight.

As IATA notes, the GDS systems used by travel agencies were created in the pre-Internet era, and are mostly limited to offering basic fares and schedules. Charging "ancillary fees" for in-flight amenities is now a widespread revenue-earning strategy pioneered by low-cost carriers and adopted by the world's major airlines – and all actual and potential costs should be presented to a client when they are choosing a flight.

The goal of NDC is to reclaim ground for travel agents lost to direct booking via airline websites with a greater scope of flight information and options to share travel preferences and social media profiles. Ultimately, this should yield more targeted marketing for airline special offers and service upgrades.

In 2013, IATA undertook five pilot projects, one in the US, one in New Zealand, one in Switzerland and two in China. The first live ticket was sold to a passenger through the NDC pilot project involving Hainan Airlines, TravelSky (the Chinese GDS) and a Chinese travel agency.

The "big three plus one"

China's current airline structure was codified in the early 1980s when ten airlines were consolidated into three groups; Air China, as the national flag carrier, based in Beijing; China Eastern Airlines based in Shanghai; and China Southern Airlines with its hub in Guangzhou. The government's objective was to create three regional airline groups with the scale and domestic flight structures to enable them, ultimately, to develop links with international carriers, implement codeshare agreements and enhance their global reach. In this way, the "big three" airlines would be able to service domestic, outbound and inbound passengers, join one of the major global alliances – SkyTeam, Oneworld and Star Alliance – and take their place among the world's leading airlines.

It's been a bumpy flight. Protectionist policies resulting in limited competition have hindered the commercialization of operations. China's airlines posted a combined loss of RMB 2.57 billion (USD 0.41 billion) in the first half of 2006, and Air China launched a lackluster initial public offering (IPO) in Shanghai in August 2006. In June 2006, Hong Kong-based Cathay Pacific and Air China concluded a complex agreement with both companies acquiring shares in the other, while rumored strategic investments by Singapore Airlines in China Eastern and Air France/KLM in China Southern floundered.

The domestic consolidations continued – with China Eastern subsuming the loss-making Shanghai Airlines in 2009 – as Chinese carriers battled high cost structures, fleet renewals and route expansions plus high oil prices and low margins. Despite the financial challenges, government protection enabled the three groups to dominate China's airline sector, and restricted the flight paths of privately owned competitors.

China's major airlines are now international players. Its top four airlines have grown 15 to 20 percent annually over the past 10 years, according to Boston Consulting Group. The national flag carrier Air China is a member of the Star Alliance network, while both Shanghai-based China Eastern and Guangzhou-based China Southern have joined SkyTeam.

Beyond the "big three," China's fourth-largest carrier and biggest privately owned airline, Hainan Airlines, is also gaining traction. The Haikou-based airline – which only began operations in 1993 with its first flight from Haikou to Beijing, and launched its first intercontinental route, Beijing to Budapest, in 2004 – has charted its way through clouded skies. Without state funding or patronage – but having famously persuaded George Soros to invest in 1995 – Hainan Airlines developed as the "outsider" of China's commercial aviation sector. Its growth was hindered by the government's policy of protecting its three major carriers from the type of shock caused by SARS, 9/11, oil price rises and the global economic crisis.

In January 2014, Hainan Airlines launched the first direct flight linking China and Bali. The airline partnered with Caissa Touristic Group to offer packages for Chinese tourists flying from Beijing. It also launched its first nonstop service to the US, to Seattle, in 2008, and has since launched flights between Beijing and Chicago, Xian and Seattle, and Beijing and

Boston, and applied to the CAAC to launch flights between Hangzhou and Paris, and Beijing and New York, Mumbai and Nairobi.

The slow take-off of China's low-cost carriers

Despite the state-favored dominance of the big three airlines and the sheer commercial doggedness of Hainan Airlines, plus an unfavorable regulatory environment, inconvenient slot times, and the vicissitudes of military control of Chinese airspace – which challenges the rapid turnaround of aircraft that is critical to the low-cost flying model – China's low-cost carrier (LCC) model has shown green shoots of development in recent years.

LCCs in China grew painfully slowly compared to South East Asia's buoyant low-cost carrier sector, but improved market penetration into China in the past five years has stimulated LCC growth. In early 2014, there were two clear market leaders: Malaysia-based Air Asia, which counted flights from 13 Chinese cities, including Beijing, Shanghai, Xi'an, Kunming, and Guangzhou, and Singapore-based Tiger Airlines, which offered flights from nine cities, including Nanjing, Ningbo, Shenyang, and Lijiang. Also operating low-cost flights, were Jetstar, which is part-owned by Qantas and flew from three Chinese cities, and Singapore Airlines' low-cost subsidiary Scoot, which flew from four cities.

These foreign-owned economy airlines are not permitted to operate domestic routes in China, but their expanding route networks feature popular Asia-Pacific destinations like Singapore, Kuala Lumpur, Bangkok, Melbourne, and Sydney. High take-up of available flights and enhanced frequencies have proven that Chinese independent travelers are progressively more comfortable with booking and boarding no-frills flights.

Carefully overseen from Beijing, China's low-cost carrier sector accounts for a very small percentage of the air passenger market, but it received a boost in October 2013 when the government relaxed rules on new private carriers and deregulated the long-standing minimum fare pricing system. A few months later, in March 2014, the CAAC simplified approvals for start-up LCCs, and set new standards for converting existing airport terminals into dedicated LCC terminals. Airports were also told to reduce landing and take-off fees, and tax incentives were offered to budget airlines. These proposals were designed to encourage Chinese airlines to launch their own budget subsidiaries.

China's figurehead LCC is Shanghai-based Spring Airlines. Founded in 2005 by the Spring Travel Agency group as a domestic budget airline, Spring Airlines has since expanded its network to more than 50 routes in China and beyond – and its focus on social media has proved popular with younger passengers who have become adept at booking online and via mobile platforms.

Spring's regional flights have been carefully selected to include destinations popular with new Chinese travelers, such as South Korea, Japan, Malaysia, Thailand, Cambodia, Taiwan, Hong Kong, and Macao. The airline wanted international routes to account for 30 percent of its network by the end of 2014, and planned an IPO to raise funds to facilitate both fleet and route expansions. It also faces competition from China's established airlines, including China Eastern and Hainan Airlines, both of which are converting regional subsidiaries into LCCs. At the end of 2013, Spring Air received approval from the Japanese civil aviation regulator to establish a joint venture, called Spring Air Japan, with flights between Shanghai and Narita, Tokyo, plus other Japanese cities.

The LCC bug seems to be catching. Shanghai-based carrier Juneyao Airlines was founded in 2005 targeting business travelers with flights across China plus Taiwan, Thailand, South Korea, Cambodia, Hong Kong, and Taiwan. In 2013 the carrier announced the launch of an LCC based in Guangzhou; called Jiu Yuan (or, Nine Yuan) Airlines, which promised to offer a large number of flight tickets to domestic destinations starting from just RMB 9 (USD1.45)

This trend has alerted low-cast airlines that don't even fly to China. In December 2013, UK-based Easyjet – which boasts an extensive flight network across Europe, plus Israel, Jordan, Morocco, and Egypt – launched a homepage translated into simplified Chinese characters, its twentieth language site. Easyjet said in a company statement that it had witnessed a 25 percent increase in bookings from Chinese passengers during 2013 compared to 2012.

GLOBAL AIRPORTS AND CHINESE TRAVELERS

The free flow of Chinese air travelers, and their high propensity to spend en route to/from China, is impacting the world's leading airports, particularly when planning for future growth. Airport expansions from Dubai, Bali and Qatar to Los Angeles, London and Sydney are taking into account potential flows of Chinese travelers, and are paying greater heed to their consumption patterns while they wait to catch a flight.

Singapore

Singapore Changi Airport reported record-breaking passenger traffic of 53.7 million in 2013. Of the ten additional routes added to Changi's international flight map during the year, seven of them – Guilin, Jinan, Lijiang, Nanchang, Nanning, Ningbo, and Wuxi – were in China, bringing the total to 31, enhancing its position as South East Asia's most connected air hub to/from China.

Hong Kong

Hong Kong International welcomed more than 59.9 million passengers in 2013, representing annual growth of 6.1 percent. Passenger traffic to and from mainland China, Taiwan and Japan recorded the most significant increases.

London

London Heathrow handled 72.3 million passengers in 2013, an increase of 3.4 percent from 2012. Total passengers from China increased 18.9 percent (compared to a BRIC average of 6.1 percent) during the year.

Paris

Paris-Charles de Gaulle Airport handled 62 million passengers in 2013 and, in combination with Paris-Orly, Aéroports de Paris broke the 90 million passenger barrier for the first time. Total passengers (including Chinese and others nationalities) flying to and from China, reached 1.49 million.

Sydney

Sydney Airport handled 37.9 million passengers in 2013, with Chinese travelers increasing by 14.9 percent year on year. A long-term expansion plan is based on a forecast of 74.3 million passengers in 2033, driven by "continued strong economic growth during the medium and longer term for China, India and for much of Asia."

MAKING PLANES FOR CHINA

The world's two largest aircraft manufacturers, Boeing and Airbus, have established operations in China. In March 2013, US-based Boeing delivered its 1,000th airplane in the country, a next-generation 737–800, to China Eastern Yunnan Airlines. In addition, the company says that more than 7,000 of its airplanes operating worldwide use major parts and assemblies from China. Boeing – whose first chief engineer in 1916 was a Chinese aeronautical engineering graduate named Wong Tsu – forecasts that China will need 5,260 new airplanes in the next 20 years to meet passenger demand.

France-based Airbus expanded into China in 1985 with its first delivery of an A310 to China Eastern Airlines, and counted more than 900 aircraft in China by May 2013. China is home to Airbus manufacturing and support operations, including its first assembly line outside of Europe, in the northeastern city of Tianjin. In 2013, Airbus signed a memorandum of understanding with China's Air

Traffic Management Bureau, under the CAAC, to assist in the process of updating the nation's air traffic management systems and improving China's air transportation efficiency.

Private jet manufacturers are also making ground in China's nascent general aviation sector. In 2013, Cessna – which has a joint venture in Shijiazhuang with China Aviation Industry Corporation (AVIC) – signed agreements with Yunnan Ruifeng General Aviation Company to deliver two Citation Mustang airplane for private charter flights, and inked a deal with Beijing-based Reignwood Group for ten Grand Caravan EX aircraft to be used for tourism services.

While foreign aviation manufacturers dominate the market, China harbors ambitions of building its own planes. Since 2008, the state-owned Commercial Aircraft Corp of China (COMAC) has been developing the C919 jetliner, designed as a competitor to Boeing's 737 and the Airbus A320. The stated target was for the 190-seat airplane to make its first flight in 2014, but industry analysts expect a delay until at least late 2015. China abandoned previous plans to build the so-called ARJ21 jetliner, but has invested heavily in COMAC and contracted aviation experts and suppliers from around the world in an attempt to fast-track the C919's take-off, although the first aircraft deliveries are not expected to begin until later in the decade at the earliest.

Airport planning for Chinese visitors: Melbourne and Copenhagen

In 2013, Melbourne Airport reached the 30 million annual passengers milestone, which was heavily influenced by China, Taiwan, Singapore, Hong Kong, Malaysia, and Vietnam arrivals, which all grew by more than 10 percent compared to 2012. Among the new flight connections in 2013 were Sichuan Airlines' first Australian service between Chengdu and Melbourne, and extra China Eastern flights between Shanghai and Melbourne during the Australian summer.

Rewind the clock to 2009, and Melbourne Airport was already receiving 11 percent of international arrivals from China – and its management recognized a need to improve the arrival and departure experience. After consulting with Chinese airlines and the Australasian Centre of Chinese Studies, the airport introduced public address messages in Mandarin, installed Chinese signage throughout the airport and provided cultural awareness training to its staff and key service partners.

Five years later, Melbourne Airport is developing its approach. "We are now moving from what we call "China ready" to "China friendly," as we continue our Mandarin signage and public announcements, we're also looking at other ways to improve the experience for Chinese travelers," says Anna Gillett, Media & Communications Manager at Melbourne Airport. In addition to Chinese cultural training for frontline staff, it also offers Mandarin lessons and some of the airport's security staff now speak Mandarin to help them assist with the facilitation of large groups and the security screening and immigration processes in general.

Across the globe, Copenhagen Airport, which provides retail staff with Chinese culture courses and offers Chinese guides, launched a Chinese language app in December 2013. The airport says the move was "essential" to attract more Chinese travelers. The app translates signs and provides directions and information about everything from menu cards and tax-free shopping to departure times and gate locations.

An airport customer survey had revealed that language is very important for Chinese travelers, who actively seek information online in their own language before traveling. They also requested more translated information and services at the airport. Around 60,000 Chinese traveled through Copenhagen last year, and the airport has recruited 17 Chinese guides who all live in Denmark. Staff working in the airport retail outlets – where Chinese visitors spend approximately three-times more than average travelers, and up to 50 percent of luxury boutique sales are made by Chinese passengers – can take classes about interacting with Chinese travelers.

"We see the app as an investment in the future, as we expect quite a large proportion of the airport's future growth will come from China and Asia," says Carsten Nørland, Copenhagen Airport's VP for Sales and Marketing.

EXPERT INSIGHT: FRANCIS CHAO, MANAGING DIRECTOR, UNIWORLD, LLC

Mr. Chao is a leading consultant on the China civil aviation market. For more than 20 years, he has provided marketing and consulting services for international aviation-related companies seeking to establish and expand their businesses in China. An expert on Chinese and international aviation regulatory systems and practices, he also produces the monthly *China Civil Aviation Report*, the only English publication focused on the China civil aviation industry.

As China moves beyond 100 million outbound travelers in 2014, can its airport system cope with sustained passenger growth?

The airport infrastructure in China should have no problem coping with 2–3 years of sustained passenger growth, as most of the airports have been designed to account for volume expansions. The main challenge is air traffic control. The military has only 20 percent of air traffic in China, but manages 80 percent of airspace, while civil aviation must fit 80 percent of China's air traffic into 20 percent of the airspace. This has seriously jeopardized the on-time operations for airlines, and overall safety within the industry.

In addition, the political system prevents air traffic controllers from directing aircraft in the way they see fit. With all the radar installations invested in during the last 20 years, China is still operating a "radar-assisted procedure control" type of operation. China's civil aviation industry has been owned and run by the state for too long, so none of the airports or airline operators is really ready for the unexpected. Emergency procedures for dealing with adverse weather, a disaster or technical problems do not meet international standards, and this is one reason for the persistent flight delays, and even partial shutdowns of Chinese air space at times.

As urban affluence increases, in which cities do you think air traffic will grow fastest over the next 3–5 years?

There are 180 airports in China serving scheduled airlines. Many of the smaller airports have grown very fast. The top 20 airports in China all witnessed growth of between two to 21 percent in 2012, and seven of them witnessed double-digit growth. Chongqing, Urumqi and Zhengzhou have been the top three-fastest growing for the last two years, and I think this will remain the same for the next few years. It's also interesting to note that Zhengzhou is now the number one cargo airport by growth rate since Foxconn – which assembles iPhones in China – relocated its operations to the city.

Do you foresee more start-up LCCs in China over the coming months?

Currently, the major low-cost airlines in China are Spring Airlines, China United and Western Airlines. Juneyao Airlines is waiting for approval by the CAAC. It is the CAAC's stated policy to encourage China's major airline groups to establish new divisions to operate low-cost airlines.

How do you see the domestic airlines versus high-speed rail situation developing?

The CAAC has issued new regulations to relax the control of airline ticket prices, which means airlines in China can now determine ticket prices that meet the competition, which includes the high-speed rail operator. In the last two years, aviation lost out to high-speed rail competition, particularly for journeys within the "two-hour train ride" category. The effect was less damaging in the "less than four hours' train ride" category. I doubt, however, that Chinese airlines dare to take on international competition at the moment, as even Chinese passengers are favoring international carriers.

Chapter 10

The Media Game: Publishing for the Modern Traveler

Publishing for the modern Chinese traveler

A few days before Chinese New Year in January 2014, I sat in the 25th-floor boardroom of a Beijing skytower. To enter the building, I passed through an achingly modern retail and business complex housing every conceivable designer brand, a Ritz-Carlton hotel and globally branded coffee shops. A circular Giorgio Armani store, sliced into four segments, embraced the central plaza. The shelves in the whitewashed waiting room were stocked with Chinese versions of glossy lifestyle magazines. I flicked through *Vogue*, *GQ* and *Self*, but was actually here to meet the editor of another Chinese edition of a major-name title: *Condé Nast Traveler*.

Launched in the US in 1987, *Condé Nast Traveler* magazine publishes international editions in the UK, Russia, India and Spain. In March 2013, the upscale travel magazine unveiled the inaugural issue of its Chinese edition, which plans to repeat the success of *Chinese Vogue*. Launched in 2005, *Vogue* has become the cornerstone of Condé Nast's publishing portfolio in China, and its editor Angelica Cheung is an inducted member of the international fashion industry elite.

The media kit for *Condé Nast Traveler China* promises content that is "tailor-made for China's growing number of culturally refined and affluent individuals seeking to satisfy their desire to discover the world's top luxury travel destinations and lifestyles." Its stated target market is high-earning 35–42 year old active travelers.

It is a sleekly managed operation. The bilingual editorial team members hail from across China. Each is urbane, engaged and eminently well traveled. During my visit, our conversation segued seamlessly from discussing design hotels in Yunnan and the best Maldivian resorts to making a hotel booking for the 2014 World Cup in Brazil, and participating in a long-distance Xi'an–Rome driving trip.

The key to producing a smart travel magazine anywhere is to understand the progressive aspirations of a discerning readership with a hunger for untried experiences. China is no exception. "The Chinese outbound market is changing very fast. Our readers want to know about new destinations, places they are unfamiliar with," says Yan Xiao, Editorial Director of *Condé Nast Traveler China*.

The editors engage a network of travel writers worldwide – I passed a US-based freelancer in the corridor – and approximately 80 percent of the content in each of the 12 annual issues is dedicated to international travel, with 20 percent allocated to China. Japan, Swedish Lapland, Phuket, Bolivia, Mumbai, and Sydney were among the destinations featured in the February 2014 issue I browsed in the waiting room.

To keep abreast of dynamic developments in Chinese outbound travel, the magazine commissions regular readership research. Recent feedback confirmed two enduring challenges. "It is still difficult for Chinese travelers to obtain visas for several countries, and there are also not enough direct flights to many of the destinations that travelers want to visit," says Yan Xiao.

The world's most influential travel readership

The arrival of *Condé Nast Traveler* underscored the importance of the travel media in China. The magazine's considered mix of outbound destinations plus hot content from China, supported by a downloadable app version, raised the stakes for homegrown magazines. Scour any roadside newsagent kiosk or airport bookstore, and you will find a host of travel and lifestyle publications. Chinese versions of familiar titles like *Travel & Leisure*, *National Geographic Traveler* and *Business Traveler* sit beside impressive homegrown publications like *Top Travel* and *Voyage*.

Launched in 2007, *Top Travel* is a monthly magazine focused on outbound travel from China. It gained credence for featuring celebrities on its covers, and flicking through the November 2013 issue, its destination coverage ranged from Algeria and the annual *sakura* cherry blossom festival in Japan to visiting the Laphroaig whiskey distillery in Scotland and touring Europe by car. *Voyage* magazine is also a leading high-end travel magazine that features famous Chinese models, such as Yin Tao, Liu Shishi and Huo Siyan, posing in exotic destinations on the cover. The 190-page March 2014 issue journeyed from Russia and Iran to Boracay and Maldives, interspersed with a round-up of the world's best river cruises, airport lounge tips for business travelers, cycling in Hangzhou and test driving a Mercedes-Benz in Inner Mongolia.

A plethora of glossy niche titles also targets the spending power of high-net-worth Chinese consumers, including *The Yachting Lifestyle Magazine*, *Bizjet Advisor*, *Global Flying*, *The Discerning Lifestyle*, and the admirably named Kunming-based *POSH*. *Shanghai Tatler* and *Beijing Tatler*, which are part of the high-society Asia Tatler series, also feature content on international travel, dining and lifestyle. Print-based media in China is also a strong adopter of mobile and tablet technology, and most magazines offer app versions, plus a strong social media presence. Traditional media has evolved in other ways, too, with established fashion and lifestyle magazines like *Elle China* now offering their own TV channel.

Luxury yachts are coveted by new China dreamers, and publishers are stepping up to tantalize them. Launched in 2004 as a spin-off from the long-established *Asia Pacific Boating*, *China Boating* targets aspirational consumers with a rich mix of imagery and information about luxury boating and yachting worldwide. Published by Hong Kong-based Blu Inc Media, its Chinese-language stablemates include *Jet Asia Pacific*, a leading regional publication for business and private aviation, and Inluxe.cn, an online showcase of designer products and services.

Foreign media owners are navigating the choppy waters of China's media market. In March 2014, US-based Northstar Travel Media, which publishes the industry staple *Travel Weekly* magazine, acquired *Travel Weekly China*, *Travel Weekly Asia* and *Events China* from a Singapore-based company with branches in Beijing and Shanghai. Published in Chinese, *Travel Weekly China* is distributed to travel trade professionals in China, Hong Kong and Macao, while *Events China* is a leading Chinese meetings, incentives, conferencing and exhibitions (MICE) title and has an events and industry awards operation.

Smaller niche publishers have also entered the fray. Founded in Shanghai in 1999, the Chinese-language *Hurun Report* cultivated its reputation as the medium of choice for Beijing and Shanghai high society and trend watchers by publishing the annual China Rich List of the country's wealthiest individuals. In 2014, luxury property developer Star River Property sponsored the *Hurun China* Rich List, and the magazine's founder, Rupert Hoogewerf, is frequently cited in international media articles related to Chinese consumerism and spending patterns.

The *Hurun Report*'s 10th annual Best of the Best awards, published in January 2014, revealed the "preferred brands of the Chinese luxury consumer." The roll call of 51 sponsors and media partners for the awards night included Emirates, Rolls-Royce, Tourism Australia, Shangri-La Hotels and Resorts and Pernod Ricard. The magazine's 2014 China Luxury Consumer Survey of affluent Chinese urbanites ranked Australia as the number one international luxury destination, knocking France (ranked second) off the top for the first time in four years. Dubai, Switzerland and Maldives completed the top five. The survey also revealed that 60 percent of surveyed high-net-worth individuals expressed an interest in owning a holiday home, and that on average a Chinese millionaire took 7.5 days of holiday in 2013.

Chinese state media is a prominent supporter of domestic and outbound tourism, and occasionally displays an admirably opportunistic eye for a story. In December 2013, as thick smog blanketed eastern China, it ran an article entitled *Great Places to Escape City Smog*. This resourceful piece of publishing was aimed at readers who "yearned for a short getaway for their lungs' sake." It featured locations spared the enveloping smog, such as the snowy peaks of Lushan Mountain, the alpine scenery near Lijiang in Yunnan province and the palm-fringed beaches in Hainan Island. Essentially, it was a standard-form travel booster for China's natural attractions spun in a rather inventive way.

Motional media is another key travel industry supporter. Television travel shows are proliferating at a rapid speed, and the viewing figures regularly top the hundreds of millions. The satellite-based Travel Channel launched China's first road-trip style TV show, called *Ride to Berlin*, in 2008, and has since signed deals with various international tourism boards to gain access to unique places of interest to film and produce extended travel content.

Young people's desire to explore new frontiers has also been inspired by the television series *On the Road*, which is broadcast online via Youku, China's equivalent of Youtube. Hosted by a young couple, Zhang Xinyu and Liang Hong, the show follows their travels around the globe, after having given up their jobs and lives in China. Divided into series of 15 episodes, the show has taken the intrepid couple to a host of offbeat destinations ranging from Somalia, Vanuatu and Russia to sailing on a luxury yacht on a journey to the Antarctic. The first season garnered over 100 million viewers and was later picked up by state broadcaster CCTV.

Publishing for Chinese travelers overseas

To coincide with the China National Day Golden Week holiday in October 2013, *Condé Nast Traveler UK* launched a Chinese-language *Expert Guide to Shopping in London*. The 100-page magazine-style guide is published twice annually, at the start of October and for China's other Golden Week holiday, Spring Festival.

The free debut issue featured Kate Moss – a widely recognized celebrity in China – plus articles and listings covering shopping, hotels and dining in London, UK style icons and select locations to enjoy afternoon tea – a social activity heavily promoted by luxury hotel chains in China that has earned "see and be seen" social status. The guide is distributed in selected London hotels and high-end stores in the capital and Bicester Village, plus inbound British Airways, Virgin Airways, China Eastern and China Southern flights from China, and among high-end Chinese tour operators.

Established international publishers are progressively publishing new products to appeal to Chinese-language readers. In Italy, the daily newspaper *Corriere della Sera*, which publishes content via a Chinese-language website, now publishes a Chinese magazine, entitled *Italian Style*, while in 2011, French newspaper *Le Figaro* launched *Paris Chic*, a free quarterly luxury magazine.

Published in Chinese, *Paris Chic* covers French fashion, cuisine, art, luxury shopping, and chic hangouts and is distributed in places in France where Chinese travelers like to visit, stay, eat, and shop. In China, the magazine is available to travel agencies and in airport lounges, and reaches the premium memberships of Chinese banks including ICBC and Bank of China. Since its launch, an iPad version has been developed, and *Paris Chic* was also a media partner of China Rendezvous, an annual showcase of yachts, private jets and luxury lifestyle products and services founded in 2010 in Sanya, Hainan Island.

PR, press trips and excessive photography

Back in 2004, one of the first terms I came to understand in the Chinese publishing industry was *hongbao*. The "red packet" of cash, usually gifted to children during Chinese New Year, had been appropriated. Chinese journalists attending hotel openings, travel-related press conferences or branding events were discreetly presented with a *hongbao* in their media pack. The event hosts defended this practice as a reimbursement for travel expenses incurred – but it was widely accepted to be an incentive payment to show up.

As international destinations, hotel companies, airlines, and travel brands court Chinese travelers, engaging the nation's travel and lifestyle media is a strategic element of tourism marketing. Since 2004, when European destinations began receiving Approved Destination Status en masse and international hotels ramped up their China roll-outs, media lunches, press conferences and travel brand parties aimed at influential editors, journalists and bloggers became an almost daily occurrence. The process began in the media strongholds of Beijing and Shanghai, and later expanded – albeit at a less frenetic pace – to cities like Guangzhou and Chengdu.

Today, Chinese travel journalists are the most in-demand group of professional people on the planet. The articles and reviews they write reach vast audiences of new and experienced travelers, while several worldly wise editors and writers produce popular online blogs that attract millions of followers. In the language of social media marketers, Chinese media figures are coveted KOLs – or Key Opinion Leaders.

The life of a Chinese travel journalist is a whirl of media briefings and press parties hosted by tourism boards, hotel companies, tour operators, and luxury brands. In addition, there will be interview requests from foreign media to discuss Chinese travel trends. Somewhere in between, it is necessary to fly around the globe researching and writing real-time travel content demanded by the consumers of China's myriad travel magazines, websites, newspapers, TV, and online travel shows.

A few years ago on a press trip to attend a resort opening in the Maldives, I sat in a restaurant eating Sri Lankan curries with two Chinese travel writers. Both were diligent and observant, but inside they struggled with a shared pressure. Their presence – and the audiences their subsequent writings, photography and social media postings can reach – was in such demand by tourism bureaus that their travel schedules would frazzle the brain of a multinational CEO. They both talked of a sense of burden, not only to accurately represent the attractions for Chinese travelers of the destinations they visited, but to constantly provide engaging insights for an evolving readership of tens of millions, spanning first-time outbounders to discerning internationalists who had lived, studied and worked overseas.

To facilitate more efficient connections with influential Chinese media, and to raise consumer awareness through targeted online and offline coverage, travel providers began – about 10 years ago – to engage specialist PR firms. Initially, those firms were based in Hong Kong, and gradually they began opening offices in China.

Among the first Hong Kong-based PR agencies to take on China's travel and hospitality market were Impact Asia, which was acquired by US-based Cohn & Wolfe in 2011, and GHC Asia. The growth in demand for expert PR, particularly in the luxury travel arena, has since resulted in more agencies founded outside of China expanding in the Middle Kingdom – including Petrie PR, Mango PR and Infinite Luxury – while locally based Chinese agencies are gaining market share.

"I always had China in the back of my mind, and we opened our first office in Shanghai in 2007, followed by Beijing in 2009," says Susan Field, founder of Impact Asia and former CEO of Cohn & Wolfe Impact Asia. "We dealt with local and international companies and they all needed the same: sound advice, a good strategy and a team that constantly looks for creative opportunities to showcase their products and services. By the time I sold the business in 2011, we had 35 staff in China."

One of the major changes during that time was the influence of online sourcing. "As the Internet became more accessible, people have become much more aware of 'what's out there' in terms of overseas destinations." says Field. "As a result, travel bookings are now increasingly made on smartphones, rather than traditional government-run travel agencies. This has been a big development for the industry."

Once a decision has been made to engage local PR specialists, creating press trips crammed with enticing story hooks is an integral part of romancing the Chinese media. "The travel and lifestyle media in China have become more experienced. They are very savvy and are looking for intriguing stories with strong narratives in interesting locations, and they also want insider information and experiences," says Gary Yu, Shanghai-based Managing Director, China of GHC Asia.

Yu says press trips are a high-priority aspect of media engagement in China, since they generate expansive coverage for a destination or travel brand. "Press trips engage journalists to create unique, insider information for their target readership. Because of this, the process has become more collaborative in recent years. We work with clients and invited media while planning an overseas press trip to make sure that it meets the changing needs of their readers," says Yu.

Consumer sentiment is shaping the travel industry in China now, and the media are seen as opinion leaders, not just information providers. "Press trips give tourism boards and host hotels a chance to sit down and talk with Chinese editors and writers and learn from their experiences, and to discuss what Chinese travelers now expect," says Yu. "The same is occurring with client campaigns. Often the media is invited to give their opinions on the format and targeting of travel promotions."

An important attribute of Chinese travel journalists is that they are constantly on the road, so they are not fazed if the next trip is to Hong Kong, Maldives or Chile. "They are happy to travel anywhere for any length of time if the story is right," says Linda Petrie, Managing Director of Petrie PR, a luxury travel and lifestyle PR company with offices in Hong Kong, Singapore and Jakarta. "Confidence in traveling has improved and language is rarely a problem for travel and lifestyle writers. They have all become experienced travelers."

A structured approach is also noted. "They like to travel in a group, and to have a fixed itinerary throughout the day and evening. This is a big difference to international media, who tend to prefer freedom to research on their own," says Petrie. "The Chinese media also enjoy guided city tours and meeting local people, such as chefs, winery owners and craftsmen. They want to get fully immersed in a destination and include personal angles in their stories." Other differences Petrie has noted include a preference to share meals together at breakfast, lunch and dinner, and the necessary allocation of "shopping time" during a trip.

Regular access to Wi-Fi is another imperative, as is a seemingly ceaseless level of photography. "The Chinese travel media doesn't like to use stock images. Editors prefer to use their own photos that have some kind of Chinese context, so you often find journalists are featured posing in each other's shots," says Petrie. "Food imagery is also often included in travel articles, and a lot of time is dedicated to getting the right shot of a local dish or delicacy."

As the Chinese outbound surge continues to develop, understanding its fragmented nature is crucial, says Sarah Curra, CEO of London-based Mango PR, which has expanded to Singapore and Hong Kong. "China is huge a country where cities sometimes have populations bigger than some countries, and there is a massive media market for both print and online. In order to penetrate China, you need deep pockets. It's better to have a clear idea of where you want to be – in terms of sector of the market and city or region of China – and then pursue it."

16 recent headlines you may have missed

Separating the rose-tinted hype from the prosaic truth is an inexact science in the tourism industry. Quite often, there is a rather disconcerting overlap. As consumers, we are easily hooked by the peachy aggrandizement because tourism providers are selling us a dreamscape, an escape from predictability, a vision of otherness. In this sense, China is the perfect storm. The world is focusing its attentions precisely because Chinese urbanites have their eyes firmly fixed on escaping the pollution, overcrowding and cut-throat commercialism of daily life.

The travel media connects these representations of the fantastical and the humdrum. Where Chinese outbound tourism is concerned, the faculty for an incisive headline and a dream-catching photo speaks louder than the text that follows. This selection of headlines from the international and Chinese travel media provides a succinct snapshot of Chinese transcontinental voyaging at this point in time.

International media

- Thousands attend event showcasing Bahamas in China.
  The Nassau Guardian

- Abu Dhabi chases more tourists from China.
  Arabian Business
- Recovering Irish tour operators eye EUR 74 billion Chinese tourist market.
  Irish Times
- Latin America lures Chinese tourists.
  CNN
- China's Big Spenders Surge Into Bali.
  TTG Asia
- No Visa for Chinese Visitors to Jamaica.
  Jamaica Observer
- Beijing couple proposes on North Pole, weds on South.
  Shanghaiist.com
- Costa Rica plans more consulates in China to attract tourists and investment.
  El Pais (Spain)

Chinese travel magazines

- De Haar Castle: The Downton Abbey in the Netherlands.
  Airport Journal (China)
- Danube Dreams.
  Business Traveler China
- Bicycling in Namibia.
  National Geographic Traveler China
- Aurora Hunting in Swedish Lapland.
  Condé Nast Traveler China
- Reykjavik: A Song of Ice and Fire.
  World of Cruising China
- Iran: Dreaming of Persia.
  Voyage China
- Algeria: The Rain Will Never Come.
  Top Travel
- Europe's Hottest Winter Carnivals.
  Kempinski Greater China Magazine

EXPERT INSIGHT: CHERRY LI, EDITOR-IN-CHIEF, GRAND HOTELS MEDIA

Cherry Li is editor-in-chief of Shanghai-based *Grand Hotels* magazine. A graduate of Shanghai Normal University, Ms Li worked as a senior hotel communications executive in Shanghai before launching *Grand Hotels* in December 2005. She developed the glossy Chinese-language magazine as a platform for luxury hotels to showcase their properties and services to Chinese customers.

What was the objective of publishing *Grand Hotels*, and has that evolved over time?

I had been thinking that a hotel is not just a building for lodging, meals and other services; but it is a kind of lifestyle. When I worked in hotel communications, I was a bridge between the hotel and the media, but the mass media wasn't able to cover many things related to a hotel. Therefore, *Grand Hotels* came into being as an alternative. Nowadays, hotels set a benchmark for the new lifestyle trend in China. We still adhere to our initial publishing objective, the only change is that we have a more diversified reach through print media, television and online.

What is the target readership of *Grand Hotels*?

We publish around 100,000 copies per issue, which are distributed to hotel professionals and in guest rooms and on the executive floors of hotels across China, plus some South East Asian and European hotels. We are also distributed to the global top 500 companies in China and the top 500 Chinese enterprises, members of foreign chambers of commerce and golf clubs, and have individual subscribers in Taiwan, Hong Kong, Macao, Singapore and South East Asia. We publish two annual special issues, for the Chinese F1 Grand Prix and the ATP Tennis Masters in Shanghai, which are big events for hotels.

Since the launch of *Grand Hotels*, the hotel industry in China has changed significantly. How have you reported these changes?

Yes, the development of the hotel industry has been dramatic, and we have continuously promoted this process and given our objective feedback. We are committed to making hotels understand the needs and aspirations of Chinese guests, and to help Chinese consumers learn about different hotel brands and services. Today, tier-1 cities are becoming saturated with hotels, so more hotel groups are eyeing the fast-growing tier-2, tier-3 and even tier-4 cities. China is a vast country, and each place has its own culture and unique history worthy of exploration, which hotels need to reflect and promote. We try to convey these exciting developments to our readers.

Another development has been the emergence of Chinese hotel brands. How do you balance coverage of these and established global brands?

As a result of strong economic development and the hotel market becoming more mature, brands like Hilton, Starwood and Marriott are everywhere in China. They have been successful in establishing their own position and earned a reputation in the minds of consumers. Like the development process in other hotel markets, China has also entered a new era of segmented competition with more personalized and precisely positioned hotels, and an increased number of consumers seeking unique hotel experiences. Chinese people are now curious about new things, and some of the emerging hotel groups in China are developing their awareness and positioning. Brand, culture and service levels will be increasingly important.

Chinese travelers are discerning in their choice of hotels and amenities. Are hotels catering to these changing needs?

Consumers from different countries should have basically the same requirements for hotels, and that is why many international hotel brands have achieved success in China. From a commercial point of view, various hotels have made adjustments in response to market needs, and this has proved quite effective. Many hotel groups are now creating brands with strong Chinese cultural and historical elements, such as NUO, which is being specially tailored by Kempinski for China. Some hotel brands also serve a cup of Chinese tea when guests arrive. In addition, some Chinese enterprises that are large owners of real estate have branched into hotel management, such as Wanda Group's Vista, Realm and Reign. J Hotels by Jin Jiang Group is deeply imprinted with Chinese culture and will open its first hotel in Shanghai's tallest building. Chinese guests also have their own characteristics, such as a preference for traveling with the whole family, and this creates special service needs. The international brand hotels in China have made extraordinary efforts, and they will continue to study the preferences of local guests to create hotels and resorts endowed with local culture and strong brand features.

Are you noticing more Chinese general managers at major hotels?

Yes. This is an inevitable trend, and it is the junction point combining a hotel brand with the Chinese market. A dozen years ago, Chinese general managers were very rare, as the hotel industry needed foreign professionals to help establish international concepts of branding and service. Since then, in parallel with the rapid development of

China's hotel industry, more local talent is now moving into management levels of major hotels, and Chinese hospitality professionals are also setting up and managing their own hotel companies.

Your background is in the hotel industry; what new things have you learned from publishing *Grand Hotels* magazine?

I was fortunate to have the opportunity to learn about the hotel industry bit by bit from an insider's perspective. Since launching the magazine, I have developed a more comprehensive view about hotels and the market – which makes me love this industry even more. The hotel industry is growing rapidly in China, and for many people it has been a familiar process of going from not understanding, to understanding. I love this industry not only because it brings joy to people, but because of the personalized meaning and purpose. Hotels are committed to providing comfortable stays for guests, and they also want to improve their service, which is hard to experience elsewhere.

Chapter 11
Smart Travel, Chinese Style: Trip Planning and New Technology

Microblogging goes mobile

"Hello my friends in China. I'm pleased to have joined Weibo and look forward to visiting China very soon." With those words, British Prime Minister David Cameron opened his personal site on the Weibo social media network – widely regarded as being China's equivalent of Twitter – before a visit to China in December 2013. The message prompted thousands of questions from Chinese netizens, on subjects ranging from tuition fees at UK universities for overseas students to whether Britain might introduce a visa-free policy for Chinese travelers.

Prime Minister Cameron's entrance into the frenetic world of Chinese social media recognized an evident truth about China today: mobile-based connections are the single most effective form of interaction. Consumer brands, retailers, tourism boards, governments, celebrities, effusive netizens, and even football clubs (Manchester United's pitch-side advertising boards reference its Weibo account launched in July 2013) all vie for attention in Chinese cyberspace via the nation's two social network mega-sites: Sina Weibo and Tencent's Weixin (popularly known as WeChat).

These two platforms have grown and thrived in a protected domestic environment where Twitter and Facebook are blocked, and while WeChat has latterly dominated, in 2014 Sina was working on new service innovations ahead of its planned IPO in the US. At the same time, brands should not overlook the Youku and Tudou video-sharing sites, which have similarly prospered from the blocking of Youtube.

To a large degree, the future of the Chinese tourism experience will overlap with technological developments that impact all global nomads. The wider availability of in-flight Wi-Fi and phone calls will be eagerly consumed, as will the advancement of mobile flight and hotel check-in services. Airlines will need to meet or beat on-the-ground quality of Internet access speeds enabling passengers to download large files and watch videos and movies on phones and notepad computers. Improvements will be made in the provision of power outlets on-board, so batteries can be revived before landing at a destination – although expect to see more widespread marketing and consumer uptake of portable power packs and personal Pocket Wi-Fi devices.

Payment mechanisms are evolving, too. Chinese consumers are following the global shift towards applications enabling settlement by smartphone and digital credit cards, though, inevitably, with a greater volume of converts. A Beijing-based company called OneCard has already staked its claim on the space by seeking crowd-funding on Demohour, China's version of Kickstarter, for its digital card that is designed to store both credit card details and prepaid membership and loyalty card details.

But for travel providers, the power, scale and diversity of social media technology in China – fuelled by the desire to share "emotion evoking" imagery and video-based content – make it the go-to marketing tool. Seamless connectivity is largely taken for granted in Chinese cities, where free Wi-Fi is widely available and 3G networks are pretty robust. In March 2014, China Unicom began rolling out its 4G wireless services in 25 cities, and aimed to connect up to 300 urban centers by the end of the year.

Content generation and sharing are so popular that in a bid to gain some ground from the social networks, CCTV collaborated with railway stations across the country during the 2014 Spring Festival to set up video recording booths, so that travelers could tell their stories and express their new year's wishes to family and friends.

The mobile content sharing revolution in China mirrors a global pattern, of course. "Every serious player in the online travel agent space is prioritizing mobile technology development and pushing hard for travelers' attention in the form of traffic, transactions and app downloads," PhoCusWright said in a November 2013 report. "The rapid proliferation of tablets, with bigger screens more suitable for comparing offers and building trips, is also helping to increase mobile's profile in online travel," the report added.

China is a keen adopter of all things mobile – and all technological things social. As a Beijing-based hospitality marketing executive friend neatly surmised "No-one I know checks personal email or sends an SMS any more. Everything is WeChat." As she said that, she produced a mobile charger from her bag and placed it on the counter of the cocktail bar. The battery in one of her two expensive smartphones had drained – fortunately, the spare handset was in action while the other was recharging. Hence, China's great societal faux pas – not being connected to social media – was avoided.

The WeChat phenomenon

Launched in 2011, WeChat hasn't just transformed Chinese social media, it has reformatted mobile peer-to-peer interactions and created a multi-functional platform to connect brands and consumers. While Weibo has a vast base of more than 600 million subscribers – about 60 million of which use it daily, including the highly coveted KOLs – and has proved a fertile medium for disseminating information and messaging, the layers of functionality offered by WeChat since it diversified from its WhatsApp style origins have made it much more than a messaging tool. The shift in social media usage from Weibo to WeChat has encouraged hoteliers and travel brands to deploy it as a sophisticated tool for customer service management and interactive market research.

WeChat is owned by Internet services giant Tencent, which was founded in Shenzhen in 1998 and listed on the Hong Kong Stock Exchange in 2004. The company's media platforms also include QQ.com, Tencent Microblog and Tencent Video. It also formed a joint venture with leading online shopping sales phenomenon JD.com which "enables JD to tap Tencent's significant mobile and Internet user base, and Tencent to leverage JD's best-in-class e-commerce services to offer superior user experiences," according to a company statement. In addition, Tencent owns a 20 percent stake in Dianping, China's largest restaurant and dining reviews website, and has incorporated restaurant reviews and a dining locator function into WeChat.

At the end of 2013, WeChat had 355 million users, a 121 percent increase on 2012. With the launch of new services, such as a video calling facility, a game center and the Weixin Payment mechanism, plus revamping its Moments wall, Weixin has evolved into a multi-functional platform that provides metrics and analytics for business accounts similar to those of Facebook.

"Alluring, aspirational and ambitious" are the three most frequently used terms related to content posting by presenters at China's social media marketing conferences. "Finding your niche, engaging your target demographic and communicating your brand stories" is another popular seminar phrase. Chinese social media users are not just seeking brand and travel-related content that engages them and is relevant to their patterns of travel, but stuff that actually lifts them off their seat, invokes their imagination and inspires them to share and discuss with friends. This is not as simple to achieve as it sounds, primarily because of the sheer volume of social media content being posted hourly, let alone daily.

The beneficial proposition of marketing via WeChat – instant, real-time access to a vast potential audience – can also be its potential Achilles Heel, says Amy Fabris-Shi, co-founder (with myself) of Scribes of the Orient, which works with travel and tourism companies on marketing and communications projects in China and worldwide. "It's important to remember that social media platforms in China are almost exclusively used on smartphones. As a result, the content, competitions or discount offers you publish aren't simply going to be found by web surfers browsing the Internet. They will be transmitted directly to people who are checking their phones constantly during waking hours."

There have been several recent cases in China where hospitality and travel companies have been embarrassed by ill-conceived content or special offers published via social media, or by disaffected staff members hashtagging the brand or senior members of the firm when posting critical messages. "Such situations can escalate very quickly into a public relations crisis, because stories go viral at rapid speed in China. Within a few minutes, you may find that you have a mountain to climb to repair the damage to your brand image," says Fabris-Shi. "While this has long been a vulnerability for consumer brands in China, travel brands are more 'on-radar' now because of heightened interest among a broadening class of travelers."

Outbound travel goes online

Internet travel planning and booking in China is expanding fast. This is unsurprising given the prevalence of Internet usage and the orbital status of online shopping. At the end of 2013, China counted 618 million Internet users (up from 564 million in 2012) – equivalent to the total population of the 28-nation EU plus an extra 100 million – according to the China Internet Network Information Center (CNNIC). Among all Internet users, 81 percent use mobile phones to get online, CNNIC said in an official statement.

A key feature of Internet expansion is the growth in smartphone ownership, and industry analysts believe this will drive increased mobile travel booking. The 2013 Ericsson Mobility Report revealed that in the first quarter of 2013, 130 million new mobile subscribers were recorded worldwide, with China accounting for 30 million. According to IPK International's World Travel Monitor, which was commissioned by ITB Berlin, from 2008 to 2012 the market share of Internet bookings in China more than doubled, rising from 19 percent to 39 percent.

Travel bookings by smartphones account for a smaller percentage in developed markets, and the Chinese are "already racing ahead," according to IPK's World Travel Monitor. The report adds that the move towards mobile booking is compressing the model of searching and booking, particularly for hotels, with around 70 percent of hotel bookings made via smartphone being decided upon within 24 hours.

"The development of mobile technology will reshape the travel industry," said James Liang, Chairman and CEO of Nasdaq-listed online travel agency Ctrip.com, as it launched version 5.0 of its mobile application in September 2013. Ctrip says the mobile app is now its pivotal booking platform, accounting for more than 35 percent of hotel bookings and 20 percent of air ticket sales in the fourth quarter of 2013.

Founded in Shanghai in 1999, Ctrip proudly claims to be China's leading online travel agency, offering over 9,000 flight routes and 277,000 hotels in 172 countries to its 60 million members and 2.5 million real time users at the end of March 2014. The company, which listed on the Nasdaq in December 2003, also has investments in travel companies in Hong Kong and Taiwan. In addition to its Simplified Chinese, Traditional Chinese and English language sites, Ctrip offers online travel sites in Japanese, Korean, German, French, Spanish, Russian, and Vietnamese.

Version 5.0 of Ctrip's mobile app was engineered to incorporate emerging trends in Chinese travel. In addition to offering individual and "group buy" hotel rooms, flight and train tickets, group tours, plus leisure activities and car rentals worldwide, it includes an expanded "last-minute deal" section and more "mobile-exclusive" rates and discounts. A "smart itinerary" function enables users to integrate holiday plans with their smartphone calendars and share with friends, while more than 60,000 destination guides and 180,000 reviews and opinions in Chinese support offline browsing and trip planning. Bookings can be made with all major credit cards, plus China-specific payment options, such as China UnionPay and Alipay.

In recent years, Ctrip's main challenger has been Nasdaq-listed eLong, which is part of Expedia, Inc. It offers more than 260,000 bookable domestic and international properties in 200 countries through its website and mobile platforms. The company's 2013 financial statement shows that mobile hotel bookings comprised more than 30 percent of total hotel room nights stayed in the fourth quarter of the year, compared to 25 percent in the third quarter. Cumulative downloads of eLong mobile apps exceeded 45 million, and eLong customers booked 25.8 million room night stays in 2013. In April 2014, eLong announced a strategic cooperation with Suzhou-based Tongcheng, which operates leading online leisure travel service, LY.com.

Counting Baidu, China's largest online search engine, as a controlling shareholder, has unquestionably assisted the growth of Qunar.com (去哪儿网 meaning "where to go"), a high-profile hybrid online site for travel searches and reviews, flight, hotel, and rail ticket bookings, and group-buying deals through its website and mobile applications. Headquartered in Beijing and originally launched as a meta-search travel site in 2005, Qunar's rapid growth encouraged Baidu to invest USD 306 million in 2011 to support its future expansion. In November 2013, Qunar raised USD 167 million through an IPO on the Nasdaq in New York. The company claimed 234 million Internet and 54 million mobile users in 2013, and a possible merger (or at least greater collaboration) between Qunar and Ctrip was a hot media topic in 2014.

From beehives to travel buddies

A common trait of Chinese independent travelers is a methodical approach to pre-trip planning and research. Before booking a trip, Chinese outbounders carefully search out the opportunities and potential dangers that await them at a new destination. Hotels, tour guides, shopping and dining options and activities are pre-selected, and itineraries are carefully pieced together.

Chinese Internet companies have responded to this craving for global travel intelligence. In addition to secure travel booking sites like Ctrip, eLong, Qunar and, more recently, Taobao Travel, information-based websites and mobile platforms integrate travel planning tools with bespoke destination guides and peer reviews and recommendations that are highly valued by Chinese travelers. Armed with a diverse library of mobile-based travel information tailored for each trip, Chinese vacationers are among the best-informed tourists in the world.

Ask aspirational Chinese travelers where they go to source travel information, and online search site Baidu is frequently cited, often followed by Mafengwo (nicknamed the Beehive 蚂蜂窝 – directly translated, it's a linguistic play, with *ma* meaning ant, *feng* meaning bee or wasp, and *wo* as nest). Founded in 2006, Mafengwo is an online repository of user-generated reviews of hotels, airlines, destinations, and offers downloadable travel guide apps. The website is also integrated with travel booking engines, like Ctrip, eLong and Agoda. Aimed at young, travel-savvy metropolitans seeking new experiences overseas, Mafengwo says most of its users are from Beijing, Shanghai, Guangzhou, Shenzhen, and Hong Kong. In 2013, Mafengwo's expansion plans were boosted by a USD 15 million cash injection from Qiming Ventures and Capital Today.

Travel planning website Qyer.com (Qiong You, 穷游网) was founded in 2004 by a Chinese student studying in Europe who chanced upon a hotel discount promotion in Switzerland and was encouraged to share information with Chinese travelers. In 2008, the company established a Beijing base and began to expand its offerings. It currently claims to offer information on around 40,000 destinations worldwide, and provides flight ticket bookings, hotel reservations and a foreign visa service.

In 2013, Qyer.com – which claims around 10 million users, around half of which access via mobile phones – hit the headlines when it received an undisclosed investment from online giant Alibaba Group, the world's largest online marketplace. Hangzhou-based Alibaba operates the consumer-to-consumer shopping service Taobao and the Tmall virtual B2C retail shopping center, the Alipay online payment platform, plus Taobao Travel, which it launched in 2010 as a competitor to Ctrip. Alibaba also invested in 117go.com (known as On the Road, 在路上), a mobile travel journal and photo sharing app, purchased an 18 percent stake in the Weibo microblogging service, and bought Chinese mapping software firm AutoNavi.

New applications are being created and funded at a heady pace to facilitate faster, more convenient travel planning. Outbound trip planning websites include Uzai.com, Weego.me, Yiqifei.com, Tuniu.com, Ukubang.com, Aoyou.com and Lvmama.com, while Alibaba and China Broadband Capital invested USD 20 million in ByeCity.com which aims to provide visas via its website and app for people who want to travel overseas.

In November 2013, Shijiebang.com, a travel services platform founded in 2012 to connect Chinese travelers to local tour companies overseas, announced the launch of its Trip Planning Assistant (TPA). Shijiebang, which counts angel investors such as Jerry Yang, founder of Yahoo! Inc, Fosun ZhongKun Capital Group and ChinaRock Capital Management, raised several millions of dollars in an initial funding round, some of which will be used to acquire mobile businesses. It launched the TPA at a seminar attended by representatives of Deutsche Zentrale für Tourismus, VisitBritain, Scandinavian Tourist Board, Brand USA, Canadian Tourism Commission, Atout France, Switzerland Tourism, Turespaña and Netherlands Board of Tourism & Conventions.

The TPA is targeted at the swelling ranks of independent Chinese travelers who require up-to-date, reliable destination information and are concerned about the high cost, and lack of Chinese customization, of tailor-made local tours. It initially signed agreements with travel providers in 20 destinations worldwide, with plans to expand. Travelers to a featured destination must complete a questionnaire about their preferred vacation activities and travel needs, and a free customized itinerary is created using information provided by overseas travel associations, tourism boards and tour operators. Shijiebang also acts as a third-party trading platform for providers of air tickets, cruise trips, hotel reservations, visa services and travel insurance.

China's emerging backpacker and budget travel constituency tends to favor Ijianren (捡人网), a website that helps potential tourists meet like-minded travel companions for both domestic and overseas travel. Meanwhile, the tourism "sharing economy" is starting to develop. In 2014, Tujia.com, an online property and accommodation rental site sometimes likened as China's version of Airbnb, raised USD 100 million in development funding.

SINGLES' DAY DISCOUNTING

Price promotions and discount offers are highly prized in China's explosive online shopping sphere. If well marketed through WeChat and Weibo, targeted offers and selective discounts offer a good opportunity for travel providers seeking more Chinese travelers. One calendar date stands out for online discounting: 11 November, known locally as 11.11 (or Singles' Day, because of the succession of ones).

On 11 November 2013, Alibaba earned RMB 35 billion (USD 5.63 billion) in one day, a cash-busting 83 percent increase on 2012, as more participating merchants offered discounted products. Around 21 percent of the day's 171.4 million orders on the Tmall.com and Taobao websites were made via mobile devices, with mobile orders totalling RMB 1 billion (USD 0.16 billion) processed in the first hour alone, surpassing the full-day total in 2012.

Earning customer loyalty is the avowed principle of the one-day mega-sale, according to Alibaba, which launched the initiative in 2009 to generate extra spending during the slow period between China National Day and Spring Festival. "Once a year, merchants will be able to take their best products and sell them for the lowest prices in order to thank consumers for their support and transform that relationship for the better," said Jack Ma, Founder of Alibaba, in an official statement.

FRANCE HITS THE HALF-MILLION ON WEIBO

In November 2013, Atout France, the nation's tourism development agency, released a statement noting that France had become the "Number one European destination on Weibo," having passed the 500,000 fans threshold. France launched its Weibo presence in January 2012, and by 15 November 2013 had accumulated 517,028 fans.

The statement noted that its Weibo haul "exceeds that of closer and more traditional destinations for the Chinese market, such as Singapore (412,465) and Japan (278,011)." Atout France accredited its achievement in widening its social media reach in China on two years of producing targeted, high-quality content to resonate with young Chinese Weibo users. This included campaigns on gastronomy, wine tourism and culture; weddings and honeymoons, and engaging the Chinese media and influential bloggers who, in turn, helped boost the distribution of France's Weibo.

Chapter 12

Keeping It Local: Fast Trains, Ski Slopes and the New Macao

Rethinking Chinese tourism on the home front

As previously mentioned China's tripartite travel industry increasingly forms a Venn diagram of contiguous influences, and each of the domestic, inbound and outbound travel sectors are undergoing an unprecedented restructure. Huge investment is a shared feature of all three sectors, as is the influence of cutting-edge technologies, the primacy of the Internet and the embrace of new leisure experiences.

Just as the rush to attract Chinese travelers has created intensifying competition within the global travel industry, China is also recognizing that its own tourism industry needs to broaden its horizons to confront the fierce scramble among Asian tourism providers for the fast-expanding volumes of intra-regional travelers.

In statistical terms, tourism within China is in a pretty healthy state. The country witnessed around 3.2 billion (primarily domestic) tourist trips in 2013, according to official figures. Sanya, Hainan Island, was the most popular travel destination, but burgeoning figures were recorded in destinations countrywide.

Inbound tourism, however, has performed sluggishly. Aggressive tourism marketing by other Asian destinations is one factor, as the majority of tourists arriving in China are from Asia – and China's own tourism promotion has been poorly conceived and delivered. Another factor has been the increased value of the RMB, which has made travel in China more expensive than competitor nations in South East Asia. A third inhibitor – and, indeed, an increasing push factor for Chinese wanting to travel overseas – is the choking air pollution that hangs for extended periods over major cities.

Nowhere is feeling the pinch more than Beijing, whose tourism reputation has been adversely damaged at home and abroad by its noxious air quality. The capital's tourism business has been largely stagnant in recent years, despite the hoped-for boost of hosting the 2008 Olympics. Beijing received 4.36 million visits in 2007, a figure not bettered until 2010, when 4.9 million visits were recorded. A record high of 5.2 million visitors in 2011 was followed by 5.01 million in 2012, dropping to 4.5 million in 2013, according to figures from the Beijing Commission for Tourism Development. The introduction of a 72-hour visa waiver program for short-stay transit arrivals failed to make an impact.

China's second city Shanghai also recorded a decline in overseas arrivals for a second consecutive year in 2013 – receiving 7.55 million overseas visitors, down 5.7 percent from 2012. Media reports in early 2014 suggested that a 72-hour visa-free stay would be extended to cruise ship passengers docking in Shanghai, although there is little evidence to suggest that it would have an effect. In 2013, a similar scheme launched at the city's airports for transit passengers from 45 countries attracted only 15,000 take-ups. Hopes are now turning to the opening in 2015 of the city's biggest tourism project, Shanghai Disney Resort, particularly for attracting visitors from Hong Kong, Singapore, South Korea and South East Asia.

If Beijing and Shanghai are struggling to sustain their tourism economies, China itself has long suffered from sterile, ineffective tourism marketing. It has relied too heavily on its one-dimensional "mass tourism" sites, such as the Great Wall of China, Forbidden City and Temple of Heaven in Beijing, Terracotta Warriors in Xi'an, the Bund in Shanghai and Three Gorges on the Yangtze River. These proved successful in attracting "first time" visitors, but little effort has been expended to diversify and drive repeat visits to explore China beyond its marquee attractions.

In early 2014, the Chinese National Tourism Administration (CNTA) sought to refresh its tourism branding by launching a new promotional campaign, entitled Beautiful China – 2014 Year of Smart Travel. Still wedded to the outdated "Visit Our Country" school of destination marketing that Chinese travelers themselves now overlook when choosing a destination, the CNTA at least unveiled an overdue new website.

Although an inbound campaign, it – like many aspects of the Chinese domestic travel industry – merits consideration from tourism providers worldwide since it provides insights into the technology-based marketing developments being adopted in China, and yields an inside track into the mindset of Chinese tourism planners. Essentially, the new marketing strategy is a further evocation of the ways in which domestic, inbound and outbound tourism planning are being integrated in China.

The new online presentation of tourism in China has clearly been shaped by the CNTA's research into Chinese travelers in the domestic and international markets. Initially, the beta version website was only available in English and Chinese. A phased roll-out added French, German, Russian, Korean, and Japanese versions. The content is richer and more visually engaging than the one-dimensional CNTA sites of before, with more consideration given to the value of imagery, plus geographic and suggested tour routes, interactive trip planning options and modifications for smartphones and tablets.

The key battleground for China's tourism planners, though, will be on the home front. Keeping domestic travelers entertained will require a nationwide build-out of tourism infrastructure to excite twenty-first century experientialists. The Chinese dreamers are no longer interested in the rebuilt vestiges of several millennia of history – their leisure time is precious, and to spend it they want interactivity, inspiration and a sense of the spectacular.

Taking the inter-city express

"Welcome to 'Harmony' … Please do not smoke within any area of the train." As the recorded on-board announcement in English and Chinese neared completion, the white, bullet-nosed China Railway High-Speed (CRH) train eased out of Beijing South Railway Station bound for Shanghai. I gazed out the window and turned my thoughts to the book on my seat table.

Anyone who has read Paul Theroux's gracefully phrased musings about his rail journeys across China in *Riding the Iron Rooster* will recall an apparently antediluvian era of transport. Inter-city train travel has changed enormously since 1988, when Theroux's account of his labored hinterland crossings was published. Indeed, Chinese train travel has changed completely since 2008, let alone 1988.

Those changes are evident before boarding. Most of my fellow passengers collect the tickets they pre-booked on the Internet at self-service machines on the station concourse. I had purchased my ticket in advance, too, but had made a journey to the station ticket booth to present my passport. Online booking has slashed ticket lines considerably, and it took less than ten minutes, a fraction of the time Theroux would have spent queuing in smoky ticket offices with no English signage.

The train in which I am traveling is a physical replica of Japan's *shinkansen* bullet trains (which were launched in 1964), although its ascribed name is definitively Chinese. "Harmony" is a Confucian allusion to the repeatedly stated objective of the previous government of President Hu Jintao – on whose watch the high-speed network was launched – to create a "harmonious society" in China.

My journey from Beijing to Shanghai, a distance of about 1,300 kilometers, took a few minutes less than five hours. The standard-class ticket cost RMB 540 (which equates to around 0.42 pence (UK) or 0.7 cents (US) per kilometer at January 2014 exchange rates). It is little surprise that taking the fast train is now widely considered a more cost-effective and convenient alternative to flying, which takes just over two hours in the air, plus the inevitable ground delays and check-in time.

Inaugurated to national fanfare in June 2011, Beijing–Shanghai is the flagship route of China's ongoing Great Railway Rollout. The Chinese government has pumped billions of dollars into its signature national infrastructure project: the high-speed rail network, and connecting the nation's two largest cities was its defining glory.

The rolling stock began shifting at speeds exceeding 200 km per hour in 2008, with the unveiling of a 28-minute connection between Beijing and Tianjin. Since then, inter-city passengers from Wuhan to Guangzhou and Nanjing to Jinan have been lining up to board trains that traverse vast tracts of this expansive nation at high velocity. By the end of 2010, 8,358 kilometers of high-speed track was in operation on inter-city routes. That figure rose to around 10,000 kilometers (or one-tenth of China's total rail network) by the end of 2013. The next official target is 18,000 kilometers by 2015.

The opening of each new long-distance route is heavily promoted. In December 2013, state media reported the launch of a fast service between Shanghai and the northern city of Harbin, just in time for its popular annual Ice & Snow Sculpture Festival. The line slashed the journey time between the two cities, from 32 hours to 13, with stops en route at Suzhou, Wuxi, Changzhou, Nanjing, Xuzhou, Jinan, Tianjin, Shenyang, and Changchun. Construction was also due to start in 2014 to link Beijing and the northern city of Zhangjiakou, two cities that submitted a joint bid to host the 2022 Winter Olympics.

Beyond the rapidity, China's trains look and feel different. The carriages are open-plan, resembling elongated airplanes rather than the iron roosters of yore, and on-board staff members have adopted uniforms and a service style similar to flight attendants. Traditional Chinese train staples, such as green tea and kettles of hot water to fill up pots of dried noodles, remain, but the attendants also offer me fresh-brewed coffee and salted peanuts. Most of my fellow travelers eschew the services offered, preferring instead to watch downloaded TV shows on their smartphones or take selfies with friends.

The train stations have changed, too. The brand new airport-sized hangars on the outskirts of major cities appear to have been constructed to cope with triple-digit capacity growth in the coming years. With the addition of a grass pitch to cover the departure lounge, some could easily host the Super Bowl or FA Cup final.

In addition to the fast-changing city skylines and the proliferation of metro networks, luxury brand stores and new apartment blocks, the high-speed train stations are the most visible signs of the colossal scale of urbanization in China. They also facilitate domestic tourism expansion. Train travel has always been the "people's transport," and now it is faster, more efficient, and better connected than ever. Although ticket prices have risen significantly in recent years, the train remains better value and more punctual than traveling by air. There are no air miles to be accumulated, of course, but travelers are willing to forgo those in favor of rapid inter-city movement.

The expansion of high-speed train travel has not been without problems. On 23 July 2011, 40 people were killed and 191 injured when a fast train smashed into a stationary train near the east coast city of Wenzhou. The State Council launched an investigation, and the government temporarily halted rail construction projects. More recently, the debts of China Railway Corp, which operates the Chinese rail network, spiralled to around RMB 3 trillion by the third quarter of 2013. Calls grew louder for the removal of its monopoly, and for private investment to be secured both for new inter-city projects and for much-needed metropolitan commuter networks in major cities.

Passengers have also complained of limited on-board facilities while zipping from city to city, including the absence of Wi-Fi connectivity, a convenience to which Chinese commuters have become accustomed on metro trains, and also the instability of China's 3G and 4G services. In early 2014, a telecoms industry alliance said it was preparing to launch on-train Wi-Fi as soon as it received regulatory approval.

Aside from the technological glitches, the advent of high-speed rail has raised the comfort levels and expectations of Chinese train travelers. While many of my fellow passengers en route to Shanghai were too young to remember the crowded, smoke-stacked trips about which Paul Theroux wrote, they will inevitably compare the conveniences of rail travel in China when they board trains on their global travels. It should be no surprise to international train operators if the home journeys are scripted more favorably in their WeChat posts.

The world of Wanda

Wang Jianlin, China's richest man and chairman of property developer Dalian Wanda Group, is determined to drive the twenty-first century tourism train in China. Wang's company, which owns more than 80 Wanda Plazas combining retail, office and residential space, and hotels across China is banking on large-scale cultural tourism projects in major cities to generate revenues of RMB 80 billion (USD 12.86 billion) by 2020.

Wanda is well positioned to dictate development in Chinese tourism – and has unleashed a cascade of investment into tourism projects targeted at domestic travelers. Its recent acquisitions include major travel agencies in Beijing and Hubei, plus UK-based Sunseeker yachts and AMC Entertainment, comprising the second-largest chain of movie theatres in North America. Foreign tourism planners may be interested to learn that movie watching in China is booming. China's 2013 box office sales totaled almost RMB 22 billion (USD 3.54 billion), 58.7 percent of which was accounted for by Chinese domestic movies, according to the State Administration of Press, Publication, Radio, Film and Television (SARFT). Spotting the growth potential, WeChat and Alipay Wallet both introduced online-to-offline movie ticket payment.

Wang also has the ability to create dramatic surprise. In 2013, he flew a clutch of movie stars including John Travolta, Nicole Kidman, Leonardo DiCaprio, and Zhang Ziyi to the coastal city of Qingdao for a gala party to announce the world's largest movie studio complex, Oriental Movie Metropolis. Inevitably dubbed "China's Hollywood," the USD 8 billion film and entertainment park is scheduled to open in 2017, and will feature state-of-the-art movie studios – with the aim of making up to 100 movies a year, including 30 foreign films – a movie-based theme park, hotels, a celebrity wax museum, and a yacht marina.

Wanda is also investing in so-called "tourism cities" in China, the first of which began construction in the northern city of Harbin in April 2013. Also under construction is the RMB 24 billion (USD 3.86 billion) Guilin Wanda Cultural Tourism City, in the southern region of Guangxi. The mixed-use development will feature a theme park, hotel, cinemas, and a shopping mall, and has a stated aim of "raising Guilin to a world-famous cultural tourism city."

One of the most ambitious projects is Wuxi Wanda Cultural Tourism City, located in Wuxi, 130 kilometers from Shanghai. Targeted to welcome up to 20 million visitors per year after opening in 2017, this mega-resort will feature a 70-hectare outdoor theme park, including a 150-meter-high rollercoaster, a film park including a 3D theater and a large stage show directed by Franco Dragone, a retail center, seven hotels, and a bar street with "more than 20 famous bar brands from China and overseas," according to a company statement.

Wang was quoted in Chinese media as saying that his objective is to create a new, more diversified business model for cultural tourism in China, arguing that the nation's approach to developing tourism facilities has been too simplified in terms of revenue structures. Viewed from inside or outside of China, the three most interesting aspects of these projects are not the scale, the cost or the ambition.

Firstly, they signify that the government is now sanctioning large real estate developments with a direct focus on cultural development and diversified consumer spending that does not just rely on brand shopping. This is a clear departure from the constructive mania of residential and mall properties and industrial facilities of the past two decades.

Secondly, such "big ticket" developments exemplify the leisure and tourism investment power that now exists in China, and which will inevitably spread overseas to destinations that are, and which will become, popular with Chinese tourists. Wanda itself is testing the waters beyond China. The firm has gained planning permission to develop two towers – including Europe's tallest residential building – at One Nine Elms in Vauxhall, London. More high-profile projects seem certain.

Thirdly, owners and developers of tourism attractions outside of China should take a keen interest in the scope and standards of facilities offered – not just because they are tailored to the preferences of Chinese consumers, but because those same tourists will take with them elevated expectations when traveling overseas as a result of the new and innovative experiences enjoyed in their own country. This point is particularly salient, since it highlights that China is now an active creator, investor – and increasingly an acquirer – of modern tourism, not just a consumer of facilities and amenities created beyond its borders.

Crossing the Tibetan Plateau

A few weeks after the Shanghai–Lhasa railway opened on 1 October 2006 (China National Day), I was commissioned by a travel magazine to take the 52-hour trip. I needed to travel incognito as, for a journalist, obtaining a visa for a trip to Tibet was, and still is, extremely difficult.

I had visited Tibet on one previous occasion, in 2005, and knew that an entry permit must be secured in Shanghai, and that traveling beyond the capital, Lhasa, was not permitted without signing up for an officially accredited tour. That was not an issue, as I only intended to stay in Lhasa for a few days, before flying back to Shanghai via Chengdu (there still are no direct flights between Lhasa and Shanghai).

The back-story of the Tibet Autonomous Region is a sensitive issue. Tibetan-Chinese history is fraught with frictions and reciprocal land battles. The defining intervention was made in 1950, when China invaded Tibet causing its spiritual leader, the Dalai Lama, to flee into exile. The Free Tibet issue has become a campaigning platform worldwide, given extra profile by celebrity activists in Hollywood. Violent protests against Chinese rule erupted in Tibet in March 2008, and Tibet is frequently "closed" to non-Chinese visitors, especially before, during and after the anniversary of the uprising, which was quelled by the Chinese army.

The nearly 4,400-kilometer train journey – which crosses seven Chinese provinces, Jiangsu, Anhui, Henan, Shaanxi, Gansu, Qinghai, and the Tibet Autonomous Region – is spectacular, particularly after exiting the city of Xi'an where the route traverses the Loess Plateau. Rounded mountains rise from flat, sandy plains, many of which have been sculptured over several millennia. Later, these mountains became atrophied, and the train clips through a broad causeway of ridges and canyons, before rising to the high point of the trip: the Tibetan Plateau.

Here, the Tangula Pass, which peaks at 5,072 meters and is claimed as the highest railway in the world, passes the shores of Cuona Lake and beside Tangula Mountain with its photogenic glacier. Back in 2006 everyone on board my train, including myself as the only foreigner, gathered at the corridor windows to take photos with digital cameras (ownership of smartphones in China then was considerably scarcer than today). The train then descended the Qiangtang grasslands to Lhasa, where the majestic burgundy and white Potala Palace, rises from a rocky plinth.

The opening of the Shanghai–Tibet railway followed on the heels of July 2006's launch of the Beijing–Lhasa route, inaugurated to great media fanfare by China's president, Hu Jintao, a former Communist Party Secretary of Tibet. China exclaimed the railway as an exemplary feat of engineering that opened up Tibet as a new destination for Chinese holidaymakers. In turn, inflated tourism revenues and job opportunities, it was hoped, might assuage anti-Chinese sentiment among Tibetans.

Since 2006, Tibet has been extensively promoted to China's new travel class as a destination offering fresh air, beautiful mountain landscapes, off-road adventure, and unique culture. Starwood's St Regis brand, Four Points by Sheraton and Shangri-La have opened deluxe hotels, an element previously missing from Tibetan tourism. In 2013, Tibet received 12.91 million tourists (including 223,000 visitors from overseas) – an increase of 22 percent on 2012, and more than triple the four million tourists in 2007. Another 230,000 visitors arrived during the 2014 Spring Festival, and 2.18 million Chinese visited in the first five months of 2014.

To cash in on the purchasing potential of rising visitor numbers, tourism officials are planning to open duty-free stores, similar to the successful luxury brand-focused duty-free malls on Hainan Island, in Lhasa, Nyingchi and at Lhasa airport. In 2014, a new railway was expected to open from Lhasa to Shigatse, extending rail access to the city nearest to Mt. Everest – enabling Chinese travelers to travel by train to the roof of the world. On this basis, the predicted 15 million annual arrivals by 2015 may prove a rather conservative estimate.

Making the New Macao, or "China's Orlando"

If the casino resorts of Macao have created the ultimate leisure-time expression of the Chinese Dream, wait until you see what is planned for Hengqin, an island off Zhuhai, Guangdong province. Promoted as being three-times the size of Macao, Hengqin is China's next man-made holiday destination – with resorts that are bigger, brassier and bolder than ever. Expect the glitz factor to be ratcheted ever higher, as Chinese tourists covet ever-grander amenities and facilities from the nation's cashed-up tourism's developers.

The inaugural opening in Hengqin, in early 2014, was the Chimelong Hengqin Bay Hotel and Chimelong International Circus World. Developed by a Guangzhou-based firm, it will open in phases, and when completed will offer nearly 2,000 hotel rooms, a conference center, a spa and an indoor water park. Italian luxury yacht maker Ferretti, now controlled by China's Shandong Heavy Industry, is building its Asia Pacific headquarters plus a yacht club in Hengqin, and Galaxy Entertainment, which operates six of Macao's casino resorts, announced in March 2014 a framework agreement for a proposed RMB 10 billion (USD 1.6 billion), 2.7 square kilometer resort development. These announcements are just the beginning.

Two key factors presage Hengqin's existence. Firstly, the Chinese government is determined to ensure sustained investment flows into large tourism projects that encourage consumer spending and create jobs. Consequently, Chinese investors are ploughing eye-watering amounts of money into facilities to ensure Chinese tourists continue spending their hard-earned currency within the nation's borders.

Secondly, it has become increasingly evident that a critical flaw exists in the Macao Plan. Despite sizeable reclamations from the sea, the shortage of available land inhibits the expansion of tourism capacity. In addition, developers and investors are eager to expand and diversify their tourism portfolios for a new generation of travel consumers on mainland territory, not just on the reclaimed colonial land masses, now known as the Special Administrative Regions of Macao and Hong Kong.

Officially explained as "covering an area three times Macao," Hengqin is connected by a road bridge to Macao. In August 2009, the State Council approved the commercial development of Hengqin as a way of "exploring a new mode of cooperation" between Guangdong province, Hong Kong and Macao. Later that year, Hengqin was ratified as China's third national-level "new development area" – placing it on an equal footing with Pudong in Shanghai and Binhai in Tianjin, both of which are lauded as paragons of China's economic opening up. Similar to Pudong and Binhai, Hengqin offers preferential tax and investment policies and easier customs clearance to incentivize the haul of investors it needs to justify its exalted status.

In addition, Hengqin offers two extra advantages: strong government support, and a beneficial location. Once the much-touted Hong Kong–Zhuhai–Macao Bridge is completed in 2016, Hengqin will be the only part of the Chinese mainland that is directly connected to both Hong Kong and Macao. An express train service linking Hengqin with Zhuhai Airport is anticipated to open in 2019.

Taking to the slopes

Beijingers have discovered a new winter weekend pastime. As the capital's offices close on Friday afternoon, young couples, families and groups of friends load up their cars and head for the mountains. During winter 2013/14, the coolest way to spend after-work downtime was not shopping at Galeries Lafayette in Beijing, brunching in a smart restaurant or visiting an art gallery. Those in the know went skiing and snowboarding.

Snow abounds throughout the long, cold winters in the mountains of northern China, yet for many years winter sports struggled to make tracks in the domestic tourism market. Ski resorts have been in operation for several years near the city of Harbin in Heilongjiang province, but facilities were considered outdated and thousands of winter tourists instead preferred the less active attractions of the Harbin Ice & Snow Carving Festival that attracts thousands of visitors each January.

Winter sports received a boost in China during the 2010 Winter Olympics in Vancouver, when China placed joint seventh on the gold medal table, with short-track speed skating star Meng Yang winning three gold medals. Four years later, as Chinese competitors prepared for the Sochi Games, winter sports had finally gained traction in the country's trend-aware leisure market. A combination of factors, including the desire to escape city living and experience outdoor pursuits, urban pollution and rising affluence, plus improved ski resort infrastructure and more attentive media coverage, had made ski-weekends a hot winter trend.

In 2010, Club Med opened an all-inclusive skiing and family holiday resort at Yabuli, 120 kilometers from Harbin, with more than 30 kilometers of skiing and snowboarding trails, plus ice skating, tubing, and sleigh rides. At Yabuli, Club Med has partnered with the Ecole de Ski Français (ESF), which has established a campus with 10 professional French ski instructors to help guests learn how to ski, snow-trek or snowboard, or improve their technique. The resort also presents nightly ski shows, with instructors brandishing fire torches showing off their skills on the slopes.

Two years later, in 2012, Wanda and five other Chinese investors, opened the first phase of the 21 square kilometer Changbaishan International Resort in Jilin province, close to the North Korean border. Translated roughly as "Forever White Mountain," Changbaishan features 43 skiing trails and a holiday village with luxury shopping, dining and a hot spring spa center, plus hotels by Park Hyatt, Hyatt Regency (the first Hyatt ski resorts outside the US), Sheraton, the Westin, Marriott, and Holiday Inn. A representative for one of the hotel operators in Changbaishan told me the resort "was booked out several weeks in advance" of the 2014 Spring Festival.

For Chinese capital dwellers, a flight is required to reach both Yabuli and Changbaishan, but with driving weekends the current choice *du jour*, three options are popular from late November through April. Option number one, being a three-hour drive from Beijing, is the RMB 6.5 billion Genting Secret Garden resort on the outskirts of Zhangjiakou. The resort was opened by Malaysia-based Genting in time for the 2012/13 ski season and promises 87 ski trails, a resort hotel and serviced residences, two golf courses, restaurants and a spa and is jointly bidding to host the 2022 Winter Olympics. Option two, Wanlong Ski Resort, is located 250 kilometers from Beijing at Honghualiang, is another popular weekend retreat, offering around 20 ski trails, a hotel and Chinese and Korean dining.

Option three, closer to the Chinese capital, and considered a training ground for novice skiers, is Nanshan Ski Village, which is a 40-minute drive from Beijing and boasts 21 relatively simple trails, plus sledding and toboggan runs, a 1,318 meter-long dry luge track imported from Germany and 20 artificial snowmaking machines.

An important factor in favor of skiing is that it is viewed as a family activity, and tends to go hand-in-hand with shopping, dining and sightseeing. Savvy winter resort investors recognize that China's early ski resorts failed because they did not offer a broad range of alternative entertainment and activities. New ski resorts are adapting the integrated resort model that has proved magnetic in Macao (without gambling, of course, which is illegal in mainland China).

Winter sports in China are not just relying on climatic authenticity. In the true spirit of inter-city Beijing–Shanghai rivalry, Shanghai has announced that a Singaporean firm will develop the world's largest indoor winter resort, named Winterland Shanghai. Slated to open in 2018, the RMB 13.5 billion (USD 2.17 billion) year-round winter sports center promises the world's longest indoor ski trail, a chalet-style hotel, plus a monorail, a retail mall, restaurants, and a 4-D theatre.

Mickey Mouse in the Middle Kingdom

"Shanghai Disney Resort is one of the largest investment projects in [the] service industry in the 30 years of China's reform and opening up. It marks the start that new sectors are being opened up to a whole new level."

Those revealing words feature on the website of the expansively titled Shanghai International Tourism and Resorts Zone – a vast tract of land near Pudong International Airport. The Shanghai Disney Resort will be the central feature of the development when it opens in late 2015, alongside, golf courses, entertainment venues and Shanghai Village – the second China luxury outlet retail center by Value Retail China, an affiliate of London-based Value Retail, which the company believes will "become the most important outlet shopping location in Asia."

For many years, Shanghai's Disney project seemed more a subject of speculation than an achievable proposition. Long touted, it encountered numerous procedural hurdles and was then delayed until after the 2010 World Expo. The groundbreaking ceremony for the 3.9 square kilometer theme park finally took place on 8 April 2011.

The first Disney resort in mainland China is a joint venture between the Walt Disney Company and Shanghai Shendi Group. It promises the familiar mix of Disney characters and attractions, two hotels, an enchanted storybook castle and the first themed section of a Disney park based on the movie series Pirates of the Caribbean, plus "exciting new elements that will be unique to the Shanghai Disney Resort" to make it both "both authentically Disney and distinctly Chinese," according to an official release.

The Disney Resort will go head-to-head with one of China's most intriguing privately funded tourism attractions: Shanghai Dream City. A joint venture between Dreamworks Animation and Hong Kong-based Lan Kwai Fong Group and CMC. Scheduled to open on the west bank of the Huangpu River in 2017, the Dream Center is touted as Shanghai's attempt to create its own Broadway or West End. The riverside entertainment district will feature performing arts theaters, music halls, an Oriental DreamWorks studio, a Kung Fu Panda themed area, a 500-seat IMAX cinema, plus restaurants, bars and retail stores.

Positioning of the Disney resort began while the site was still congested with cranes and construction workers. At the end of 2013, it signed an agreement for ICBC to become the Official Retail Bank partner. This is a tactical play from both sides. ICBC will install ATMs throughout the resort and gain exclusive branding rights at the Garden of the Twelve Friends, which promises 12 mosaic murals, each depicting the 12 signs of the Chinese zodiac using famous Disney characters. Shanghai Disney will benefit from huge exposure to the client base of ICBC, ranked the largest bank in the world by market capitalization.

The Disney Resort in Shanghai will also compete with its more established counterpart in Hong Kong. Hong Kong Disneyland reported a record net profit of HKD 242 million (USD 31.2 million) for the fiscal year ending September 2013, during which it received a total of 7.4 million visitors, thanks to a growth in visitor numbers from China. The theme park, which opened to underwhelming reviews and initially disappointing visitor figures in September 2005, also announced plans to open a third 750-room resort-style hotel in 2017.

Chapter 13

The Resort Revolution: Chinese Weekenders in Search of Style

Luxury by the lakes

Located 160 kilometers west of Shanghai, the city of Huzhou is rarely visited by foreign tourists. Indeed, even though its undulating landscape boasts natural hot springs, tea plantations and bamboo groves, several friends in Shanghai questioned why I wanted to visit. Then I showed them a photo of the Sheraton Huzhou Hot Spring Resort. They smiled.

I arrived on a cool winter morning, via a 30-minute train journey from Hangzhou, and a 25-minute taxi ride through dusty industrial outskirts. After leaving the vast new train station, my cab passed several servicing facilities for global automobile giants. The grimy air was redolent of China's southern manufacturing heartlands. It seemed absurd that I would shortly arrive at a holiday resort described in a press release as "the most architecturally innovative property in Sheraton Hotels' global portfolio."

Sheraton's China portfolio is adding a clutch of eye-catching hotels and resorts, notably the lakeside Sheraton Bailuhu Resort, Huizhou, in southern Guangdong province, which is being built into the hills surrounding a lake, and the soaring Sheraton Taizhou Wenling residing beside a river in Zhejiang province, and which is set to be completed in 2019.

As my taxi plunged on, we turned onto a new highway that forged a path towards green hills and away from grimy industry. As the landscape flattened, the 101-meter high, horseshoe-shaped resort emerged from the cold waters of Lake Tai. It's a bold architectural statement. Designed by Zaha Hadid's protege Ma Yansong, it has been said to resemble both an ancient Chinese arched bridge and the mouth of a fish.

Pulling up by taxi is unusual, because the 282-room resort has been built to cater for China's new urban demographic: self-drive vacationers. Affluent families and young couples from Shanghai and the cities of Zhejiang province escape high population densities and polluted urban skies to arrive en masse by car on weekends and Chinese holidays. Once the car keys have been deposited with the bellboy, guests enter a lobby decorated with a curtain of Swarovski crystals, and floor-to-ceiling veined marble and jade quarried from Italy, Pakistan and Afghanistan.

From my lake-view room, I spotted the 39 lake-front villas and yacht marina that were under construction, while the grass turf of the ring-shaped "wedding island" was being readied for a high-society marriage. These images were offset by a picturesque backdrop of traditional wooden fishing junks hired by the local government to cruise close to the shore for added photogenic value.

The photo options are intensified at night. Standing in the icy wind and rain, I watched playful neon patterns arcing around the façade of the hotel and reflecting in the darkened waters of the lake. "Images like these are what Chinese smartphone users crave," says Stephanie Choi, Director of Sales and Marketing at the resort.

More than 1,200 kilometers north of Huzhou, one of China's most anticipated resort projects prepared for an Autumn 2014 opening. Framed by mountains with views of the Great Wall of China, Kempinski Yanqi Lake is a 14-square-kilometer, multi-purpose resort about an hour's drive from Beijing. Scheduled to open in phases it will ultimately comprise a see-it-to-believe-it circular 306-room hotel, nicknamed "The Sunrise," on the shore of Yanqi Lake, plus 12 boutique hotels on an offshore island and a State Guest House for visiting government VIPs and political leaders.

At the heart of the resort is a conference center large enough to host the 2014 Asia-Pacific Economic Cooperation (APEC) Leaders' Summit, while a spa, 14 restaurants and bars, a yacht marina, 18-hole golf course, and spacious wedding facilities have been designed to cover a range of clientele bases.

"For Kempinski, this is our flagship project in China, which we expect is going to be for China what our Emirates Palace is in Abu Dhabi – a magnificent resort for hosting heads of state delegations, global politicians and celebrities. It will be the modern face of China for important visitors hosted by the government, and we believe this will give the resort huge credibility in the market," says Michael Henssler, President of Kempinski China and Managing Director of Key International Hotel Management Ltd, a joint venture between Kempinski and Beijing Tourism Group.

The rise of the lifestyle resort

Projects like Kempinski Yanqi Lake and Sheraton Huzhou are not just noteworthy for the outreach of international hotel brands into lesser known corners of China that would have been unimaginable a decade ago. They offer world-class resort locations, architecture and amenities to broaden the tourism experience base of Chinese travelers. The "resort concept" is today's go-to buzz phrase in Chinese hospitality.

The triangular area between Shanghai, Hangzhou and Nanjing features an impressive portfolio of lifestyle-oriented resorts, including Amanfayun, Fuchun Resort and Four Seasons West Lake in Hangzhou, Naked Retreats and Le Passage Mohkan Shan in Moganshan, and Sheraton Hot Spring Resort Huzhou.

Resort developers are also moving into quaint tourist-friendly canal-side locales, such as Shaoxing and Zhouzhuang. Meanwhile Hyatt Regency opened the first resort on the island of Chongming, near Shanghai, which is promoting itself as an eco-friendly weekend destination offering natural wetlands, a migratory bird reserve and organic farms.

Elsewhere, Anantara Xishuangbanna Resort & Spa offers 80 deluxe rooms and 23 pool villas amid primeval forests of scenic Yunnan province, the first China resort by Six Senses is located at the gateway to the Qingcheng Mountains near the United Nations Educational, Scientific and Cultural Organization (UNESCO) World Heritage & Natural Cultural site of Dujiangyan in Sichuan province.

But it's not just the deep-pocketed international hotels chains that are creating China's Resort Revolution. Forward-thinking entrepreneurs are playing their part by designing and building "lifestyle hotels," which are distinct from branded chain hotels in terms of style, design, products, and service.

The attraction of a lifestyle hotel is neatly summarized as "a place where guests can seamlessly connect, a setting where guests can become part of an experience by interacting with the people that live there as well as staff and a place where design adds to the uniqueness of the adventure," according to *A New Breed of Traveller: How Consumers Are Driving Change in the Hotel Industry*, a report published in November 2013 by HVS, a leading hotel and leisure consulting firm.

Sustainable luxury in rural China

On a sunny afternoon in October 2009, South African entrepreneur Grant Horsfield and his Hong Kong-born architect wife Delphine Yip-Horsfield stood in a field flanked by forested hills and tea plantations near Moganshan – a three-hour drive from Shanghai – and planted a tree.

They were not alone in that bucolic corner of Zhejiang province, however. As the tree planting was completed, the generous applause of a gathering of local government officials, business owners and the media echoed around the valley. We had all just witnessed the groundbreaking ceremony for an eco-themed resort called Naked Stables Private Reserve, the first of its kind in China.

The Naked story had begun a couple of years earlier, when the couple purchased a handful of farmers' cottages in a village on the slopes of

Moganshan, a photogenic mountain region clad with bamboo groves and tea fields that had been used as a weekend retreat for European and Chinese city elites during Shanghai's decadent 1930s Paris of the Orient era.

Yip-Horsfield restyled the cottages adhering to stringent eco-friendly principles and a rural-chic theme, and Naked Retreats was born. In addition to vacationing weekenders, Naked Retreats attracted corporate teambuilding clients from Shanghai and Hangzhou for its verdant scenery, connections with local culture, hiking and cycling, and lakeside yoga. It even offered a British Army-style fitness boot camp. The seeds were sewn for a new China-made eco-resort concept.

At a drinks reception following the groundbreaking ceremony, a beaming Horsfield told me that the couple's second resort project, Naked Stables Private Reserve, would "adhere to the world's highest environmental standards, and prove that 'Made in China' can provide luxury and sustainability while supporting the local economy."

The Horsfields' "sustainable luxury in nature" gambit has proved a winning bet. Not only did Naked Stables Private Reserve become the first resort in China to achieve the LEED (Leadership in Environmental & Energy Design) Platinum Certification, it also became a poster child for China's leisure revolution. Guests escaping the frenetic city life in Shanghai, Hangzhou, Suzhou, and Hangzhou jump in their cars at weekends and head to Naked Stables, where they can stay in tree-top villas, enjoy horseback riding, tea picking or secluded fishing trips. Less adventurous guests relax in the spa or sip locally grown green tea beside the infinity pool. As darkness falls over the forest, Michelin-starred chef Stefan Stiller prepares degustation dinner menus in Kikaboni restaurant.

The resort's success, Horsfield says, has hinged on a reappraisal by travel-savvy metropolitan Chinese of how and where they wish to spend their time outside of work. "There has been a radical shift among younger people in the large cities towards enjoying nature, breathing fresh air and trying out new leisure activities," he says. "In the last couple of years, spending money on luxury experiences instead of spending on luxury products has become a noticeable trend, both in China and overseas."

In the second decade of the twenty-first century, urban leisure spenders are demanding challenging experiences. "We hit the market at exactly the right time," says Horsfield. "The old Chinese model of selling tickets for mass tourism sites has become outdated. People want to try out new things and visit different places. They are buying items like mountain bikes, tents and horses and heading out of the cities. Eco-themed tourism is becoming very popular, but there are virtually no resorts in China for people to enjoy the natural environment."

As a result, Naked Retreats, known in China by its local brand name 裸心是, meaning Naked Heart, has charted an expansion path. In addition to its two Moganshan resorts – Naked Home (which is being expanded and renamed Naked Castle in late 2014) and Naked Stables Private Reserve – the company is designing and building, and will operate, a small portfolio of new luxury rural resorts across China. Naked Hill is slated for Shaoxing, Naked Spring will open in the hills near the city of Yiwu, Naked Wall is pending near the Great Wall of China at Badaling, and Naked Island will be created at Taihu Lake.

The objective is "to build a scaleable Chinese brand with resorts near the main cities of Shanghai, Beijing and Hong Kong that could, in around five years time, go international," says Horsfield. "Brands are the future in China, and we want to establish a strong presence, not just be a translation of a western brand."

Managing the pace of expansion in a nation where action today is preferred to waiting until tomorrow is critical, he adds. "People are spotting the appeal of our resorts, and because we design, build and manage each one, we have become the number one option for anyone who wants to build a resort. We get a call at least four times a week from a different developer somewhere in China asking us to plan a resort for them."

A frisson of French chic in the country

Born in Hong Kong and educated in the UK, Pauline Lee Peres and her French husband Christophe were tiring of urban life in Shanghai, so they decided to purchase some land in a Zhejiang province tea valley and build a country getaway for their young family. Several coincidental twists and turns during construction resulted in a total rethink, and Le Passage Mohkan Shan was born.

Le Passage Mohkan Shan is a distinctive proposition. Lee Peres calls it "a French luxury country house hotel in a verdant Chinese valley." The heart and soul of this elegant mini-resort is French, and designing and building it was a labor of love. But the owners also worked tirelessly to ensure its authentic look and feel, rather than tailoring the design to the Chinese market. Leisure seekers flock to Le Passage largely because it feels like a small pocket of France in the Chinese countryside. "Affluent Chinese from the big cities are now looking for unique places where they can drive and stay, eat great food and enjoy themselves. We have created a place that delivers the kind of experiences they are seeking," says Lee Peres.

It could have been different. The couple had built a small house on an isolated patch of land they had rented, and were about to renovate an adjacent barn into a larger home when they received a knock on the door in 2008. Government officials from Moganshan stopped by to ask if they would be interested in building a hotel, which could be integrated into a plan to develop the area as a tourism destination and stimulate the local economy. In return, the couple would be able to acquire the land. "We thought about it carefully, because we had never planned to open a hotel," says Lee Peres. "The idea gradually crystallised in our minds, and for both of us, it became a dream we wanted to pursue."

The hotel – the name of which, Le Passage Mohkan Shan, refers to the historic English translation of the place known today as Moganshan – soft-opened in 2011 with nine rooms, and has since expanded to 29. "Every aspect of the hotel was designed by Christophe, whose grandparents owned a small hotel in the Pyrenees," Lee Peres says.

From day one, the aim was to be "a gourmet destination." The couple hired a Shanghai-born executive chef who worked for Mandarin Oriental in London to elevate the standards of the kitchen and restaurant with the ultimate goal of gaining a Michelin star accreditation, and built an impressive cellar of fine wines. Later, in spring 2014, Le Passage opened a French gourmet cooking school.

The resort's French-styled offerings have struck a chord with affluent weekenders.

"Money isn't an issue for Chinese guests and families that stay with us, especially on weekends," says Lee Peres. They aren't looking to stay in one place for five or six days, that is not a concept they understand. Short getaways are what they want, and for people living in nearby cities like Shanghai, Hangzhou, Ningbo and Nanjing, Moganshan is becoming their own version of The Hamptons."

Managing the entire project themselves gave the couple time to thoroughly assess their target market and their positional approach. "We started our marketing in January 2013, and focused squarely on the Chinese media," says Lee Peres. "Social media is also very important in China. Visitors take more photos than we could ever expect from our own photographer, and they re-post them via Weibo and WeChat. You can't create publicity like that. It's a phenomenon."

Initially, Lee Peres noticed two distinct guest profiles, sophisticated consumers with overseas travel exposure who were possibly educated abroad and take international business trips and are very familiar with five-star hotels. Then there were very wealthy guests, with plentiful money to spend and a desire to enjoy great French cuisine, try a French cooking class, sip fine wines on the terrace and live the experience. "The more affluent the guests, the more likely they are to drive themselves, as they like to enjoy their cars," says Lee Peres. "One client called us the day before to ask if the road to our hotel was good enough to drive his Bentley."

Le Passage's client base has since embraced newer niche segments. "A lot of Chinese mountain biking groups are enjoying the Moganshan scenery at weekends, and this brings younger guests to dine or stay with us," says Lee Peres. The opening in 2013 of a high-speed rail station at Deqing, at the base of the Moganshan mountains, has also made access easier for weekend train trippers. "The train reduces the distance," says Lee Peres. "Nanjing is a three-hour drive, but it takes just one hour by train, and Ningbo is now only half an hour away on the train."

Chapter 14

Economics in Action: Business Travelers Explore New Frontiers

Chinese capital takes flight

In early 2013, I attended a networking event hosted at a downtown Kuala Lumpur nightclub. While I was talking to a friend on the outdoor terrace, a Chinese gentleman in his late thirties approached our table. He wore an expensive suit and a beguiling smile. Urbane, well-educated and speaking fluent English, Dr. Wong explained that he was visiting KL on business. An economist by training, his profession was investment banking or, more accurately, investment research.

Employed by one of China's flourishing finance houses, Dr. Wong flies around the globe researching real-time economic studies and forecasts for Chinese investors, and seeking out potential acquisition targets for clients. In the past year, he claimed to have visited 30 countries, and his schedule over the next three months would take him to South America, Europe and West Africa. I asked him in which countries his clients were most keen to invest. "It depends on the business, and the opportunities we present to them," he beamed. "But we have had a lot of interest for projects in Peru recently. Also Spain, because there are some good deals to be made there."

Speak to any seasoned banker or investment analyst and they will tell you that Chinese corporate cash – in addition to the bond holdings and nearly USD 4 trillion of foreign exchange reserves held in Beijing – is coursing through the veins of the global economy. Between 2000 and 2012, China's economy tripled in size, and it overtook Japan to become the world's second-largest economy behind the US. It is commonly assumed that if you pricked the international finance system with a needle, it would soon start to bleed red and gold.

Economic expansion has been accompanied by rapid urbanization and infrastructure investment, plus rising incomes, greater mobility and the postponement of certain life stages, such as getting married and having children. Research by McKinsey & Company predicts that around 850 million Chinese (or 60 percent of the total population) will live in urban areas by 2020, up from 650 million in 2001.

While valid concerns exist about the disturbing levels of local government and corporate debt in China, and the possibility that the Chinese Economic Bubble could burst, Corporate China has entered an acquisitive phase, and its cash-loaded radar has a wide focus. In turn, this is fuelling China's corporate travel sector.

Lenovo recently added Motorola's handset division, which it bought from Google, to the 2004 purchase of IBM's PC operation and the server business it captured in January 2014, and Shuanghui purchased Smithfield Foods for around USD 7 billion. Volvo is now owned by Geely, which also purchased the company that makes the famous London black taxi cab, and Dongfeng Motors claimed a stake in PSA Peugeot Citroen. Bright Dairy bought a controlling stake in cereal maker Weetabix, Dalian Wanda Group snapped up AMC Theaters while China's sovereign wealth fund took a ten percent share in Heathrow Airport Holdings. The brouhaha in 2005, when Chinese white goods manufacturer Qingdao-based Haier, China's largest home appliance maker, attempted to purchase US-based Maytag and state-owned oil company CNOOC's bid to buy US-based Unocal, seems like a distant era.

More than 20,000 Chinese enterprises were operating in nearly 200 countries and regions by the end of 2013, according to the Chinese Foreign Ministry. Bullish analysts believe this represents a basement-level statistic, while even bears are persuaded by the potential spread of China's flight of capital even if they can't agree on its flight paths or long-term landings. Although China still receives more foreign direct investment (totaling USD 117.6 billion in 2013) than it delivers in outbound investment, the gap has closed significantly. Non-financial overseas investment jumped from USD 59 billion in 2010 to USD 90.2 billion in 2013, according to China's Ministry of Commerce, suggesting parity may not be far away.

Although the Chinese currency isn't officially exchangeable, RMB notes can be cashed in for local currency in most Asian nations and RMB-denominated financial products are being traded with increasing global freedom. One of the decisive factors for the establishment, in September 2013, of the Shanghai Free Trade Zone (FTZ) – the first in mainland China – was to facilitate higher levels of cross-border settlements using the RMB. Several cities in China have applied to set up their own FTZs. At the same time, the international network of Chinese bank branches is growing and foreign banks and retailers are scrambling to integrate with the China UnionPay card payment system.

Chinese companies are bidding for, and winning, construction and engineering projects on every continent. Chinese contractors earned more than USD 137 billion in 2013, according to the China International Contractors Association. Beijing Construction Engineering Group's participation in the GBP 800 million expansion of the UK's Manchester Airport and China CAMC Engineering Co's contract to build an airport at Pokhara, Nepal, are merely scene-setting deals. Meanwhile, utilities and telecoms contracts, railway network expansions, sports franchises, pharmaceutical firms, hotel companies, and mid-range retail brands are high on the wish list of Chinese buyers.

Property and land-related businesses retain a particular allure. Chinese investors are purchasing businesses worldwide, from deluxe apartment complexes in London to wine chateaux in France, and from a tract of land in the Lao jungle to build a casino resort to the proposed development of a shipping channel through Nicaragua that would render the once US-owned Panama Canal a quaint twentieth-century relic.

The planet-wide dispersion of Chinese capital isn't restricted to corporate purchases, financial trading and government debt purchases. Private wealth is also being redirected overseas. A study by the Center for China & Globalization think tank estimates that China's wealthiest citizens shipped out assets totaling around RMB 2.8 trillion (USD 0.45 trillion) in 2011. The study divulged that Hong Kong, the US and Canada were the preferred destinations of what it calls "investment emigration." During 2014, Australia and the UK were among the other nations making headlines regarding the policy of investment visas for Chinese travelers pledging to invest or purchase assets above a minimum threshold.

New World for Rosewood, Fosun and Club Med

With Chinese capital eyeing asset purchases across the globe, the hospitality industry is viewed as a strategic play that buys into the likely prospect of future outbound travel growth from China. Hotels are also a highly-prized, status-yielding asset.

In 2011, Hong Kong-based New World Hospitality acquired US-founded luxury hotel chain Rosewood – whose collection of historic properties includes Rosewood London and The Carlyle in New York. The company has since changed its name to Rosewood Hotel Group, and is targeting accelerated international expansion across its three brands: Rosewood Hotels & Resorts, New World Hotels, and the fast-growing Pentahotels mid-range marque. In mid 2014, Rosewood's portfolio encompassed 44 hotels in 15 countries, with 30 more properties in development.

Established in 1979, the Rosewood brand opened a deluxe hotel in Beijing in 2014, with planned China openings to follow in Chongqing (2015) and Haitian Bay, Hainan Island (2017). Beyond China, it has confirmed signings in Phuket, Phnom Penh, Bangkok, Jakarta, Bali, Dubai, and Bahamas. It also hired Karl Lagerfeld to design two suites for the legendary Hotel de Crillon in Paris, which was built on the Place de la Concorde in 1758, came under the Rosewood umbrella in 2013 and will reopen in 2015 after a major renovation.

Another intriguing play was the decision by Shanghai-based Fosun, which has made a succession of international acquisitions, to invest in French-based resort company Club Med. Modern Chinese tourism was founded on package holidays, a concept that still pertains today, although Internet booking, less Byzantine visa procedures and digital consumer marketing have made independent travel the preferred choice for travelers with overseas experience.

But China's overlapping relationship between domestic and outbound tourism – largely directed by the state-mandated holiday system and reduced or absent private paid leave entitlements, meaning that holidaymakers have restricted windows for overseas travel and therefore spend a significant proportion of their leisure time and disposable income inside China – gives concepts developed and proven overseas and adapted for China a fighting chance. The possibility of success is heightened if they target family travelers and happen to be backed by a large Chinese company.

Fosun seemed to fit the bill. It is China's largest private conglomerate, and initially purchased a 9.96 percent stake in Club Med. Three years later, in 2013, France's AXA Private Equity (now renamed Ardian) and Fosun, together with the managers of Club Méditerranée (Cub Med) filed a takeover bid. The move was challenged in 2014 in a Paris court, and by a large share buy-up in Club Med by an Italian investor.

Founded in France in 1950, Club Med rode the crest of a new travel wave in Europe during the 1970s: the all-inclusive package holiday. It operated holiday resorts across the Mediterranean where guests paid a fixed price including accommodation, meals and drinks, activities and entertainment. It appealed to travelers wanting to experience overseas travel but preferring resort-style vacations at a clearly defined "all you can eat, drink and do" cost. Club Med adapted the concept to ski resorts and then to long-haul destinations, including Tahiti, Mauritius and the Caribbean. Now it is taking on China, which is likely to become its second-largest market, after France, by 2015.

Club Med opened its first resort in China at Yabuli in 2010. Located in the snow-capped mountains of north-east Heilongjiang Province, Club Med Yabuli was launched as "China's first international all-inclusive ski resort." Three years later, the company opened Club Med Guilin, among the picturesque karst landscapes of Guilin, in southern China. Club Med's first beach resort in China, on Dong'ao Island in the South

China Sea – an hour from Hong Kong, Macao and Zhuhai – opened in 2014. The oceanfront resort features one of the largest Club Med sports academies in the world, with activities including water-skiing, sailing and banana boating, plus the BBQ-Donut, "a new-concept floating a barbecue and dining table in the middle of the ocean." It also planned to launch a new brand targeting China's weekend vacationers.

Launching all-inclusive resorts in China is Club Med's approach to engaging experience-hungry domestic travelers, and upselling those who enjoyed the holiday to try one of its 80 resorts worldwide. The essential elements for achieving this goal are locations in places of exceptional natural beauty and accommodations and facilities that deliver high levels of comfort and style. A third, equally important, element is a diverse range of activities that appeal to the Chinese penchant for international allure with distinctive Chinese elements. For every pole-dancing class, jet-ski ride and high-wire trapeze act, there is a karaoke club, rooftop tai-chi and mahjong table. Dining is also heavily accented with Chinese flavors.

The contrasts with 1970s Mediterranean and Caribbean beach holidays do not end there. Club Med is itself an entirely different company. Its shift east was directed by the softening of its traditional French, European and North American markets. But moving into China also saw the composition of the company change, with a Chinese firm, Fosun, becoming the guiding hand for Club Med's China-focused future.

Investing in outbound markets

Cross-border capital accounted for nearly 30 percent of global hotel investment in 2013, largely driven by outbound finance from the Middle East and Asia. New sources of cross-border capital are emerging with funds being allocated to Asian hotel assets. China, inevitably, is lining up to play a greater role.

"The Chinese government's announcement in 2013 to provide better access to state bank financing for private investors will make it easier to invest offshore. This is expected to result in more mainland Chinese groups emerging as hotel investors not only across Asia, but globally," says Frank Sorgiovanni, Head of Research at JLL's Hotels & Hospitality Group in Asia.

Chinese outbound real estate investment totaled USD 4 billion in 2012, and doubled to around USD 8 billion. That figure is projected to increase to around USD 10 billion in 2014, according to JLL. Hitherto, the hotel acquisition targets have been relatively clear-cut. "Chinese investors have been mostly interested in long-term investments in prime-quality assets in mature, highly transparent markets," says Sorgiovanni. "Singapore, Sydney and Hong Kong have proven highly desirable, to the extent that some Chinese investors are asking us to approach owners whose hotels are not even for sale."

All three locations are highly desirable destinations for Chinese travelers, and the SGD 1.14 billion (USD 0.9 billion) purchase of the 309-room Grand Park Orchard in Singapore, which includes the Knightsbridge retail podium, by Bright Ruby was the largest single real estate acquisition deal in Singapore's history.

The investment outreach of Chinese companies is a relatively new phenomenon. "You never heard of mainland Chinese capital until perhaps the last five years. Now institutional investment and REITs (real estate investment trusts) from China are looking to diversify," Sorgiovanni says. "We will probably see them shifting into newer markets like the Maldives, which has a number of well-developed, high-performing resort assets in the USD 50–100 million range, which is considered a small price by such investors. Tokyo is another market to watch, particularly in the lead up to the 2020 Olympics."

A potential hindrance to Chinese hotel investment could be market buoyancy. "Hotels as an asset class have been performing quite well, so a lot of owners have been reluctant to sell," says Sorgiovanni. "In Singapore, you also have the issue of a limited pipeline, and this is creating a lot of pent-up demand. When The Westin Singapore opened in 2013 it was sold within a month."

Another predicted play could see international hospitality chains becoming investment targets. "It is highly likely that more hotel and travel brands will be bought by Chinese buyers. Global branding fascinates Chinese investors, and they may look for companies to purchase that will fit their portfolio expansions," says Sorgiovanni.

Branding and corporate travel

A considerable amount of nonsense is talked about an alleged lack of brands in China. The argument goes something like this: Chinese companies only invest in the hard operational aspects of their business, and pay little heed to their own soft brand value. Consequently, Chinese companies buy international assets as a way of internationalizing a business that otherwise would struggle to gain recognition from investors, consumers and the media. This is increasingly a fallacy.

Brand consultants are in the business of corporate whirl-spinning, and will readily bamboozle listeners with long, detailed presentations about the origins, attributes and sustainability of "a brand's DNA." A pretty simple indicator of global brand strength is often missing from their lists, reports and strategy documents: overseas IPOs. Listing a company overseas earns investor credibility and market brand status that no amount of brand consulting can ever achieve.

It is for this reason that Chinese executives, no matter whether their company is ranked as a headline "name of recall" in consultancy reports, are rushing to foreign bourses to expand their brand reach. In early 2014, two of the most eagerly anticipated IPO announcements were by online trading monolith Alibaba and social media network Sina Weibo. It would be hard to argue that either are not ambitious brands. Indeed, Alibaba's stated reason for raising IPO funds was to become "a more global company."

Chinese companies have started to become more aggressive in selling into global markets. Names like Lenovo, Huawei, Alibaba, Geely, Haier, and Wanda are increasingly internationalized, while Yingli Solar was a high-profile advertiser at the 2014 World Cup in Brazil – and this is driving the outbound corporate travel sector. Testing the China branding waters, Millward Brown's selection of leading Chinese brands *(Brand Z Top 100 Most Valuable Brands in China* report, 2014) featured several names – such as China Mobile, ICBC, Tencent, China Construction Bank, Baidu, Agricultural Bank of China, Bank of China, PetroChina, Sinopec, and China Life – that should, by now, be readily recognizable in global boardrooms and university lecture halls. Further down the list are travel-related brands Air China, Ctrip, Hainan Airlines (which has a stated ambition to become a global top 50 companies by 2030), China Eastern Airlines, China Southern Airlines, CITS, Home Inn, and Hanting.

Global branding and business travel are big buddies in the modern corporate world, especially for Chinese conglomerates seeking to "go global." Just consider the reverse situation a decade ago. Global brands seeking to break into China were often hampered by having either no or only an insufficient on-the-ground presence. The key to connecting with clients, suppliers and consumers was hammered home zealously at business conferences in China during the last decade: to succeed in China, you must expand your in situ network, and key executives must visit the country frequently. Doing business in China means exactly that. It was for that precise reason that international hotels and airlines began expanding in China, to cater for foreign corporate travelers flocking in the thousands to the Middle Kingdom. As the capital flows reverse from East to West, the same precept applies.

China is poised to overtake the US as the largest business travel market in the world as early as 2015, according to the Global Business Travel Association (GBTA). The GBTA's *BTI Outlook – China 2014 H1 Report*, published at its annual conference in Shanghai in April 2014, predicted that Chinese business travel spending would grow 16.5 percent in 2014, to USD 262 billion (RMB 1,610 billion). In 2015, it expects travel spend to accelerate slightly, with growth reaching 17.8 percent.

In 2013, China remained the second-largest business market in the world, although it gained additional ground on the US (the spending differential fell from USD 66 billion in 2012 to USD 47 billion in 2013), according to the GBTA report. Concerns exist, however. International business travel was beset by tepid growth between 2011 and 2013, although the GBTA projected outbound business travel spending to grow 15 percent in 2014, followed by an 18.9 percent jump in 2015, when Chinese business travelers are expected to spend USD 13.3 billion on outbound trips (see Table 14.1).

Table 14.1 China RMB appreciation versus international currencies, 2004–2014 (value of RMB, 1 January each year)

Year	GBP	USD	EUR	AUD	JPY
2014	10.04	6.05	8.32	5.40	0.06
2013	10.14	6.24	8.24	6.49	0.07
2012	9.77	6.29	8.16	6.42	0.08
2011	10.29	6.59	8.83	6.74	0.08
2010	11.04	6.83	9.79	6.13	0.07
2009	9.89	6.83	9.54	4.81	0.07
2008	14.51	7.30	10.66	6.38	0.07
2007	15.31	7.82	10.31	6.16	0.07
2006	13.88	8.07	9.56	5.91	0.07
2005	15.89	8.28	11.20	6.47	0.08
2004	14.80	8.28	10.43	6.24	0.08

Source: XE.com.

On 21 July 2005, the Chinese government removed the RMB's peg to the US Dollar, which had been in place since the Asian financial crisis. China's exchange rate moved to a managed floating exchange rate based on a basket of currencies. Previously, the RMB had been pegged at 8.28 to the US Dollar.

Since 2005, the Chinese currency has appreciated considerably against the US Dollar, the Euro and the British Pound giving Chinese travelers extra spending power when visiting countries using those currencies. However, the impact of currency appreciation on Chinese outbound travel is unproven. For example, the Australian Dollar remained relatively stable against the RMB during the last decade, yet it witnessed a large rise in Chinese travelers.

Banking on business events

During March and April 2013, the Chinese arm of US-based Amway organized one of Asia's largest incentive trips of the year to Taiwan. Around 12,000 sales representatives from China – in five separate groups – enjoyed an expenses-paid, four-day trip to Taipei, with excursions to Hualien, Kaohsiung, Sun Moon Lake and Alishan Mountain. The guests stayed in five-star hotels, and were treated to banquets and gala performances by Taiwainese pop stars. Almost a year later, in February 2014, more than 6,000 Chinese guests from Nanjing-based Joymain International Development Group attended an incentive travel program in Bangkok and Pattaya.

Business events tourism, commonly known as MICE, is a strengthening driver of spending in both China's domestic and outbound travel sectors. Virtually every deluxe hotel or resort opened in China features extensive meetings, events and weddings facilities. The corporate market is buoyant, as international and Chinese companies seek to incentivize greater staff productivity and loyalty in cut-throat employment markets, and Chinese companies seek to internationalize their products and services. The government sector, which was a well-oiled engine for the MICE industry over the last decade, is moving into reverse, however. The Chinese government's well-publicized crackdown on junket spending has impacted high-end hotels and restaurants that counted city governments among their best clients.

Beyond the mainland, meetings and incentives groups are spreading their wings. Macao, Hong Kong and Hainan Island are popular destinations, and tourism boards across Asia Pacific are dedicating considerable resources to niche MICE promotions in China.

In December 2013, the Taiwan External Trade Development Council unveiled a three-year plan to make the island a leading Asian MICE destination. A key part of its strategy included promotional road shows in China and inviting Chinese media and potential buyers on familiarization trips. The Malaysia Conference & Exhibition Bureau's Twin Deal program offers two packages of rewards, such as Malaysian cultural performances for gala dinners, team-building activities, city tours and shopping vouchers, for incentives planners and event participants in key inbound markets, including China.

The media, too, is increasingly MICE-friendly. Asia-based publications like *MIX Meetings*, *CEI Asia* and *MICE Biz*, a bilingual (English and

Chinese) magazine published by the Hong Kong-based *South China Morning Post*, report on the regional diversification of this high-revenue branch of business travel. Each title has a strong focus on China, both as a destination for MICE events and as a source market for outbound MICE groups traveling to Asia-Pacific destinations.

Australia is a coveted destination for MICE groups from China, and the Gold Coast has assiduously promoted its attractions in China and other key regional markets. In recent years, it has hosted several large Chinese groups, including a Toyota incentive trip in 2011 for 600 participants, and the 2007 Amway Greater China Leadership Seminar for 5,793 guests.

"We recognise that the Chinese MICE market is a powerful one, with incentive groups in abundance," says Anna Case, Director of Business Events, Gold Coast Tourism. "We were one of the first Australian destinations to establish an office and a promotional program in China, and we have four staff, including two in China, dedicated to promoting the Gold Coast."

Generally speaking, Chinese MICE groups prefer to visit in the first and final quarters of the year, and Surfers Paradise is the number one location choice. "Beach and beachside activities are extremely popular, as are shopping and day trips to Dreamworld, Warner Bros Movie World and Sea World," says Case. "Recently, there has been an evolution in the requirements of Chinese incentive groups, with more of an emphasis on teambuilding and CSR activities, such as dune restoration or a visit to Currumbin Wildlife Sanctuary Animal hospital."

Corporate China heads to Milan Expo

The 2010 World Expo in Shanghai was the largest global tourism exhibition in history – and its singular target for the 192 participating countries was the New Chinese Traveler. The Shanghai Expo broke attendance records, attracting 72 million mostly Chinese visitors. Having demonstrated its rise in the world, Shanghai handed the baton for the five-yearly global showcase to Milan, which is hosting the 2015 Expo Milano, before the show moves on to Dubai in 2020.

Expo Milano is expected to be another strong showcase for Chinese businesses and travelers. Indeed a stated pillar target of the 2015 Expo organizers is to attract one million Chinese visitors across the six-month event. Another key objective is to use Expo Milano 2015 as a platform for "close cooperation between Chinese provinces and Italian regions ... to strengthen exchanges and to promote business opportunities."

Milan is investing around EUR 3 billion in the hope of attracting 20 million visitors to the 420-acre Expo Park and to the city itself, the second most popular Italian destination after Rome, which welcomes around eight million visitors annually. A large part of the funds will be channeled to build two new metro lines connecting the airport and city to the Expo Park. It has also commissioned Walt Disney Company Italia to create the Expo mascot in the same year that the Walt Disney Company will open its Shanghai Disney Resort.

The Milan Tourism Board is preparing for the influx of Chinese visitors. Its website is produced in eight languages, although only three are highlighted on the main menu bar: Italian, English and Chinese, and a downloadable city guide is offered in Chinese.

In November 2012, China signed up not just to participate at the Milan World Expo, but also to host the event's second-largest pavilion, spanning 4,590 square meters. "China will be a very relevant country for Expo Milano 2015," said Giuseppe Sala, CEO of Expo 2015 at the signing of the pavilion agreement. A few months later, Chinese real estate giant Vanke signed up as the Expo's first corporate pavilion occupier. As part of its initial EUR 3 million investment, Vanke has hired Studio Daniel Libeskind to design its pavilion, and will participate in 2015 Expo promotional roadshows in major Chinese provinces.

A third pillar of the Chinese presence at Expo Milano will be the China Corporate Pavilion. Showcasing "Made in China" products, it will be the first overseas Expo that Chinese companies have attended as a collective group. China will also provide a stage for its emerging Chinese fashion designers in a city renowned worldwide for its sartorial passions.

The Chinese travel dream: business or pleasure?

Milan, a quintessentially European city of architecture, arts and culture, fashion and cuisine, is a fine setting to depart the Chinese travel story. As discussed throughout this book, it is an evolving story about people, about travelers, about a desire to see, witness and explore by traversing previously closed borders into a world that welcomes their arrival like never before.

It is a story infused with the trimmings of the twenty-first-century Chinese Dream – increased urban affluence, work-life balance, cutting-edge technology, access to aspirational destinations and experiences, high expectations, branded purchasing, lifestyle and dining, and lavish capital investment. Essentially, it's a vision of a better, more globalized future.

In its broadest sense, Chinese travel is about international economics. In the post-2008 world order, governments of developed and emerging economies recognize that tourism is a high-potential growth sector – a channel for improved consumer spending, enhanced tax receipts, more inbound investment and new job creation. The world's tourism economy is being reconfigured and new source markets are being courted and embraced. The richest pick is China, because it is sending more travelers to spend more money in more destinations than any other country.

Will the inexorable rise of the Chinese traveler continue? Throughout history, China has always been, and remains, a difficult country to predict. Continued internal economic and social stability are critical factors for the global financial system not just for international tourism. But what the revolutionary changes over the last decade have shown is that the assimilation of domestic, inbound and outbound travel has created a powerful economic structure. Chinese tourism is a highly integrated, well-financed and knowledge-driven force that is driving new policy approaches by governments and tourism providers at home, across Asia and worldwide.

After almost three decades as the world's factory for manufactured goods, China is developing a new service-driven production line. Outbound tourism, and the related investment flows, is emerging as China's next big export sector.

Index

Australia   3, 18, 42, 43, 46, 47, 64–65, 68, 89, 90, 106–108, 116–117, 162, 212, 220
Air China   6, 21, 90, 148–150, 217
Approved Destination Status (ADS)   17, 18, 19, 165
Association of South East Asian Nations (ASEAN)   42, 105–106

Bahamas   66, 128, 168, 212
Bali   5, 6, 38, 43, 49, 81, 82, 83, 86, 90, 101, 119, 149, 152, 212
Bangkok   1, 12, 29, 145, 150, 212, 218
Beijing (Peking)   3, 5, 6, 7, 8, 11, 14, 20, 21, 24, 25, 30, 31, 33, 34, 39, 40, 49, 60, 67, 70, 73, 74, 77, 82, 90, 93, 98, 102, 104, 108, 111, 113, 115, 117, 120, 121, 126, 127, 133, 139, 146, 147, 148, 149, 150, 159, 162, 165, 166, 181, 186, 188, 189, 194, 198, 206, 212
Brazil   8, 83, 160

Cambodia   43, 99, 151
Canada   18, 31, 46, 110–112, 130, 212

Chengdu   3, 13, 30, 33, 38, 60, 66, 73, 102, 111, 113, 117, 126, 128, 133, 147, 155, 165, 193
China Eastern Airlines   21, 90, 148–150, 153, 164, 217
China National Day   5, 21, 26, 35, 51, 163
China National Tourism Administration (CNTA)   1, 20, 37, 114, 187
China Southern Airlines   21, 148–150, 164, 217
China UnionPay   6, 9, 69, 75, 78, 121, 179, 211
Civil Aviation Administration of China (CAAC)   21, 143, 158
Chongqing   8, 33, 73, 126, 147, 157, 212
Club Med   212–214
Copenhagen   154–156
Cruise Travel   93–94, 101–102
Ctrip   6, 22, 179, 180

Dalian   9, 33, 73, 126, 147
Dalian Wanda Group   9, 88, 93, 137, 172, 191–193, 197, 210
Disney Resort (Shanghai)   199–200

Europe 3, 15, 22, 78, 109–110, 161, 169, 209

France 5, 12, 18, 42, 90, 162, 183, 213

Germany 7, 18, 47
Golden Week 4, 5, 8, 17, 31, 35–37, 51, 81, 85, 95, 163
Guangzhou 3, 20, 30, 33, 34, 36, 38, 39, 60, 70, 73, 76, 102, 111, 113, 117, 126, 147, 148, 150, 151, 165, 181, 189

Hainan Airlines 6, 90, 137, 148, 149, 150, 217
Hainan Island 5, 24, 66, 79–94, 100, 126, 128, 137, 163, 164, 185, 195, 219
Hangzhou 13, 33, 39, 73, 74, 126, 135, 161, 201, 205
Hawaii 48, 79, 80, 89, 90, 94, 109
Hengqin 86, 195–196
Hong Kong 3, 5, 6, 15, 16, 19, 24, 28, 32, 35, 39, 42, 43, 50, 52, 67–78, 93, 94, 102, 108, 109, 114, 129, 131, 134, 144, 145, 151, 152, 162, 166, 167, 170, 196, 200, 206, 212, 214, 215, 219
Huzhou 201–202

India 42, 45, 83, 91, 159
Indonesia 15, 42, 45, 90, 91, 140
International Air Transport Association (IATA) 21, 142, 144
Ireland (Republic of) 112–113
Italy 42, 43, 45, 48, 94, 164

Japan 5, 11, 18, 31, 62, 90, 94, 114, 127, 151, 160, 161, 184, 210
Jin Jiang Hotels 135, 139–141, 172

Kempinski Hotels 138–139, 172, 202
Kenya 18, 117–120, 123
Kuala Lumpur 3, 100, 150, 209
Kunming 7, 73, 128, 147, 150, 161

Langham Hotels and Resorts 131–133
Le Passage Mohkan Shan 203, 206–208
London 3, 15, 71, 77, 101, 127, 129, 131–133, 134, 137, 152, 163, 212
Los Angeles (LA) 10, 90, 114–116, 152
Low-cost Carriers (LCCs) 150–151, 157–158

Macao 3, 5, 15, 16, 19, 29, 32, 35, 39, 50–66, 75, 86, 144, 151, 162, 170, 196, 214, 219
Malaysia 15, 17, 31, 43, 45, 61, 63, 84, 86, 94, 109, 150, 151, 169
Maldives 32, 49, 82, 86, 89, 91, 94, 128, 134, 161, 162, 165, 167
Mandarin Oriental Hotel Group 133–134
Mauritius 87, 99, 128
Mercedes-Benz 6, 22
Melbourne 15, 106, 116, 150, 154–155
Meetings, Incentives, Conferences & Exhibitions (MICE) 84, 162, 218–220
Milan (World Expo 2015) 220–221
Myanmar 42, 105

Naked Retreats 203, 204–206
Nanjing 8, 24, 26, 33, 39, 73, 150, 189, 208
New York 71, 101, 109, 127, 131, 150, 212
New Zealand 3, 18, 31, 42, 45, 100, 106–108, 148
Ningbo 9, 26, 73, 98, 150, 208
NUO 138–139, 172

Oxford 12, 121–122

Paris 5, 24, 45, 71, 78, 101, 129, 134, 152, 164, 212
Peninsula Hotels (The) 130–131, 142
Peru 18, 45, 123, 209
Philippines 31, 56, 62, 86, 90

Seoul 90, 127
Seychelles 82, 87, 92–93
Shanghai 3, 7, 11, 20, 25, 30, 33, 34, 39, 40, 50, 60, 67, 70, 73, 78, 82, 90, 93, 94, 98, 100, 101, 102, 104, 108, 111, 113, 115, 117, 126, 127, 133, 134, 135, 139, 140, 144, 147, 148, 150, 162, 165, 166, 170, 181, 186, 188, 193, 194, 196, 198, 199, 201, 205, 211, 220
Shangri-La Hotels and Resorts 129–130, 162, 194
Shenzhen 20, 30, 33, 34, 39, 73, 76, 77, 126, 181
Singapore 1, 5, 15, 17, 42, 45, 57, 59–60, 61, 64, 77, 84, 94, 145, 150, 152, 167, 170, 184, 215
South East Asia 15, 17, 42, 94, 123, 150, 170, 186
South Korea 5, 18, 19, 29, 31, 45, 63, 64, 90, 94, 102, 114, 119, 151

Spain 6, 18, 42, 94, 159, 209
Spring Festival 4, 5, 6, 22, 31, 35–36, 67, 81, 93, 95, 163, 194
Sri Lanka 19, 60–62, 94
Starwood Hotels and Resorts 85, 127–128, 171, 194
Suzhou 33, 40, 73, 74, 78, 189, 205
Switzerland 45, 109, 120–121, 148, 162, 181
Sydney 10, 47, 48, 65, 103, 112, 116, 130, 150, 153, 160, 215

Taiwan 5, 6, 29, 31, 35, 68, 131, 144, 151, 170, 218
Tasmania 107, 116–117
Thailand 5, 10, 17, 19, 29, 31, 42, 56, 86, 94, 97–98, 109, 151
Tianjin 3, 33, 40, 73, 93, 102, 126, 128, 136–137, 153, 189, 196
Tibet 5, 193–195
Tokyo 40, 62, 90, 127, 151, 215
Tourism Law of the PRC 26–29
TravelSky 21, 148

United Kingdom (UK) 12, 18, 19, 30, 46, 47, 48, 66, 68, 77, 88, 90, 121, 123, 159, 163, 174, 212
United States (US) 7, 15, 18, 22, 31, 46, 47, 66, 68, 71, 90, 99, 108–109, 132, 148, 210, 212

Vietnam 15, 31, 44, 61, 94, 119

Weibo 8, 113, 117, 119, 128, 130, 174, 183, 216
Weixin (WeChat) 8, 104, 117, 119, 130, 133, 174, 176–178, 183, 191

Winter Sports 36, 111, 120–21, 196–197

Xi'an 7, 20, 74, 82, 128, 150, 186

Xi Jinping (President) 26, 87

Zambia 11, 18
Zhengzhou 22, 23

Printed and bound by CPI Group (UK) Ltd, Croydon, CR0 4Y